SUB/VERSION

SUB/VERSION

Lorna Irvine

ECW PRESS

CANADIAN CATALOGUING IN PUBLICATION DATA

Irvine, Lorna, 1936–

    Sub/version: Canadian fictions by women

Bibliography: p. 181
INCLUDES INDEX.

ISBN 0-920763-03-0 (bound). – 0-920802-99-0 (pbk.)

1. Canadian fiction (English) – Women authors - History and criticism. *
2. Canadian fiction (English) – 20th century - History and criticism. *
3. Feminist literary criticism – Canada
4. Feminism and literature – Canada
I. Title.

~~PS8089.5.W6I78 1986~~   C813'.009'287   C86-093273-7
PR9188.I78 1986

Sub/version has been published with the help of a grant from the Canadian Federation for the Humanities, using funds provided by the Social Sciences and Humanities Council of Canada. Additional grants have been provided by The Canada Council and the Ontario Arts Council.

Designed by The Dragon's Eye Press.
Typeset by ECW/ PRODUCTION SERVICES, Oakville, Ontario.
Printed and bound by Hignell Printing, Winnipeg, Manitoba.

Published by ECW PRESS, 307 Coxwell Avenue, Toronto, Ontario.

Copyright © 1986 by ECW PRESS.

ACKNOWLEDGEMENTS

I am particularly indebted to the National Endowment for the Humanitites for a grant that made it possible for me to do the research for this book; to the Canadian Embassy in Washington for a Faculty Enrichment Grant that helped defray the expenses of my research in Canada; to Carleton University in Ottawa for facilitating my work; and to George Mason University for allowing me freedom from my teaching responsibilities. I would also like to mention the Association for Canadian Studies in the United States, which keeps those of us living outside Canada informed and excited about Canadian studies, and individual people I have met through that organization and with whom I have talked at length about Canadian literature: Cathy Davidson, Lee Thompson, Ted Davidson, Bob Thacker, Paula Gilbert Lewis, Karen Gould, Mary Jean Green, and Jane Moss. I had help from George Mason students who devoted a semester to the study of Canadian women writers and who helped me to clarify many of my ideas.

A version of Chapter Two entitled "The Here and Now of Bodily Harm" was presented at the National Women's Studies Association Conference in 1983. Chapter Six is a longer version of "Politicizing the Private: Sylvia Fraser's *Pandora*" which was first published in *Mosaic* in 1984. A number of points in Chapter Eight were originally put forward in *World Literature Written in English* in 1982.

for Neil, Michael, and Kerri

Contents

Introduction 1

1. The Hieroglyphics of *Mrs. Blood* 21
2. Atwood's Parable of Flesh 37
3. Delusion and Dream in Thomas' *Blown Figures* 55
4. Sisterhood and Secrecy in
   "Its Image on the Mirror" 73
5. Women's Desire/Women's Power:
   The Moons of Jupiter 91
6. *Pandora* and the State 111
7. Maternal Vitality in Gallant's Fiction 131
8. Colonial Metaphors:
   The Honeyman Festival and *Lunatic Villas* 149

Notes 171
Selective Bibliography 181
Index 187

Introduction

"For what we are asking be scrutinized are nothing less than shared cultural assumptions so deeply rooted and so long ingrained that, for the most part, our critical colleagues have ceased to recognize them as such. In other words, what is really being bewailed in the claims that we distort texts or threaten the disappearance of the great Western literary tradition itself is not so much the disappearance of either text or tradition but, instead, the eclipse of that particular form of the text, and that particular shape of the canon, which previously reified male readers' sense of power and significance in the world."

— ANNETTE KOLODNY
"Dancing Through the Minefield"

In "Freedom of Interpretation: Bakhtin and the Challenge of Feminist Criticism," Wayne Booth focusses on one of the most provocative of current problems in literary studies: the degree to which sexual ideologies determine the limits, the metaphors and the interpretations of literature. Booth argues that the denial of social and political influences on textual representation reveals a blindness no longer even peripherally defensible; he then attacks his colleagues who persist, "not often in the presence of women," in castigating the feminist critique as absurd because "if you took it seriously you would have to repudiate almost the whole of Western literature and most of the rest of the world's literature too." Flying in the face of such rationalizations by acknowledging that current research indicates a need for the massive overhauling of traditional canons, Booth announces his affiliation with feminist revisionists:

> I finally accept what many feminist critics have been saying all along: our various canons have been established by men, reading books written mostly by men for men, with women as eavesdroppers, and now is the time for men to join women in working at the vast project of re-educating our imaginations.[1]

Booth's conversion may be somewhat belated. Nonetheless, feminist critics agree that the re-educating of the literary imagination is the major task of the new feminist theory. Nor is there any argument about the masculine dominance of language, and therefore of the ways in which experience is translated. Male stories have traditionally defined the fictional imagination. Roland Barthes eulogizes the "pleasure of the text" as "an Oedipal pleasure (to denude, to know, to learn the origin and the end), if it is true that every narrative (every unveiling of the truth) is a staging of the (absent, hidden, or hypostatized) father,"[2] and the writer as "someone who plays with his mother's body in order to glorify it, to embellish it, or in order to dismember it, to take it to the limit of what can be known about the body."[3] Indeed, the story of the father dominates men's literature. Thus, as Barthes claims, for men, the "[D]eath of the Father would deprive literature of many of its pleasures. If there is no longer a Father, why tell stories?"[4] Freud's scenario of cultural development, the "rebellion of the sons against the father" is, as Norman Brown emphasizes, "not an historical explanation of origins, but a supra-historical archetype; eternally recurrent; a myth; an old, old story."[5] The story is old, this story of loss and of the discovery of the law. It has dominated the acquisition of language, the psychological shift marked by Lacan from imaginary to symbolic structures. The child's development, then, metaphorically male, is linked through

Freudian theory to the past by a steady succession of literary works from Greek to contemporary times. Women writers have also attempted to use this seminal story, transposed as the father-daughter story, often as their entrance into masculine narrative structures. In *Monsters of Affection*, Dianne Sadoff traces its frequency in nineteenth-century fiction, indicating the ways in which George Eliot, for example, attempts to appropriate the father-son story by changing her name. Yet Eliot simultaneously subverts that story, denying paternal precedence, questioning the "authority of her fictional fathers,"[6] binding them finally not to justice but to an idiosyncratic moral law, an alternative story. Thus, in spite of the fact that Eliot imagined "the traditions of storytelling as patriarchal and genealogical," believed the authority of narration to belong to male narrators,[7] and created stories often dramatizing paternal engendering, her work inevitably reveals conflicts and repressions that signify the narrating daughter. Indeed, as Sadoff argues, "the paternal thematics and narrative sequences of the self-engendering writer who fathers himself in language can only be metaphorically — perhaps literally — a masculine activity. The woman who writes encounters a different father, a different desire." Sadoff believes that the paternal metaphor fails the daughter and occasions writing fraught with ambivalence. Different from her father, but "like her mother, whom she perceives as lacking significance,"[8] the daughter often learns to construct narrative divided against herself.

However, other writers, argues Sadoff, attempted to recognize and somehow appropriate a female heritage. Although Charlotte Brontë, like Eliot, feared female authority, she struggled to articulate the female voice and to subvert the male gaze, usurping masculine power by becoming a spectator rather than a spectacle. Nonetheless, in a phallocentric system, neither Brontë nor Eliot was able to create a narrative structure that demonstrates female desire. As a result, doubling dominates the discourse. In Lacanian terminology, this doubled discourse, because it belongs to the psychic imaginary, is constituted by alienation from the self. Other critics agree. Images of madness, represented, for example, in Gilbert and Gubar's *The Madwoman in the Attic* as exorcisms in the woman author's search for an authentic story, become a common signal of desire.[9] Thus, women's writing, particularly in the nineteenth century, seems frequently dominated by the imaginary, by mirrors in which the self is reflected back as the other. At the same time, like a number of other critics of Brontë's work, Sadoff shows that Brontë also attempted to master language as a woman. In *Villette*, Lucy Snowe "alters the psychoanalytic paradigm of language and culture acquisition"[10] because she uses language and imagery appropriate to women. Furthermore, the novel addresses the issue of female mastery, thereby partially liberating the author from a dominating desire for the father.

It is not my intention, in this introduction nor in the studies that follow, to construct a detailed comparison of male and female narrative patterns, but rather to investigate what it means, in the second half of the twentieth century, after the modern novel has helped alter certain traditional, familial patterns, for women to write stories. During the past two decades, the problem has received considerable attention. Scholars whose critical fields vary from linguistics to anthropology, from psychology to sociology, have contributed to a rapidly expanding study of gender, to the ways in which writing and reading interact with experience. Many of these studies stress perceptual change. Thus, for art historian John Berger, vision becomes both theme and metaphor, and self-consciousness about various "ways of seeing"[11] becomes a necessary approach to the interpretation of art. Berger connects economic and sexual ideology and insists that an observer looking at a man recognizes power, a power that, whether threatening or supportive, remains extrinsic to the individual man. Such is not the case with women. Metaphorically immanent and spatially restricted, women, says Berger, have been trained to see themselves through masculine eyes; that is, to split themselves in order to view themselves objectively. It stands to reason, then, that narrative patterns will reflect this vision.

Current feminist critics certainly recognize a radical split in female representation. They recognize, too, as Berger postulates, that women have developed tactics to insure their survival in a "limited space" that is frequently under masculine control and reflected through masculine imagery. Obviously, the cost has been high. Yet critics like Sadoff, who points out that "in Freud's masculine and patriarchal view of a paternalistic culture . . . the daughter has no function; unlike the son, she cannot question the father's authority, nor can she as an adult free herself from her self-definition as a daughter,"[12] nonetheless discover, even in nineteenth-century fiction, narrative patterns that reflect female desire and even female mastery. It seems reasonable to assume that women's narrative patterns in the twentieth century should even more dramatically reflect the cultural ebb of paternal authority. Thus, although, as Berger points out, masculine perspectives overtly dominate culture, women have developed highly sophisticated strategies for survival. In fact, as newly reissued out-of-print texts reveal, and from the careful textual feminist analyses that accompany their resurrection, subversive stories seem to characterize female texts.I believe it to be their dominating characteristic. When read from an enlightened point of view, such subversion effects a fictional break-down of reified male perspectives and often reveals a story that dramatizes the authority of female characters. Indeed, such revised readings have far-reaching results. As Booth and Kolodny make clear, they force the questioning of established canons; even more dramatically, they suggest changes in literary definitions of realism itself.

Such questionings are, of course, fraught with difficulties. Because the female body has been traditionally imagined as immanent and its potential for abstraction limited, feminist critics have been accused of a multitude of sins, ranging from triviality to fallacious logic to failure of humour. The work they discuss, so often about women, also falls under a barrage of criticism for its assumed irrelevance or its peripheral importance. Although recent critical articles sometimes attempt to code more blatant sexist remarks, well-known critics, male and even sometimes female, nonetheless persistently imply that women writers do not focus on the major issues; do not, at least seriously, venture into the arcane depths of politics and philosophy; do not introduce, into the enclosed and confining structures of the home, the outer world. Descriptions that suggest suffocating female prose abound. Jane Austen's novels are often cited as examples of a perfected smallness; that white spinster, Emily Dickinson, is held up as a ghostly reminder of the frightening peculiarities and personal limitations of the female writer. Twentieth-century writers as varied as Virginia Woolf, Sylvia Plath, and Anne Sexton, lumped together by many critics, exemplify an instability peculiarly exacerbated by the stress of artistic composition. Furthermore, we are repeatedly told that women writers seem unable to create realistic male characters. And it is true that many do avoid or minimize male characters, choosing to develop, for purposes of placing in the foreground otherwise unnoticed female characters, single-gendered landscapes symbolically foreign and therefore virtually inaccessible to the untrained male reader. As a result, feminist critics who choose to concentrate attention on such apparently idiosyncratic and limited texts fall under double attack: they glorify the trivial and sacrifice aesthetic criteria for suspiciously political ends.

Without doubt, we do no service to feminist criticism by pretending problems do not exist. Sometimes, the tone and substance of feminist analysis assume the very faults attacked, recreating, from texts that may well encourage readers to do so, a monologic rather than a dialogic imaginative experience. In translating masculine perspectives into feminine ones, such criticism misreads cultural signs and limits the universe it has attempted to open, thus becoming neither competent analysis nor good feminism. Biased readings efface other important textual issues.

Indeed, by concentrating only on female perceptions, or by showing their superiority to male perceptions, a critic can present analyses that, while politically interesting, may be theoretically insipid. Such circumvention of the multivarious activities of the text also frequently encourages the blandest of readings. Unlike the "triumphant wrestling with the greatest of the dead"[13] that Harold Bloom delineates as the poet's greatest creative impetus, these flattened readings suggest limitations that misrepresent the struggles present in women's narratives.

Feminist readings can also become monotonous, dependent on a limited number of core works that are repeatedly quoted as illustrations of female development and female difference. Because women writers have idiosyncratic problems with the establishing of an authoritative voice, they tend to reach outside the claustrophobic, suggestively maternal enclosures of the literary text to substantiate metaphor with experience. They want to give credence to their literary worlds. Furthermore, because female authority tends to be questioned, women critics feel the need to rely on theory that, in the newly developing field of feminist studies, has a limited number of elucidations. For example, two of these, Nancy Chodorow's *The Reproduction of Mothering*[14] and Carol Gilligan's *In a Different Voice*,[15] both works of remarkably astute scholarship and of considerable social and psychological significance, are quoted in almost every serious feminist analysis. One of the results of such repetition is, not surprisingly, considerable uniformity in the issues being isolated and in their explication. Chodorow's study of female boundaries and Gilligan's of women's moral choices sometimes determine the interpretations of the stories being investigated and although the texts may be from different countries, may have contradictory theses, may present female characters in a variety of shapes and articulate them with a multitude of voices, the critics tend to reduce women's writing to singularity. This reduction is precisely what must be avoided.

Then, too, practitioners sometimes elide the divisions between sociopsychological studies and literary analyses, thereby conflating human beings and literary characters. In *Women Writers and Poetic Identity*, Margaret Homans argues that "[T]he call for a women's language that, on the model of a single-sex society, would be free of masculine fictions about women" is "an anachronistic dream"[16] because we now know that language is dual, built on contrast and conflict. Furthermore, Homans stresses literary language's fictiveness. Because women writers and their critics frequently attempt to avoid fiction by approximating the truth, the conflation of "word and referent, of signifier and signified"[17] collapses the structures of rhetoric without coming to terms with their relationship to masculine authority. Such conflations hamper the work of serious literary theory by introducing a prescriptive base. Instead of allowing the critic to work outwards from the text, they suggest the rules of the game, the arguments that must be made if the analysis is to pass as feminist theory. Thus, although inter-disciplinary concerns have been an exciting and necessary part of the new feminist theory and have made it possible to break out of a circle that simultaneously puts forward and then silences women, literary structures are, in numerous ways, self-contained and need idiosyncratic explication as well as a carefully controlled application.

Finally, and perhaps most damaging, insistence on difference can lead toward the solidifying of what has already proved to be an unsatisfactory gender division. Since women's texts have traditionally been isolated from mainstream literature and have been marked by the assumed insignificance of the female voice, we must ask ourselves what can be gained by separating women's and men's writing. In the introduction to *The Future of Difference*, the book's editors summarize some of the arguments against emphasizing gender. Most of the arguments are from the early 1970s, when it seemed apparent that "difference from men meant inequality and continued oppression for women."[18] Yet as the decade continued and more work was done on women's issues, a new rationale evolved. Many feminist scholars began to see that women's differences from men were precisely what needed illumination. As it turned out, that illumination has been remarkably liberating. Whereas the annotation of the wrongs done to women under patriarchal systems, or the detailed contrast of male and female perspectives, exacerbated stereotyping, analysis from a "woman-centered perspective" has "created an increased willingness to contemplate the varieties of female experience," as well as a "freedom to look at male experience as different, or even deviant, from what in this view is considered central, or normal."[19] Literary studies concentrated on woman-centred perspectives have, in fact, proved enlightening because of the articulation of the female voice, and also because of the revelation of structural variations that result from different perspectives on the world.

What, then, constitutes a feminist theory directed towards the explication of narratives? Certainly, feminist critics need to address the problematic issue of a masculine-dominated language in which many of the major religious, cultural and literary stories have been designed to clarify the male ego. Feminist theory has split on this issue. French critics, concerned with the repression of the feminine, rely on analytic methods that isolate psychic symptoms, such as the gaps and silences that signify the absence of the female voice in texts or the textual eruptions and incongruities that signify the return of the repressed. Much critical effort is devoted to what is perceived as deconstructing the dominant masculine discourse. On the other hand, North American critics, more pragmatically, tend to appropriate that discourse to elucidate the suppression of the female. This difference in critical focus affects how we read texts and how we talk about them. In "Her Very Own Howl," Margaret Homans sums up the perplexing ambiguity that faces the woman writer and critic:

> A woman novelist's ability to represent verbally her response to exclusion from the dominant discourse does not at all disprove the thesis that women's silence serves as the basis for the operation of language. Such an ability is constantly undermining itself: in the very act of asserting through capacious representation the adequacy of language, these novelists betray their anxieties about its sufficiency.[20]

For example, Homans analyzes Monique Wittig's *Les Guérillères*. She argues that the novel — multicentred, narratively disruptive, consciously building idiosyncratic structures — reveals the "dependence of both writer and reader on the system of representation that her characters are represented as demolishing."[21] *Féminine écriture* cannot divorce itself from traditional discourse. On the other hand, the American novel *The Bleeding Heart*, by Marilyn French, explores "a vast range of women's experiences" and creates women characters who, "unlike their literary foremothers, do not appear to be silenced at all."[22] In fact, Homans believes that North American writers often use "women's exclusion from language as one of their significant themes."[23] This example of the difference between a heavily theoretical discourse and a more pragmatic one also demonstrates the current general critical distrust, in North America, of deconstruction, and of the linguistic uses made of psychoanalysis. The majority of North American critics favour an applied criticism over abstract theoretical constructs.

It seems to me that feminist criticism can situate itself quite firmly at the juncture between theory and practice. We might therefore answer the question as to what to expect from it in the words of the collective group of women responsible for the writing of "For The Etruscans": that it is the possibility of a real dialectics that attracts numerous critics, that the feminist critic can suggest "a vision which men have barely glimpsed of what dialectical thought is really about — a total, specific, feeling and thinking subject, present in her interaction with 'objective materials,' overcoming the division between thought and action."[24] Whether women can effect a critical union between a separated thought and action is certainly open to question. Yet, metaphorically, women's texts frequently postulate such a union. Thus, Homans suggests that feminist critics might begin dialectically with analyses of women's ambiguous relation to hegemony as it is reflected in the language and structure of their works. Shared attitudes toward oppression suggest to Homans a possible union of French and North American theory. Not surprisingly, that union functions best in the work of women writers in countries dominated by other countries, writers who have, therefore, "besides gender, another reason — either race or nationality — for linguistic alienation."[25] In such work, language, structure and content combine to reveal "the experience of both participating in and standing outside the dominant culture." Such work, "(ambiguously) non-hegemonic,"[26] most fully demonstrates the various ways in which women's texts stand both inside and outside dominant cultures.

For Canadians, this "experience of both participating in and standing outside" the language of their own country which, in its turn, dramatically reflects colonial positions toward dominating countries like England, France, and the United States, influences, in idiosyncratic ways, the metaphors and structures of their literature. For example, the frequent construction of covering stories — that is, stories that disguise hidden narratives — certainly seems politically characteristic of dominated people. In Canada, the covert story most often signifies nationalist concerns about the intrusions of an overwhelming American power. Recognition of much tension in this respect is apparent, for example, in the work of the Canadian writer Dennis Lee, who has analyzed the influence of what he believes to be a dominating Americanism on the Canadian imagination, and who has documented the peculiarly inauthentic voice Canadian writers have had to adopt in order to be heard by a wider community. What he calls "colonial space," and what he deciphers as muteness in the midst of a barrage of language, combine to separate the writer from his own story — for Lee, the story of the father — and, metaphorically, feminize the creative imagination. Colonial space forces silence. Lee's own numbness, his sense of inauthenticity, of powerlessness, his physical constriction, his apparent loss of the past, his assumed victimization coalesced, during the 1960s, around a failure of language: "To speak unreflectingly in a colony, then, is to use words that speak only alien space. To reflect is to fall silent, discovering that your authentic space does not have words."[27]

Lee's silence and his subsequent recovery, a peculiarly "visceral" process, is remarkably similar to that described by many women writers. Yet women also remain ambiguously situated within such power structures. For one thing, feminization, assumed by the male writer in a colonial situation to be synonymous with powerlessness, does not have the same political implications for women. Although, within gender divisions, femininity connotes passivity, within political-nationalist structures it suggests, as I think it does in Canada, an entirely different approach to governance. Furthermore, narrative traditions become problematic in terms of gender. Whereas Lee acknowledges still the standard story, the story in which a "colonial writer finally comes to know *his* house, *his* father, *his* city, *his* terrain,"[28] the woman writer has a quite different story to tell. Her story, the story of feminization, can, on one level, be perceived as another version of the colonial story. But it can also articulate a female voice that politically and culturally personifies Canada.

This tension has propelled Canadian women into the writing of fiction. It has also created fictional patterns that, while diverse, rely extensively on covert stories. Thus, although both male and female writers in Canada construct narrative patterns somewhat different from those that dominate American literature, women's narratives, often covertly, more commonly stress gender issues. Culturally and sexually, their fictions quite naturally introduce a new world mythos that rejects "westering," with its self-conscious individualism. Indeed, many Canadian works translate what is perceived to be American aggression and domination into metaphors of masculinity, metaphors that also inform the critical work of such American writers as Leslie Fiedler when he describes the frontier experience as "leaving the domain of the female."[29] Although Canadian writers in general often illustrate adventure and escape differently from American writers, women writers more consistently than male writers situate and celebrate a maternal domain that presents an alternative structuring to that of patriarchal systems. As a result, within already established patterns of colonization, or at least of economic and political domination, women writers find that subversive language powerfully connects their cultural and psychological situations, their positions as Canadians and as women.

The subjects and themes of their literature also significantly mark their writing. Adrienne Rich argues for the political importance of the contextual shift that results from the foregrounding of the female body because its repossession "will bring far more essential change to human society than the seizing of the means of production by workers." Feminist criticism helps to elucidate the meaning of this body. For Rich, to imagine a world in which "every woman is the presiding genius of her own body," that body traditionally seen as "virgin wilderness to be exploited and assembly-line turning out life," is to imagine a profoundly creative world. The very meanings of "sexuality, politics, intelligence, power, motherhood, work, community, intimacy" and "thinking itself will be transformed."[30]

Such massive cultural shifts do not happen instantaneously. But without efforts to re-educate the imagination, it is doubtful that they can happen at all. Many contemporary critics of various persuasions isolate specifically the need to read gender differently as the process of re-education begins. Booth suggests that readers begin to question the "we" of literary response and interpretation; Kolodny suggests that critics examine "the dilemma of the male reader who, in opening the pages of a woman's book, finds himself entering a strange and unfamiliar world of symbolic significance."[31] Scholes suggests that we open up a code that is "both unconscious in its operation and powerful in its action, for it derives its energy from a deeply felt male fear of female sexuality."[32] And Cixous suggests that "[M]en still have everything to say about their sexuality, and everything to write. For what they have said so far, for the most part, stems from the opposition activity/passivity, from the power relation between a fantasized obligatory virility meant to invade, to colonize, and the consequential phantasm of woman as a 'dark continent' to penetrate and to 'pacify.'"[33]

Feminist theory helps, then, to familiarize readers with narrative structures that reflect women's bodies and that consequently emphasize female space and time. Although the overt narrative may appear simple — that is, may fail to establish competition, aggression, voyeurism, individualism, and apocalypse, themes frequently central to masculine narrative patterns — women's novels, like the ambiguous positions of women within social structures, operate on various levels. On one level, the story may seem passively situated within dominant patterns as, for example, Jane Austen's *Emma* has seemed to many critics politically conservative in terms of marriage. On other levels, women's stories, often less obviously, establish their female characters as historically connected with the female past and in control of a language that contradicts numerous of the allusions of the dominant language. Irony often pervades the tone, while social and political critiques resonate throughout. Narrators and authors of such texts develop exceedingly complicated voices, sometimes using distance to reveal the absurdity of rigid gender definition, as Austen often does; at other times merging with the characters to give emotional depth to the subversions posited.

Without doubt, such reading is difficult. The symbols, even the structures of subversive fictions are foreign to competent readers who have been trained in a dominantly male literary tradition, as well as to uneducated readers, who rely directly on the symbols and codes of their surrounding cultures. Gender limits need total translation. Indeed, male readers are not alone in the difficult task of reading women's fiction. Trained in the same universities, by the same professors, to revere the major texts of a patriarchal system, women too are often unable to read such texts. Although they are more likely to recognize the real-life situations that often form the content of women's narratives — the lying-in room, the hospital room during a mastectomy, the female wing of a psychiatric ward, the home filled with the unavoidable noises of children, the kitchen — they have not been trained to interpret these spaces symbolically, nor have they learned how to recognize their structural significance. To place in the foreground what has been treated as trivial poses a major problem in interpretation.

To learn suitable interpretive strategies is difficult, largely because men and women superficially speak the same language, as do Americans and English Canadians. Furthermore, the practice of sexual discrimination is so fully a part of our lives that it is virtually invisible. In *The Sceptical Feminist*, Janet Richards insists that to recognize sexual injustice "for what it is is to have a view of the world which is radically different from that of most people." To many critics, as Richards further argues, because "[T]he feminist sees what is generally invisible, finds significance in what is unremarkable, and questions what is presupposed by other enquiries," the feminist seems to be "imagining the non-existent, making a fuss about nothing, and gratuitously instigating disturbances in the foundations of society."[34] The logical dilemma a feminist critic must constantly combat is just here: that without a feminist view of experience and without a critical recognition of alternate structures, what is isolated and stressed may seem trivial to the uninitiated, perhaps even dishonest. In the heavily coded female text, the usual story can often be found easily. Because we are familiar with the myths presented, can recognize allusions to patriarchal religions, know well the major writings that are bound to resonate throughout (for example, in English-speaking writings those of Shakespeare and Milton) the stories can be glossed in the most conventional ways.

To teach the reading of covert stories seems, then, a major task of feminist theory. Metaphorically, "ways of seeing" will thus be altered. For example, in his essay on the uncanny, Freud demonstrates that children characteristically worry about their eyes, a worry apparently provoked by a morbid fear of injury. Extending such fears to include myths, dreams and fantasies about the eyes, Freud explains the anxiety — the fear of going blind, for instance — as "often enough a substitute for the dread of being castrated."[35] Intricately connected with doubling and splitting, this dread certainly pervades literature from Sophocles to Shakespeare to Joyce to Pynchon. Yet the imagery of eyes, with its metaphoric connection to "ways of seeing," can be differently explicated in female texts. Theorists suggest that women do not function, as men seem to, in a dominantly scopic mode. Instead of reflecting the problematic issue of castration, in the female text images of eyes seem often to signal covert readings and the need for clear sight.

The narratives discussed in this collection reveal linguistic, structural and thematic subversions signalled by various methods. To pursue a little further the imagery of eyes, for example, is to discover the signalling of subversion. Indeed, repeated emphasis suggests the importance of clear reading and the possibility of misreading. Certain themes affect character, setting and plot in various of the stories. Blind male characters appear; other characters possess different kinds of distorted vision; darkness frequently closes over the narrative events; mirrors reflect endless complications. Other devices also alert the reader to alternate stories. Voice is emphasized. Narrators and central characters draw attention to the fact that stories are being told, sometimes by splitting and doubling, allowing description and commentary to function together; at other times by didactic tones meant to help readers achieve a new perspective. Silence and noise contrast to elicit ironic attitudes to the traditional conflict between the word and the silent woman. Images of disguise imply hidden stories; game imagery implies authorial manipulation. The reader is taught to take women's texts seriously, to recognize not just the surface of the female body but its hidden meanings.

Generally, the discussions that follow use different kinds of feminist theory to emphasize the variety and the complexity of a number of stories written by Canadian women. Organized to move from fairly introverted reflections of the female body and psyche to concerns with relationships among women to broader social and cultural issues, the essays that make up the collection are also close readings of specific narratives. They are not meant to be exclusive. Obviously, I have paid particular attention to images and themes that clarify female characters and address theoretical issues appropriate to female narrators and authors. Furthermore, each of the essays reflects on the others. For example, the emphasis on sisterhood in "Its Image on the Mirror" also illuminates Rennie and Lora's relationship in *Bodily Harm*.[36] The affection between Roberta and Valerie in Munro's "Labour Day Dinner" reflects the camaraderie of Harriet and Marshallene in Engel's *Lunatic Villas*. Similarly, although I emphasize revisions of western myths in *Mrs. Blood*, such revisions occur in each of the narratives so that, for example, the more social concerns of *Pandora* resonate historically because the novel also retells the myth of Pandora. Finally, although I usually concentrate on one or two works by a particular author, extensions to other work by that same author, occasionally made explicit, are also implied throughout.

More specifically in terms of themes, the ambiguous body limits illustrated in *Mrs. Blood*, the first novel I discuss, and the narrative's metaphoric allusions to fullness and emptiness, speech and silence, appear in all the stories discussed. So too does the struggle to achieve a female symbolic language. In *Mrs. Blood*, allegory dominates and becomes a split dialogue between two parts of a woman's psyche. Both psychologically and culturally, such a dialogue questions woman's place in the literary text. As a representative female hero, Isobel struggles against a system designed to trivialize her experience and her voice, a system that she increasingly demonstrates to be absurd. Consequently, as they do in this novel, the psychological and social problems addressed in each of the narratives require a double reading. On the one hand, the stories show conventional gender problems in recognizable ways. For instance, some of the female characters seem relatively passive; they function outside the major public spaces, remain responsible for the nurturing of children, verge on madness, find their work secondary to their personal lives, fear male violence, suffer masochistic tendencies and so on. On the other hand, when female perspectives become central and female struggle significant, the particular shifts to the universal. Generation then becomes symbolically complex, affiliation politically necessary and nurturing physically meaningful. Because generational continuity dominates the structure of many women's lives, so it does the content, the structure and the metaphors of their literary works.

Bodily Harm, the second novel discussed, also allows conventional readings of gender hegemony. Rennie Wilford, as a number of critics have noted, can be interpreted as simply another passive and victimized female character and the novel as another diatribe against male dominance. Yet such readings ignore the importance of the genre — the mystery — the extraordinarily complicated spatial and temporal structures of the text, and the irony of the ongoing political parallels. Certainly, Atwood has anticipated a conventional reading of the novel. Part of its irony depends on it. Thus, like the usual mystery, *Bodily Harm* holds back information, obliges the reader to solve problems, and posits a victim. Yet, feminized, the secret plot subverts traditional narrative pattern, for what is hidden from the reader accustomed to regular plots is, in fact, its central subject. That subject is the female body. To discover its meaning requires a new way of seeing that extends the narrative act. Indeed, in Atwood's novel, the teller seems to have designs on the reader, designs that ultimately trap the reader within the female psyche. Similar traps exist in the fictions elaborated following *Bodily Harm*. *Blown Figures*, "Its Image on the Mirror" and several of the short stories in *The Moons of Jupiter* thus continue to vocalize the usually silent; they force repressed material into the open and insist on idiosyncratic female perspectives on experience. Furthermore, in each of these stories, conflicts between overt and covert stories partially determine the subject matter, while metaphorically and structurally illustrating certain splits in the female personality.

However, not all of the stories treat secrecy metaphorically. In *Pandora*, the subject of the sixth chapter, the reader is more openly instructed to understand the female voice and more directly helped to revise traditional mythologies. This novel also reveals the surfacing of repressed material, but its political aims seem more direct. It subverts the patriarchal family while offering a possible feminist solution. The girl at the centre of the story assumes a voice and a space that conflict with traditional assumptions about the sound and the place of female characters. Indeed, as her heroism develops, like a ground bass, the old myths of Pandora and Eve disrupt the text and enter the fictional world. As a result, peculiar discrepancies occur. As in some of the stories that appear in *The Moons of Jupiter*, female sexuality and power play off against each other, suggesting new answers to what women desire. The narratives include instructions to assist in reading the female text and they also analyze their composition in cultural terms. And, in chapter seven, I show how both "The Pegnitz Junction" and the Linnet Muir stories of *Home Truths* dramatize ways in which the author effects the surfacing of submerged plots by demonstrating co-operation between writer and reader, between teller and listener. Gaps and fissures symbolize the political silencing of women's narratives, although in these stories their presence is articulated and the reader is given material with which to fill the gaps. That fleshing out occurs also in two of Engel's novels, *The Honeyman Festival* and *Lunatic Villas*, the last to be discussed in this collection, where enclosed female worlds are not isolated and peripheral, but come to symbolize the whole culture.

While each of these novels and short stories obviously contrasts activity and passivity, victors and victims, within gender dichotomies, each also treats many of the different splits ironically. As a result, the language used, suppressed, has evolved in subversive, often coded ways, announcing itself through metaphors that, like *memento mori*, alert the reader to underlying themes. Peculiarly ambivalent tensions between the seen and the implied, between the manifest and the latent, between what is assumed and what is, further stress subversion. Annis Pratt insists that "even the most conformist of women authors admit elements of intellectual, erotic, economic, and spiritual rebellion into their narrative structures."[37] Rebellion there certainly is. Yet there is also an implied network of initiated readers who understand the perspectives taken, the assumptions made, and the structures used. For them, hidden stories seem relatively manifest.

Furthermore, each of the narratives presents the woman's body as its central locus, metaphorically creating out of that shape its narrative structure. Berger suggests that women are "depicted in a quite different way from men — not because the feminine is different from the masculine — but because the 'ideal' spectator is always assumed to be male and the image of the woman is designed to flatter him."[38] Literary female characters often thus respond to the male gaze. But in these stories, the female body is not voyeuristically observed and thus objectified; instead, it looks outward and sees not itself reflected, but a multi-various world. As illustration, *Mrs. Blood* and *The Honeyman Festival* establish a rhythm of events that reflects the physical changes of pregnancy as well as various manifestations of the cultures in which Isobel and Minn find themselves. *Bodily Harm* and *Blown Figures* use the bodies of the central characters to represent metaphorically, among other suggestions, the text itself. Womb and breast become actively descriptive. The title *Lunatic Villas* memorializes a building project conceived and executed by a woman; the novel investigates a variety of maternal functions, not the least of which is a mother country's relationship with her colonial daughter as that daughter attempts to mature. With their emphasis on mirrors and with their attention to the female voice, Mavis Gallant's stories also construct patterns meant to fill certain of the gender gaps and fissures in the cultural text with formerly invisible characters, and such Munro stories as "Dulse" and "Hard Luck Stories" experiment with connections between women's passion and their narrative distancing. *Pandora* suggests in poignant physical detail a young girl's blossoming sexuality which includes her attraction to other female bodies, the "budded mystery" of chests, warm bellies, powerful thighs, and vulnerable genitals. Celebration and festival surround what has too long been cloaked in mystery.

As well, the central characters and narrators of these fictions, when interpreted as everywoman, become culturally significant. As female characters they represent their space and time, are not perceived by their authors as the "other" and are allowed to undergo socially important tests that mark them as heroes. Thus in Thomas' work, the heroic physical struggle of giving birth realistically and metaphorically illustrates an intellectual struggle to create resonant narratives; Rennie Wilford's victimization by a repressive regime is paralleled by a mental struggle that gives creative pattern and structure to the woman's novel. In *Pandora*, the narrator presents the *bildung* of Pandora as a series of active tasks against which the girl pits herself, and which she successfully accomplishes. Again, Pandora's development marks out social and cultural steps toward female participation. Marian Engel's Minn and Harriet both represent motherhood but, unlike their nineteenth-century prototypes, are active rather than reactive, are frequently introspective rather than altruistic, and have achieved distinctive and varied voices in the place of silent suffering.

Thus, as we read these stories, we discover repossessed voices, the physical presence of women's bodies, and the female character as representative rather than peripheral or idiosyncratic. The creative act becomes dramatically subjective. Beginnings and endings change. Matrilineal, these stories ignore patriarchal inheritance, and revise the intricate legal and cultural history that has structured western culture. Their writers allow their female characters to see the world differently; what they see becomes their narratives. Furthermore, each communicates its share in the development of a complex female aesthetic in which, contrary to many narrative patterns where women, if allowed to journey at all, are punished according to the audacity of their attempt, female characters successfully complete both physical and spiritual journeys that afford them greatly increased personal knowledge. Indeed, what the uninitiated reader may perceive to be minimally important adventures, peripheral to the major crises that constitute history and that effect political action, for the initiated, move into the foreground, politicizing the most idiosyncratic events of the female life. This particular subversion seems fundamental. As Booth suggests: if understood, it alters the nature of the imaginative act.

Finally, each of the stories addresses the issue of female creativity: its authenticity, its authority, its stance. Annis Pratt suggests that "[W]hen a woman sets out to manipulate language, to create new myths out of old she transgresses fundamental social taboos in that very act."[39] Such transgressions seem constantly to bemuse the writers of these stories as they attempt to create narrative patterns that authentically echo the voices of women. Often, they direct attention to the problem through narrators or central characters who are themselves writers and who thus are able simultaneously to demonstrate and analyze women's writing. In *Mrs. Blood* and *Blown Figures*, Isobel's character splits precisely along these lines, an acting self and a writing self; in *Bodily Harm*, Rennie indicates the changes that occur as she alters from a writer of superficial magazine articles to a committed political writer; Linnet self-consciously experiments with genres and forms in Gallant's *Home Truths*; Harriet, the "Depressed Housewife" columnist of *Lunatic Villas*, like Rennie, learns, as the novel progresses, why she must develop a serious voice. Female writing is also imaged in distinctive ways — blood marks on sheets — as well as psychologically illustrated in the context of stories about the tensions between writing and loving that inform many of Munro's fictions.

For female writers, the act of writing seems carefully self-conscious. It also seems politically crucial. Toward the end of *Archetypal Patterns in Women's Fiction*, Pratt celebrates the continuity and consequent authority that she believes finally distinguish women's writing:

> Women novelists . . . have dug the goddess out of the ruins and cleansed the debris from her face, casting aside the gynophobic masks that have obscured her beauty, her power, and her beneficence. In so doing, they have made the woman's novel a pathway to the authentic self, to the roots of our selves beneath consciousness of self, and to our innermost being.[40]

Not much has been said about the importance of the current women's movement. It seems clear, by now, that gender arrangements are radically changing as a result of this movement. What seems most significant is stressed by Kermode in a different context, when he writes that "discoveries about the nature and possibilities of narrative may, perhaps must, take place at times when there are in progress reevaluations of much larger cultural scope,"[41] and by Booth when he says that "[P]erhaps it remains true that the freedom to make new interpretations by exercising freedom from old methods and assumptions is more important in some epochs than in others."[42] We seem to be living in a transitional epoch. It is essential that we learn to read the signs.

Chapter One

The Hieroglyphics of *Mrs. Blood*

If the Grail were a purely Christian Vessel, it ought not to behave like a mere food-providing talisman; if it were a mere food-providing talisman, it ought not to be surrounded with the atmosphere of mysterious sanctity besetting the holiest relics.

— JESSIE WESTON
The Quest of the Holy Grail

HIEROGLYPHIC: *an ancient mode of writing, made up of figures of objects directly or figuratively representing words or letters or even syllables; a figure, device or sign having some hidden meaning; a picture representing some word or notion it does not directly represent; sometimes used humorously to suggest characters or writing difficult to make out.*

Writing by women is hieroglyphic. It implies an ancient connection that stretches back into a time that images female consciousness. Termed by Annis Pratt an "unvention" whereby western women writers discover "a repository of knowledge lost from Western culture but still available to the author and recognizable to the reader as deriving from a world with which she, at some level of her imagination, is already familiar,"[1] this connection resonates in ways that may be only superficially recognized, even by women readers. It needs further elucidation.

Women's writing pictures the body directly and figuratively. Like that body, its surface disguises what culture has kept hidden: the gaps, the fissures, the holes that signify textual repression. Often hieratical, the markings that denote the female body insist on sacred interpretation. Thus, in that shift from picture to written sign, from body to text, the priests have guarded the representation of women. Interpretation falls to them. Words, letters and syllables assume levels, become the matter of exegesis, and the female body holds together, symbolically, the carnal and the sacred. In itself, it remains mysterious, magical, hidden, infinitely interpretable: powerless. As object, it cannot speak. Gradually, the hieroglyphics assume another meaning; what they picture is no longer what they represent. As the poet suggests in Margaret Atwood's "Foretelling The Future," historically "it doesn't matter how it is done":

> whether it is some god
> blowing through your head
> as through a round bone
> flute, or bright
> stones fallen on the sand
>
> or a charlatan, stringing you
> a line with bird gut,
>
> or smoke, or the taut hair
> of a dead girl singing.[2]

The woman's body becomes a metaphor.

But in this literature written by women, as Atwood's poem announces, "the moon seen from the moon / is a different thing."[3] Thus, in the various fictions discussed here, the crucial problem of alternate representation, reflected, as it is, in political and economic terms as well as in aesthetic ones, undermines masculine control. Just as Dennis Lee has discovered that colonization affects the whole of a culture's "verbal imagination, from single words through verse forms, conventions about levels of style, characteristic versions of the hero, resonant structures of the plot,"[4] so feminist critics are discovering that the absence of women's perspective within the culture, within the critical community and within the fictional universe affects contexts, and also affects the very structures of narratives. Such awareness already dominates commentary on French-Canadian literature by women. In "Setting Words Free," Karen Gould insists that what "the modern dominant male discourse has successfully avoided naming is a complex nucleus of (unarticulated) feminine perceptions, aspirations, desires, emotions, and fantasies that form the core of a vision and state of being which many feminists in Quebec and elsewhere believe is qualitatively different," and that "the absence of a language capable of representing crucial aspects of the feminine psyche and condition has grim consequences for all of us."[5]

Gould asserts that the women of French Canada are triply colonized but that they have become politically influential in opening up "new avenues in textual experimentation, theoretical discourse, and dramatic presentation."[6] Behind them, they have the impetus of the French feminist movement, the theory of *l'écriture féminine*. According to French-Canadian writer Madeleine Gagnon, women proclaim their female bodies every time they write; at the same time, they undertake to erase the long-standing misconceptions and harmful stereotypes that have traditionally interfered with their self-expression. For such critics, female writing becomes important not just because it breaks through stereotypes but because it reveals the female body from the inside. Like Gagnon, Hélène Cixous privileges female *jouissance* and insists on a profound difference between male and female expression that allows the "woman's body, with its thousand and one thresholds of ardor" to "make the old single-grooved mother tongue reverberate with more than one language."[7] Such feminist theorists are establishing new paradigms, to use Thomas Kuhn's concept, and are dropping bombs into established literary canons. It is difficult enough to understand what it means to inscribe femininity, and to revise Lacanian theory to alter the privileged place of the Name of the Father, and to deconstruct texts so their hidden stories, their hieroglyphics, are exposed. But contemporary feminist theorists also have considerable difficulty identifying inherently female texts. Cixous projects such texts into the future by announcing in "The Laugh of the Medusa" that "with a few rare exceptions, there has not yet been any writing that inscribes femininity."[8]

Nonetheless, a number of English-Canadian women writers, like their Francophone sisters, are struggling to enunciate the meaning of femininity. Less overtly political, however, such writers favour covert structures, stories that disguise subversion. Often, the stories imply conformity. Despite the absence of the kind of political rhetoric that appears in Quebecois works like Louky Bersianik's *L'Euguélionne* and *Maternative* or in Nicole Brossard's radically structured texts, English-speaking women writers are discovering how to write their way out of colonial spaces. Their narratives emphasize gender and articulate, from the perspective of female characters, their sense of physical dispossession; they encourage overt representations of their own spaces. Indeed, for literary characters like Audrey Thomas's Isobel Carpenter or Margaret Atwood's Rennie Wilford, even the uninformed reader senses that "under the surface alienation and the second-level blur" of words, there is "a living barrage of meaning,"[9] meaning that teems toward words that name a different world. How much more significant this new naming becomes for an informed reader is evident in novels like *Mrs. Blood*, where covert significance has escaped general reading and has allowed a decade of general obscurity. Recent feminist approaches have helped it speak again, an exegesis that interprets the hieroglyphics that are its text.

Audrey Thomas has been endeavouring to write the female body into new literary metaphors since the publication, in 1967, of her first collection of short stories, *Ten Green Bottles*.[10] The first story of this collection, "If One Green Bottle," is a striking practical demonstration of *l'écriture féminine*, a story that foreshadows the dominantly feminist texts to follow it. The unnamed narrator, everywoman, records her disjointed and agonized thoughts as she struggles to give birth to what will be a stillborn baby. The consequent joining of creation and destruction, of life and death, precisely grounds in the female body all of civilization and its discontents and gives narrative structure to what lies beyond the pleasure principle. The female body is both the page on which the story is inscribed and the author of its events and characters. Furthermore, the conflation of inner and outer illustrates Pierre Macherey's description of the critical endeavour; the critic must "realize that the work has no interior, no exterior; or rather, its interior is like an exterior, shattered and on display."[11] The alternations between the story in the womb — the bottle — and the impinging narrative of exterior events, make "If One Green Bottle" a metaphor of the shattered textual interior posited by Macherey. Its literary production becomes both metaphor and demonstration.

Spatially, the story is a geography of the pregnant female body, the "damp smell of coming rain, the overripe smell of vegetation" (p. 6); "the eyes half blind with water . . . the waves breaking over the head" (p. 11). Temporally, it is a matriarchal history, a network of daughters, mothers and grandmothers, a network powerful enough to authorize the narrator's revision of general cultural history. Thus fragments of myths, legends, the Bible, dramas, novels, even nursery rhymes appear, radically altered, entirely from a woman's perspective. Jonas-like, the narrator peers from between the whale's teeth and speaks from the other side of the mirror of the birth of Christ: "And Mary, how did she take it, I wonder . . . . And the days were accomplished. Unfair to gloss that over . . . to make so little of the waiting . . . the months . . . the hours. They make no mention of the hours; but of course, men wrote it down" (pp. 8, 9). By altering masculine genealogies and rhetoric and by questioning the nature of authority, the narrator produces a female Word that issues from the orifices of the female body. Mouth and vulva, thresholds between interior events and those of the outer world, equally proclaim femininity. Filled with ellipses, spasmodically jerked back and forth between inarticulate pain and stream-of-consciousness articulation, even structurally, the story demonstrates the last moments of pregnancy. It is presented as an epic struggle with a female hero, female tasks, and a female journey. When it is over, a new Noah has settled on Ararat: "The battle over . . . the death within expelled . . . cast out . . . the long hike over . . . Ararat. Sleep now . . . and rise again from the dying fire" (p. 16).

But this short story is only the forerunner of a much more complicated illustration of the same theme, the novel *Mrs. Blood*, published three years later. The narrator, Isobel, a writer, lives in Africa with her husband, Jason, and their two children. Told in three parts as a dialogue between two representations of the narrator, Mrs. Thing and Mrs. Blood, reminiscent of medieval dialogues between body and soul, the novel charts the long days of waiting before the birth of a dead baby. Part One, the longest of the three parts, takes place in the hospital where Isobel fluctuates between consecutive narrative (the story of her current life in roughly chronological order) and bizarre fantasies, all of which relate somehow to blood. In the second part, Isobel has returned home, still precariously pregnant. The dialogue continues until, at the end of the section, she begins to bleed again and is rushed back to the hospital. Part Three, very short, is almost all spoken in the voice of Mrs. Blood. The baby dies. As in "If One Green Bottle," inner and outer are conflated and story and interpretation seem interchangeable. Most important, like the short story, *Mrs. Blood* is a radical female text, a text that, in the words of Mary Jacobus, illustrates "the transgression of literary boundaries," the "moments when structures are shaken, when language refuses to lie down meekly," when "the marginal is brought into sudden focus" and "intelligibility itself refused."[12] What a shaking of structures and of language, what a battering of intelligibility go on in Isobel's head: "This is my body which was riven, my body which was roven — my flesh all scattered and tattered and torn, and Rosie is the riveter who nailed me there as a totem in front of the door" (p. 59).

The subversions of this text are fairly complicated. It is clear that, like the second and third parts of the novel, the first part operates on a series of levels that can best be described as allegorical. However, although metaphors signal allegorical meaning throughout, its exegesis is hardly conventional. Because it is dominated by the female body and thus the female psyche, the novel requires careful reading. Each level of exegesis illustrates the splitting signalled by the schizophrenic narrator, and also the struggle to write her own body that is, I suggest, the novel's central theme.

On a literal level, the antagonisms between men and women, muted in actuality but persistent in memory, create pervasive divisions. As Isobel lies in her hospital bed she remembers the cruelty of an earlier lover. She hears him talking to his friends, describing women as obscene, disgusting, expendable; the sexual battle stimulates their conversation, makes it erotic. She remembers, too, the disgust for women's blood of another lover. Wandering through a Japanese garden where they have just made love, the man looks at the goldfish: "'Ugh,' he said. 'They look like blood-soaked bandages'. . . . What d'you know of blood-soaked bandages?' I asked and spoiled his poetry" (pp. 23-24). Not surprisingly, Isobel's hospital room is presented as a female enclave. Watched over by the nurses — the symbolically named Esther, Grace, and Alexandria — she lies protected, harbouring "the child, my nutmeat, my centre, my dying darling" (p. 26). The main gynecologist of the hospital intrudes with every entrance, his white rubber boots pounding, his contempt for women blatant. Even her husband Jason's visits "are becoming impossible" (p. 95) because they disturb the placidity of an isolated female world; Isobel resents his "muffled excitement" (p. 95), his masculine ignorance of female suffering, his lack of concern for it.

Apart from the literal level of male and female tensions, the novel also operates at another level, the allegorical, where the signs of the text assume less easily decipherable meanings. In Part One of the novel and elsewhere, the story illustrates a persistent concern with writing; with deciphering hieroglyphics, and also with creating them. The "white page" is alluded to in a variety of ways (for example, the white hospital sheets) as are the marks that colour it. Isobel's own whiteness contrasts sharply with the blackness of those around her. Thus, in spite of her inclusion in the womb-like room, she remains an outsider, a foreigner, a white woman being looked after by black women. Her difference is pronounced. The ritual African ceremonies that would end her isolation and that figure so powerfully in *Blown Figures*, the final novel of the trilogy, evade her: "I would like to really know them, but I sense that they are only as verbose as they are because I am a stranger, and they are young and romantic. So I must arrange the snippets of information I gather on a thread of the purest conjecture" (p. 84). Indeed, Isobel suffers a knowledge of what her community assumes to be white cultural superiority and what she believes to be her inferiority to the black women around her. Her weakness, exaggerated by her white skin, makes her difference embarrassing. Like a narrative filled with secrets, black and white also describe the conflict experienced by the narrator in connecting words with her experience. The colours are a metaphor for writing.

The novel presents a moral landscape, a romance controlled entirely by the female body. Set in Africa, its landscape evokes a heart of darkness now perversely feminized. Sometimes, in the sickened vision of this Fisher Queen, it becomes deadly. To a woman in Isobel's condition, sexuality can seem diseased; the female sexual organs appear like a Venus flytrap, "mouth open wide to catch the unsuspecting guest" (p. 107). Warm, sticky smells, swollen flowers, flatulent frogs, the monotonous beating drums, even the greedy vultures seem extensions of a female body that struggles with death.

The imagery is organic. Opening and closing, filling and emptying, each movement charts an ancient journey. The blood-red hibiscus that decorates the fringes of the narrator's vision duplicates the female sexual organs; body and plants metaphorically join. Isobel imagines herself "wilting on a too thin and bloody stalk" (p. 29) and the surrounding world, as it did for Conrad's Kurtz, becomes a mirror of an inner narrative: "And that spring I noticed for the first time that the street-lamps looked like onions growing the wrong way up and wilting in the sun. Or chive plants gone to seed" (p. 28). The narrator exhibits concern about what is felt rather than about what is seen. Women have too often been described as "the object of the male gaze." In this novel, seen through a woman's eyes, the narrator makes a narrative structure of the evolutions of her own body; the evocation of the unsettling Alice-in-Wonderland shifts of her body's boundaries and her translation of physical sensation into language insist on active control, on authority, in ways denied to more lyrical descriptions of the joys of motherhood. She refuses even the "impossible syllogism"[13] of Julia Kristeva's symbolic motherhood.

Myths merge. Rites of passage and portions of the Grail legends make of *Mrs. Blood* a repository of cultural fragments and a newly organized narrative of them. In her psychologically active moments, Isobel writes of herself as a hero, a journeyer through wasted lands where the path is narrow and where she is followed by "whatever it was that I had felt behind me, stalking me, for all those years" (p. 12). Her major tasks are to keep from shedding blood and, like Noah, to preserve in the ark of her body the life she carries. Her goal is the same as it was for some of the knights of the Holy Grail — to bring life to the wasteland, to preserve the fish. More traditionally, she becomes the Grail, a bottle wherein are preserved secrets that, like "grenades" (p. 103), could blow apart the present as well as the past. Thus she fluctuates. Sometimes she rewrites with her blood, the journey of the hero; sometimes she is the blank white page on which the story is inscribed. In this novel, blood and milk form the words of the story, mingled as in one of Isobel's recollected stories. She remembers driving with her father and seeing an accident, a "milk truck on its side and another car smashed underneath it and blood and milk together running all across the road" (p. 20). The text is marked by the secretions of the female body.

As Jessie Weston diagrammed,[14] the romance of the Grail merges with ritual. At what Frye calls the anagogic phase, Isobel, representative of all women, illustrates Christianity, the religion of her childhood. But the religion evoked is a religion of the female body and of the woman as creator. Isobel's voice is the priest's, is Christ's: "'Take this,' I said, 'in remembrance of me'"(p. 26); her body is the "broken altar" (p. 92): "And no one will assay to touch me because of the shards which gleam greenly against the white altar and the wine shall run over and down and expire in a hiss when the sun sticks his finger in the window. Drops of red pain, rivers of pain and the earth outside rusty with blood. This is my body" (p. 99). Isobel imagines the African nurses passing her bloody nightgowns from hand to hand, participating in a ritual of blood. The drama of birth and death and sacrifice is thus feminized, articulated entirely by the female voice. The female body becomes a metaphor for religious sensibility and a correlative for the rituals that accompany it. No Mary, Isobel revises the Christian structures that insist on passive, virginal motherhood, on a female body that is no more than a receptacle for male continuance.

The first section of *Mrs. Blood* ends in a series of fragments that symbolize the deconstruction that has dominated the text. The levels of the allegory cross through each other and the problem of female writing, the need for a new *logos*, dominates. Hieroglyphics mark the grave of a mother whose absence in the family remains a "wound" (p. 123). A sign advertising the forthcoming performance of two musical bands merges with female body rhythms; the musical programme is entitled "The Mid-Month Blues." A photo-printing establishment is named the "Deo Gratias Studio" and an advertisement for the return of lost keys metaphorically signifies Isobel's simultaneous desire to keep her secrets locked inside her (to keep the baby safe and the narrative silent) and to open the safe (to let the baby out and to let the narrative speak). Other themes — the relationship between moral and physical health, the rationale of casual victimization — also crop up. They are fragmented. As the section ends, Isobel's narrative is both penance and therapy.

Part Two is told from Isobel's own home. Because the bleeding has stopped, the doctors allow her to leave the hospital. She is still pregnant. The double voices that have thus far constituted the narrative continue, and the allegory established in the first section is refined and extended. History forms the literal base, Isobel's past. She attempts to reconstruct her mother's life, particularly the moment Isobel was born: "'When I had you,' Mama said, 'they put a bit of gauze over my eyes. I think they did it always, then. Just to make sure everything was all right, you know, before they let the mother see her baby'" (p. 138). This repetition — Isobel describes her own figurative blindness and agonizes over the welfare of her baby — gives Isobel a genealogy that further accounts for the splitting and doubling of the narrative voice. Her physical reality continues to be stressed, the marks of her womanhood, its hieroglyphics. Menstruation is one of these marks. She remembers the old Sears Roebuck catalogues, with their advertisements for "[S]anitary napkins in bulk" (p. 158); an episode from the sixth grade when a student discovers a dirty Kotex under her chair; her cousin's tears because she got her period the morning of her wedding. In Africa, the country of taboos, she remembers silent Canadian taboos on menstruating and pregnant women. She cannot recall seeing a pregnant woman when she was a child.

Other memories introduce other kinds of realities. Isobel recalls a summer spent working in a mental institution, a period of her early life described in considerable detail in the middle novel of the trilogy, *Songs My Mother Taught Me*.[15] References to the mad women give resonance to the split between sanity and insanity, a split dramatically present throughout *Mrs. Blood*. The references also remind the reader of the damage that can be done to the female body by cultures that do not value it. Isobel includes herself in the condemnation: "And they weren't really women to me, you know, just screaming, kicking monstrosities or parodies of human beings"(p. 172). Now that she is suffering, Isobel is able to sympathize with the plight of such women; she gives them a voice. She knows that beneath the skin — in the womb, for example — life goes on, that, as the narrator of *Bodily Harm* announces in a variety of ways, " . . . things here aren't always what they seem to be and one must behave accordingly" (p. 11). Just as women's bodies harbour secrets, so do their narratives.

The second section also concentrates on the act of writing, on what it means to translate the idiosyncratically female event of pregnancy into narrative. Isobel self-consciously draws the reader's attention to the creative verbal act at the opening of the section when she announces that she is going to "begin at the new beginning" (p. 131). Edward Said demonstrates convincingly that such announced beginnings have certain psychological intentions, for they involve reversal, a "change of direction" that "constitutes an authorization for what follows from it."[16] By attempting to change direction, Isobel endeavours to substantiate her precarious pregnancy through narrative structure. She alters the story and changes its direction. She also more consciously struggles to overcome her fear by cleverly manipulating language, "[C]ontrolling the panic by speaking in careful sentences" (p. 196). Yet in spite of Mrs. Thing's attempt to narrate the story, the voice of Mrs. Blood breaks in, out of place, sometimes irrational, wild. For Mrs. Blood, words and fragments of sentences assume terrifying meanings, meanings dominated by her body: "*Avez-vous du pain?*"; "*Ne rien insérer.*" Even the dictionary harbours evil meanings; the word "grave" metamorphoses into "gravid" (pregnant), then into "grieve." Unconscious and conscious associations intersect and the manifest narrative collides with the latent.

Repeatedly, then, Mrs. Blood deconstructs the well-formed sentences, the structured narrative. Her voice fills the gaps she creates with apparently disconnected images and thoughts, with bits and pieces of literary texts, signs seen, newspapers read, a veritable babble of tongues. In Part Two, the novel continues to exemplify the blending of story and interpretation that characterizes *Bodily Harm*, *Pandora*, and *Lunatic Villas*. Like the exegesis of mediaeval manuscripts, marginal textual commentary insists on allegorical meaning. This meaning I want to define as female narrative. Such a narrative displays the joining of inner and outer in a number of literal as well as metaphorical ways. It depicts ambiguous body boundaries; therefore the textual boundaries are also ambiguous. It connects physical with linguistic signs and foregrounds the female body within cultural and religious codes.

The landscape of the novel reflects the narrator's moral state. Blood-red hibiscus flowers metaphorically illustrate an invisible interior, a female space: "They have opened too early and too wide and all their energy has been sucked out by the sun" (p. 154). Isobel's dreams become grotesque. They are filled with images of dismemberment and decapitation, of infants torn apart, of voices shrieking in the night. She fears that she will bear a deformed baby. The outer world confirms her inner terrors. Newspapers repeatedly describe malformed babies; for example, a two-year-old girl was born, like Krishna, with too many arms and legs. Her neighbours discuss a Mongoloid child who will probably not live to be twenty. Around her, like a mediaeval woodcut, "the landscape drips with poison" (p. 140), and sexual disease runs rampant. As her journey continues, images of fish signal the Grail story and remind the reader of the fish's importance to the early Christians. These images — like the images in T. S. Eliot's *The Wasteland* — suggest regeneration. Sometimes Isobel imagines herself as a fish, life-giving, making love, "smooth, from the waist up to the shoulder and over into the neck" (p. 181). She often imagines the baby as a fish, swimming in its mother's womb. Once she recalls Jason's anxiety to get away from the hospital where he visits her after the birth of their first child, their daughter, Mary. She likens Jason to the "Japanese fishermen who will frantically cut their lines rather than touch the dreaded wolf fish" (p. 183). Toward the end of Part Two, a crude drawing of a fish appears on the page and an advertisement for the State Fishing Corporation reminds us that "Good fresh fish gives you / Good eating / Good health / Good value" (p. 191). The narrative of pregnancy becomes the romance of the Grail; mother and baby are the major actors.

In other bizarre moments, Isobel seems both prophet and scribe: "I heard a voice from heaven, saying unto me, Write" (p. 151). The Word, the *logos*, becomes increasingly feminized. Rejecting Pauline strictures about female silence, rejecting Eve's role as subservient to Adam, Eve's interpreter, Isobel insists on direct access to the spiritual realm; she therefore insists on the right to interpret. She does not deny moral and spiritual necessities; rather, she redefines them. In her revision, life and death assume immediate physical presence and the symbolic has a bodily base: "'Today,' he said, 'we will discuss the symbolic significance of the bloody and bawd of Christ, that is to say, bloody Mary, who propelled Him, shrieking, into the musty straw and thought all over that which had just begun'" (p. 193). Like a recitative, Isobel's servant, Joseph, asks: "Hey, Madame, how is your body?" Echoing sexually suggestive remarks about women, this question underlines the culturally central role of the female body. Isobel does not accept her womb as a passive receptacle; instead, she describes the female body as the hero of a complex odyssey. At the anagogic level of the allegory, the female body (interpreted by men and therefore unable to speak for so many centuries), the traditional root of all evil, the physical carrier of all sin, is redeemed. As they must if life is to continue, the physical and the spiritual unite. In the female body, such union occurs.

Part Three is the shortest of the three sections. The voice of Mrs. Thing is heard only once; Mrs. Blood speaks nine times. Images shift, condense, reform. Yet although the inner narrative is brief — a few hours that complete the months of waiting — Mrs. Blood nonetheless evokes a whole, complex culture, of which the focal point is the merging of life and death in the chiasmus of a woman's bearing a dead child. An intricate mythology of death extends space and time; ceremonial ritual stresses the significance of Isobel's struggle. The landscape remains menacing and, as this journey draws to an end, increasingly surreal. Isobel imagines "[E]verywhere red mouths opening and closing, and the smell from the frangipani tree presses down" on her face and chokes her (p. 206). Snakes slide through the grass; puff adders hide in the trees; soldier ants swarm; a plucked hibiscus looks like a "fresh clot" (p. 206). Vultures hover, both inside and out, and language slips from one meaning to another. Bizarre and malevolent linguistic transformations occur: the word "vulture," for example, metamorphoses into the word "vulnerable." Fireflies turn into evil spirits. Isobel's memories metonymically reflect her womb: a white Cortina with red upholstery, a pale-green bottle, a little ivory box.

Fragments of literary works, of the Bible, of newspaper articles, of old songs continue to flash through her mind, not haphazardly; their appearance is dictated by her constant awareness of the loss of blood. Each fragment speaks of death. "Did ya ever think / When a hearse goes by / There's comin a time when you're gonna die?" (p. 210). Geraniums, flags, a man with "[E]yes like rubies" (p. 210) all red, reflect a landscape of the womb, the other side of the mirror. The recitative, "listen, I think I'm bleeding," blends into a wasteland where the floods are turned "into a wilderness" and the watersprings dried up (p. 212). Logic breaks down and the flow of consecutive narrative stops. Prayers for the dead float in and out of the narrator's consciousness, mingling with past scenes of imagined or real events. Ironic reversals infect the language and homonyms describe Isobel's latent anxiety: "It is very meat and write so to do" (p. 212). Like Christ, she suffers the pangs of hell and, like him, journeys to the underworld. On the third night, it is over. Like a dried and wilted flower, Isobel survives in a dessicated land. Movie-reel images speed up as bits and pieces of the narrative of pregnancy rush through her mind.

The reader is completely given over to an unconscious that is a language. The various levels of the allegory condense and the doubled narrative voices fuse into a single voice. Culture coalesces around women's experiences. Excerpts from "The Song of Solomon," from the Shakespearean tragedies, from folklore, from the *Duchess of Malfi*, from airplane manuals, from past events document the odyssey of pregnancy. Nothingness dominates: Lear's "nothing will come of nothing"; the recurring French mailing instruction, *"Ne rien insérer"*; a recollection of a happier past when "we held hands in a movie called 'The Man Who Never Was'" (p. 216-17). Isobel's boundaries shift: "Jason, my love, I am not what I am" (p. 218). Appearance and reality merge, as do the open and the secret. The contents of the text have been revealed. A psychic economy infuses the imagery: "Look to your house, your daughter and your bags. Thieves! Thieves!" "PAY UP OR DIE" (p. 218). The concluding pages of the novel posit a literal base for the various condensations and displacements. At last, Isobel articulates the *lex talionis* that underlies the allegory she has structured: an early abortion that, like the abortion in Margaret Atwood's *Surfacing*, has propelled her quest. Isobel pays a life for a life.

What is the reader to make of *Mrs. Blood*? I have argued that the novel illustrates exactly what it means to write a female text. In *Mrs. Blood*, a woman physically dominates space and time. She is able to produce and structure language that describes her desires, even her body. By re-enacting the complex cycle of the Grail from a female perspective, Mrs. Blood alters the quest narrative. Both Quester and Fisher, carrying in her body the secret of the Grail ("I keep my secrets hidden, like grenades, beneath the pillow," [p. 103]) she connects human life with the land and defines women's blood as the origin and preserver of the human race. She becomes the hero of her own drama and visits her own female underworld, where the souls of the damned — the women in the madhouse — warn her about the pitfalls of female existence.

In complicated ways, Isobel's story is also a spiritual odyssey, a re-telling of the Bible. Women are the major actors in the drama of retribution and salvation. Isobel assumes responsibility for her own guilt. Even transubstantiation is feminized. She imagines the mother addressing her new-born infant with Christ's words: "This is my body which was given for thee. Feed on me in thy heart by faith and by thanksgiving" (p. 183). The Old Testament also is rewritten. Unlike

Milton's Eve, whose duplicity made her the mother of lies in a patriarchal tradition, Isobel, a committed writer, alters the nature of the conflict between fiction and reality and refuses Adam his monopoly on the Word. As she experiences and interprets the literary traditions of her culture — Greek mythology, the epics, the Old and New Testaments, the Grail cycles, the dramas of Shakespeare, Milton's *Paradise Lost* — Isobel provides imaginative resources for the female voice, a voice that now sounds in the twentieth century. To Hemingway's male universe, she responds to the woman writer: "But you want to be a writer. Stay. Why nervous in a clean, well-lighted place?" (p. 81).

By turning into narrative episodes an event usually perceived singularly and in silence — the months of pregnancy — the narrator has used *Mrs. Blood* as a metaphor for the act of writing. The narrator's demonstration of the translating of private communion into public communication, of facing the fear of failure symbolized by the still-born baby, of opening the self to the prying eyes of the reader, are a detailed example of the labour of literary production. No other human event can so accurately describe a writer's experience. The condensation of birth and book works; what a male writer can symbolize only through castration, what John Irwin in his study of Faulkner sees as "a kind of alternative suicide," an "act of autoerotic self-destruction,"[17] for the woman writer becomes an extension of her own body. Indeed, so important is the connection that Susan Gubar insists that "[T]he startling centrality of childbearing in the *künstlerromane* of women represents a response to the hegemonic texts and contexts of our culture that either appropriate the birth metaphor to legitimize the 'brain children' of men or, even more destructively, inscribe female creativity in the womb to insult women whose productions then smack of the mere *repetition* of *reproduction*, its involuntary physicality."[18] Pregnancy is actually and metaphorically central in women's narrative.

By insisting on the broadening of symbolic language, *Mrs. Blood* makes a political statement. In *The Political Unconscious*, Fredric Jameson argues that "since . . . the cultural monuments and masterworks that have survived tend necessarily to perpetuate only a single voice in this class dialogue, the voice of the hegemonic class, they cannot be properly assigned their relational place in a dialogical system without the restoration or artificial reconstruction of the voice to which they were initially opposed, a voice for the most part stifled and reduced to silence, marginalized, its own utterances scattered to the winds."[19] Thomas's text responds to such a statement. As in the recurring words, "there's no nice way to say this," words recalled by Isobel from the ending of a love affair, the novel is an allegory of the fears, sorrows, and pains of women, as well as their survival, an allegory that revokes women's culturally assumed silence and marginality. Although the stillborn baby and the psychological return of Isobel's earlier abortion are at the journey's centre and evoke fears of narrative failure, Isobel orders her experience and turns it into legend. The space is not always clean, and it certainly is not well-lit. It is, however, the space from which all stories and all story-tellers originate.

Chapter Two

Atwood's Parable of Flesh

I think "feminine literature" is an organic, translated writing . . . translated from blackness, from darkness. Women have been in darkness for centuries. They don't know themselves. Or only poorly. And when women write, they translate this darkness.

— MARGUERITE DURAS

Isn't the final goal of writing to articulate the body? For me the sensual juxtaposition of words has one function: to liberate a living past, to liberate matter.

— CHANTAL CHAWAF

Like *Mrs. Blood*, *Bodily Harm* operates on a series of increasingly complicated levels that require decoding and that covertly appeal to an initiated reader. The novel deals with female bodies in various degrees of dismemberment, with doctors, with hospitals, and with blood. These images suggest gendered narrative structures. The same splits that dominate Thomas's novel are developed in Atwood's novel. The dialogue between the ego and the id that gives peculiar resonance to the female voice in *Mrs. Blood* also appears in *Bodily Harm*. The novels complement each other. In *Mrs. Blood*, Isobel Cleary retells patriarchal stories by inverting their mythologies; Rennie Wilford, the narrator of *Bodily Harm*, suggests a new story that can be constructed from the ashes of the old. Isobel maintains her connections with the world of the fathers — Jason is not cast off — but Rennie declares out-and-out war. The text of *Mrs. Blood* assumes and feminizes the spiritual narrative of guilt and redemption; *Bodily Harm* radically swerves from it, and suggests its demise.

Significantly, both novels are textual metaphors of the female body. Stylistically dominated by structures that suggest the physical patterns of female life and by images that focus aesthetic attention on feminized landscapes, the two novels are also contextually female, specifically because they present the world through female eyes. This contextual shift has massive ramifications. It subverts patriarchal history and denies to the male gaze the right of interpretation. Indeed, both novels demonstrate the meaning of looking outward from the inside of the female body, radically revising John Berger's observation that "[T]he surveyor of woman in herself is male: the surveyed female."[1] At the same time, in semi-didactic ways, the reader of these novels is given a demonstration of the reconstituting of female characters. Isobel and Rennie are stripped, peeled layer by layer, turned inside out. This uncanny opening up of character is announced by the various ghosts that fade in and out of the central characters' purview like so many repetitions of former selves, the stereotypes of conventional female characters.

The two novels, then, are radical in fundamental ways. Their material — for example, Rennie's mastectomy and Isobel's miscarriage — is heavily coded and becomes interpretively dense when read metaphorically. Their insistence on female space and on matriarchal structures argues for cultural and historical revision. The movement from the traditionally split female voice to a single-voiced narrative reporting illustrates a juncture in each novel's political and sexual structure. Because both writers finally perceive the female character as unified, and because that perception necessarily insists on cultural assimilation, the divided character is buried and a subversive but unified character is created. Atwood's novel also reveals, subversively, certain characteristics of Canada.

With the opening words of the novel — "This is how I got here" — the reader of *Bodily Harm* is drawn into a labyrinthine plot that uses the themes and images of earlier Atwood novels, poems, and criticism to make a radical statement about female sexuality, the political body and the female text. Quite different in tone from *Mrs. Blood*, *Bodily Harm* entices and entraps. It is not specifically exegetical and, although coded, it does not rely on established cultural mythology. It is a terrifying novel, a mystery, a ghost story that systematically confuses characterization, persistently turns the screw of the plot, clouds the setting, and obfuscates the genre. Surrealism embues the reported events, making ambiguous the temporal orientation and the location. Although the opening sentence certainly implies a specific time (the present) and space (here), the novel is created in a nightmarish landscape that condenses the various characters and displaces the emotions of the situations described. Throughout, the twists and turns of the plots and sub-plots run through each other and intermingle, while the repetition of words and images evokes ritual in ways that seem to suspend chronological movement. Italicized language fragments, apparently disembodied, pierce the text, drawing to the reader's attention the peculiar balance between first- and third-person narration and the problematic narrator. At the same time, they signal a possible "here" and "now." It is a heavily coded novel that articulates and attempts to liberate the female body.

The major plot of *Bodily Harm* is superficial and overtly traditional. The young heroine, Rennie Wilford, is passive and consequently victimized, then rescued by male interference. The plot gives a deceptive order of development to the recorded events. Rennie is presented as the central character, a free-lance journalist of only mediocre ability, a writer of trendy and superficial articles. The novel appears to be her story. It is told sometimes in the first person, sometimes in the third, a splitting of subject and object that increases the aura of mystery. For example, Rennie first tells a story of a man who enters her apartment and leaves a coil of rope on her bed as a reminder of his visit. She and the reader interpret this breaking-and-entering as a crime against her body, a crime that introduces, at the beginning of the novel, the paranoia that persists throughout. The crime fits into a metaphor that works throughout the novel, which uses the game "Clue" in different combinations in each of the book's major episodes. The reader becomes involved in strategies that imply undetected messages.

Not long after the break-and-enter episode (although the chronology seems distorted), Rennie is offered a chance to write a travel story for

Visor, a magazine directed to male readers. She accepts the assignment, flies to the Caribbean island where she is to do the piece and arrives at the Sunset Inn. (The name, as it turns out, is ominous.) For the next six days — the time is rather carefully noted — she travels around the island and meets people until, apparently inadvertently, she becomes involved in a revolution. During the early morning of her seventh day on the island, and following a night of violent revolutionary outbreak, she is arrested. She suffers for about two weeks in a poorly run and terrifying Central American prison. She is finally rescued by a member of the Canadian diplomatic corps, then put on a plane to Canada. Once home, she becomes, as Audrey Thomas comments in a review of the novel, like the Ancient Mariner, "a sadder but wiser person."[2] Obviously, the narrative plot emphasizes the possibility of rescue, specifically the rescue of a female character by a male character. An acceptable plot; a politicized romance; a story about victimized women, about strong men, about foreign places. A woman's story!

Certainly, the reader learns more about Rennie than my summary suggests. Because she constantly reflects on the past, large segments of the novel are presented as flashbacks that tell other stories about other lives. One story describes Rennie's relationship with Jake, a man who has been living with her but who has moved to a new apartment before the novel begins. Connections like this figure in many contemporary romance stories. Rennie also describes her operation, a partial mastectomy. Daniel, the doctor who performs the operation, figures dominantly in her fantasy life: as she explains, his is the first face she sees when emerging from the anaesthetic, and he has been imprinted on her. This plot characterizes a more specialized romance, the doctor story. Rennie also gives the reader enough autobiography to allow a certain *Bildung*, the revelation of her early life in the small town of Griswold, where she and her mother lived with her mother's parents, a patriarchal grandfather who is also a doctor and a somewhat querulous grandmother. Memories of the grandmother flit in and out of the novel. Like movie fade-outs, segments present the grandmother's disintegrating image, her disappearing hands.

The stories of two other women are also included in the text. Jocasta is a Toronto friend of Rennie's and Lora is a woman whom Rennie meets on the island. Lora becomes Rennie's cell-mate in the last section of the novel. Because the novel's present events and characters merge with characters and events of the past, the novel's several plots, all of them women's, seem to be condensed and displaced. Rennie's operation, the grandmothers on the island of St. Agathe, the sexually violent men, the doctors, the various brutal beatings assume the resonance of recurrence rather than the thinness of singularity. As a result, the texture of the novel is peculiarly dense and the sense of buried information persistent.

The themes and images of the superficial stories of *Bodily Harm* allow for coherent literary interpretation; they satisfy demands for immediate analysis. The novel addresses itself to the nature of violence, to victimization, to women. The epigraph, which is from *Ways of Seeing*, insists that the reader pay attention to these themes: "A man's presence suggests what he is capable of doing to you or for you . . . . By contrast, a woman's presence . . . defines what can and cannot be done to her." Berger's aesthetic theories thematically and structurally resonate throughout the novel. He argues that "the entire art of the past has now become a political issue,"[3] that woman's self has been split in two, that "From earliest childhood she has been taught and persuaded to survey herself continually,"[4] that women in the western tradition "do to themselves what men do to them."[5] In *Bodily Harm*, female bodies are not whole but are presented in parts; they are constantly subjected to the male gaze and tend to be in competition against each other. Newspaper articles describe "those women they were always finding strewn about ravines or scattered here and there" (p. 23); Jake gets sexually excited by imagining intercourse as pretended rape; taxi drivers and policemen make constant sexual innuendoes; a deaf and dumb man on the island seems on the verge of attacking Rennie; the Toronto policemen's pornography museum displays women's bodies as maps of violence; men freely beat up their wives; attacked by the male guards in the prison, guards to whom she has been giving sexual favours in return for help, Lora is mutilated. Rennie's summary of the situation is inspired by her sexual involvement with Paul, whose boyish pride in his gun fills her with terror: "She's afraid of men and it's simple, it's rational, she's afraid of men because men are frightening" (p. 290).

The novel describes the sexual battlefield; it also comments on Canadian nationalism, a theme that crops up in everything Atwood writes. In the opening sections of *Survival*, Atwood discusses the ways in which victimization dominates the Canadian imagination and offers her thematic study as "a map of the territory."[6] She uses, as a dominating question, Northrop Frye's frequently quoted statement about Canadian literature, that the major question is "Where is here?"[7] The opening sentence of *Bodily Harm* seems designed to alert the reader to the novel's interest in Canadian nationalism and to certain of its political intentions. The refrain "the sweet Canadians" is reiterated by the shrunken Fisher King, Dr. Minnow, and carries different meanings at different points in the novel. Sometimes it implies the naïvety of Canadians, a theme given physical representation through the character of Rennie who, like the narrator of *Surfacing*, seems often to represent the country in which she lives. Like Canada, Rennie is perceived by many different characters as naïve, politically shallow (or at least uncommitted), obscurely old-fashioned. Toward the end of the novel, Paul says about her: "For one thing you're nice . . . . You'd rather be something else, tough or sharp or something like that, but you're nice, you can't help it. Naïve. But you think you have to prove you're not merely nice, so you get into things you shouldn't" (p. 150). At another point, an old American couple questions Rennie: "You're Canadian, aren't you? We always find the Canadians so nice, they're almost like members of the family. No crime rate to speak of at all. We always feel quite safe when we go up there" (p. 186).

By dramatizing Rennie's involvement in the political affairs of a country about which she knows so little, the novel ironically attacks Canadian simplicity. Far from keeping her safe, her ingenuousness is responsible for her ultimate victimization. Not even Canadians can exclude themselves from contemporary political violence; nor can they placidly castigate other countries for encouraging such violence. As Dr. Minnow says to Rennie: "'Everyone is in politics here, my friend . . . . All the time. Not like the sweet Canadians'" (p. 124). Later he says, "'There is no longer any place that is not of general interest . . . . The sweet Canadians have not learned this yet'" (p. 135). At the beginning of the novel Rennie emphasizes her own neutrality — "she needs it for her work . . . . Invisibility" (p. 15). But she is embarrassed by the Canadian official with his safari jacket and attempted neutrality. As she watches him following Dr. Minnow out of the room, she thinks of him allegorically as "the neutral-coloured Canadian" (p. 191). The text itself seems to represent the Canadian flag by reiterating, in different combinations, the colours red and white.

Like most contemporary fiction, *Bodily Harm* draws attention, self-consciously, to the act of writing, and dramatizes the creative process. Because the main character is a writer, the novel's spatial and temporal ambiguity evokes the actual space and time of the writing act. The small spaces and short moments of time that punctuate the novel like clockwork, and that suggest certain painful physical problems, resonate with the efforts of composition. At the beginning of the novel, masculine and feminine readers (and, by extension, writers) are contrasted. Rennie has been associated with the "Relationships" column of a magazine called *Pandora*; allusions to Pandora's box (thinly disguised here as "Lora's box") constantly keep before the reader the ways in which the myth denigrates women. Rennie presently works for a magazine called *Visor*, whose readership is predominantly male. As a writer, Rennie refuses to be taken seriously; she insists that she is interested in writing "trendy" articles. Her frivolity is misleading. Like every other stance in this novel, it is a defense. One of the poems from Atwood's *True Stories*, a collection published the same year as *Bodily Harm*, emphasizes the kind of shift experienced by Rennie, from believing in the existence of some "real story" (p. 64), superficial, easily digested, to her acknowledgement of the unreliability of narrative:

> The true story lies
> among the other stories
> ....
>
> The true story is vicious
> and multiple and untrue.[8]

The poem alerts the reader to the uncoding process necessary to a reading of *Bodily Harm*; to a reading of the textual body and therefore of the body of the novel's major female character. The themes that emerge from a superficial reading of the novel — the victimization of women, Canadian nationalism, writing — significantly connect with all of Atwood's work and with the works of countless other contemporary writers. Yet these themes do not in any immediately accessible form, explain the novel. They do not clarify its geography and history or situate the italicized voice or account for the peculiarly evasive shifts of perspective. They do not explain the emphasis on the unreliability of narrative or unmask the radical statement at the novel's core.

Each of the novel's ambiguities seems to document the symptoms of women's narrative dilemma. *Bodily Harm* is replete with secrets that pull against straightforward interpretation and cloud the novel's major themes. Rennie admits that "she no longer trusts surfaces" (p. 48) and announces that "almost nobody here is who they say they are at first" (p. 150). She fears a "faceless stranger." Her paranoia determines much of the narrative movement and is sometimes associated with specific characters (for example Paul) and at other times is merely a focus for free-floating anxiety. Rennie's stories dominate the text but, as the novel progresses, it becomes increasingly clear that her reading of events is erroneous. In some fundamental way, she is blind. She plays "Clue" poorly: "What has she done, she's not guilty, this is happening to her for no reason at all" (p. 286). The failure of reliable narration affects the reader. As I suggested about *Mrs. Blood*, narrative expectation necessarily falters in the woman's text. Readers do not have sufficient clues. This difficulty is dramatized in Atwood's novel. It is difficult to discover the space, the victim and the weapon of the crime that seems to be at the centre of Rennie's experience. Even the crime is unclear.

Most problematic is the time of the novel's action. As with many novels, this temporal ambiguity results partly from a reliance on recollection. In *Bodily Harm*, recollected stories interfere with the forward narrative movement and even break up the written page. Like the dismembered bodies, the text itself seems repeatedly torn apart. But temporal ambiguity is also contextually important. Early in the novel, Rennie admits that she has "stopped thinking in years" (p. 11). Indeed, as the novel progresses, it seems likely that she has stopped thinking in terms of time at all. Unable to assume a future ("'I'll tell you about it sometime,' he says, assuming the future; which is more than she can do" [p. 47], she admits: "There's the past, the present, the future: none of them will do" (p. 282). Time, always critical for the constructor of stories, disintegrates completely. The novel's opening sentence, with its apparently assured present tense, is a cover, a secret. Near the end, the sentence — "This is what will happen" (p. 293) — parallels the opening sentence — "This is how I got here" — and insists on temporal confusion: it stops the novel by casting the narrative into the future tense. Indeed, even the narrative closure that would be allowed by projected fantasy is questioned, for present, past and future continue to cross through each other: "She will never be rescued. She has already been rescued" (p. 301). Time is like the time of dreams or nightmares, like the nightmares described in Atwood's poem "Postcard":

> Time comes in waves here, a sickness, one
> day after the other rolling on;
> I move up, it's called
> awake, then down into the uneasy
> nights, but never
> forward.[9]

Vertical movement perplexes the novel throughout.

There is another ambiguity in *Bodily Harm*: the novel's space. It once again draws attention to the question asked of Canadian literature by Frye and Atwood: "Where is here?" The reader's attention to space is insisted on visually by repeated references to enclosed rooms that are being threatened or that reflect damage. The small apartment bedroom that contains the first of the novel's stories has been violated, a physical violation that is emphasized by Rennie's offer to show the investigating policemen her mastectomy scar. That violation is thematically repeated throughout the novel. The enclosed cabin of the plane Rennie takes to the island is connected with her damaged body: as she enters the cabin, "she's afraid to look down, she's afraid she'll see blood, leakage, her stuffing coming out" (p. 22). Later, a man breaks into Rennie's motel room in St. Antoine, "sliding himself into the bathroom like an anonymous letter" (p. 158). Lying in her room with her hands across her chest, Rennie listens to sounds from the next room; her eavesdropping is enforced by spatial constriction. The neighbouring couple's lovemaking combines torture and sex and the sado-masochistic ritual emphasized by a disembodied italicized cry — "*Oh please*" — a cry repeated in other places in the novel, an ambiguous fragment that leaves in doubt the identity of the speaker, the person being spoken to, and the situation and time of the utterance, is an important potential clue to the problems in deciphering the novel's puzzles. Other confined spaces — the cellar Rennie was locked into by her grandmother, the basement apartment described by Lora — condense into descriptions of boxes and into more pointed statements, such as Jake's assertion that women "should all be locked in cages" (p. 73).

Fear of enclosure invokes a death-like claustrophobia, which affects the novel's tone. That claustrophobia is dramatically present in the five-by-seven foot jail cell where Rennie and Lora are incarcerated during the insurrection on the island. The effect of the cell is so powerful that the reader is encouraged to make a more complicated interpretation of the meaning of the novel: that the stories that make up the text emerge from the cell's particular space. Such an interpretation accounts for the kind of story-telling that dominates *Bodily Harm* and for the temporal confusions that occur, the novel's virtually unpunctuated days. In the novel there is only one space, and the only protection against insanity is the creation of stories. The interpretation would also account for the thematic centrality of physical brutality — most often the suggestions of rape — and would explain the insistence on spatial metaphors that connect women's bodies and enclosures. The ambiguous italicized words are given terrifying power when we assume that the novel's confusions and false leads culminate with Rennie's physical crisis, which is brought on by seeing a man (Paul? the Prince of Peace? the deaf and dumb man? the faceless stranger?) tortured by the prison guards in the yard of the prison: "She has been turned inside out, there's no longer a *here* and a *there*. Rennie understands for the first time that this is not necessarily a place she will get out of, ever. She is not exempt. Nobody is exempt from anything" (p. 290). One of the novel's spatial limits is the prison cell, and one of its temporal limits is the day Lora is beaten. The novel's political violence is imaged in sexual attack; its failed narrative logic is imaged in the dismemberment of the female body. This condensation helps to account for Rennie's inability to separate "here" and "there," "inside" and "outside," and encourages at least one answer to the textual "Clue" game (which reminds us of the terrifying closeness between games and national and sexual politics): the guards in the prison with the penis-gun and the victim, Lora.

The disembodied voice of the novel, with its splits, its mysteries, its secrecy, remains insistent. "This is how I got here." The novel and its central character demand interpretation, need further stripping, become "a peeled snail,"[10] a "new kind of centerfold."[11] Other spaces come into focus. On the first page of the novel, Rennie sees her old Chinese neighbour raking the earth into "a raised oblong" (p. 11). Asked by Rennie what he dreams about, Paul answers, "a hole in the ground, with the earth that's been dug out" (p. 249). The assassinated Dr. Minnow lies in his coffin. The measurements of the jail cell assume different meanings and become the measurements of a grave. The novel becomes a matter of life and death, the game increasingly deadly. The reader is asked to imagine Rennie in a hospital room, another small space, a room where she undergoes an operation for breast cancer. So pervasive is this space in the themes and images of the novel that it also suggests a "here." The space assumes the novel's time and helps to account for the repetition of dreams, for the recurrence of the question, "What do you dream about?" and for the nightmarish confusions of the plot.

Rennie's stories, which are perhaps metaphors for women's stories in general, imply a slipping in and out of consciousness, mirrored by the events occurring in the operating room. All the events and images of the novel are displacements and condensations of her anxieties about the operation. Rennie thinks of her grandmother looking for her hands; the grandmother seems a projection of Rennie, a foremother whose fears of dismemberment foreshadow Rennie's. In one of her dreams, which apparently occurs at the Sunset Inn, Rennie dreams of gardens, of her mother who "can't take care of anything" (p. 115), of hummingbirds and of her grandmother. As she struggles to wake from the dream, Rennie is in "a long white cotton gown," although she insists she is not in a hospital. Like her grandmother, she is looking for her hands. Again she drifts into sleep and again struggles into consciousness: " . . . this time she's really awake. It's dawn, the noises are beginning, the mosquito netting hangs around her in the warm air like mist. She sees where she is, she's here, by herself, she's stranded in the future. She doesn't know how to get back" (p. 116). Combinations of waking and sleeping, of dreaming and experiencing, of sensory condensation and displacement disguise time and space. The anaesthetic, the mosquito netting, and the mist illustrate Rennie's confused senses and clouded eyes. Atwood's sign system implies another variation of the metaphoric game of "Clue": the doctor in the hospital room with the knife and the victim, Rennie.

Like the picture-puzzles of Freud's dream texts,[12] *Bodily Harm* creates perplexity by disguising time and space and by representing the same thoughts in a number of different ways. Lost gardens and grandmothers, which existed somewhere in the past, mingle with an indecipherable present and future. Toward the end of the novel, space and time become increasingly ambiguous and the characters condense, split and reform more frequently. From the jail cell, Rennie allows her thoughts to wander wildly; she wants an end to stories. We recall the opening oblong mound. She thinks of Paul; then of the doctor, Daniel; of Daniel's hands; of "Daniel . . . enclosed in a glass bubble," herself on the "outside looking in": "From here it's hard to believe that Daniel really exists" (p. 284). But the real focus of her attention is always her "nibbled flesh." She assures us that "nothing has happened to her yet, nobody has done anything to her, she is unharmed," then admits that "[S]he may be dying" (p. 284). The novel's dedication to Jennifer Rankin, 1941-1979, resonates. Hospital bed and jail cell reverberate. So does Rennie's obsession with her body. There is an insistent accumulation of clues: "Rennie opens her eyes. Nothing in here has changed. Directly above her, up on the high ceiling, some wasps are building a nest. . . . Pretend you're really here, she thinks. Now: what would you do?" (p. 284). Where is "here"? No passage precisely answers that question. Yet in the cell and in the hospital bed, both with their suggestions of the grave, Rennie needs to distance herself from her body, to pretend, to become a serious writer.

Such condensed images inevitably create a surrealistic, rather than a realistic, landscape. The hummingbirds in the dream of her grandmother, the wasps building their nest on the ceiling, the sounds of the air-conditioner in the hospital room, the drafts from open windows in Rennie's dreams, the ride in the airplane where "[T]here's too much air conditioning, wind from outer space blowing in through the small nozzles" (p. 301) merge into one image — something cold, humming somewhere above Rennie's head. Even the clothing of the novel assumes various meanings: the safari jacket worn by the Canadian-government official looks like a doctor's uniform; the uniforms of the stewardesses on the plane, and the waitresses at the Sunset Inn are similar to nurses' uniforms. Rennie almost always wears white: "a plain white cotton dress" (p. 59), a "white shirt and a wrap skirt, also white" (p. 203). The bed in which she sleeps with Paul has been "expertly made, hospital corners firmly tucked in" (p. 203). Rennie remembers a dream she had during her night with Paul; she describes "another man in bed with them; something white, a stocking or a gauze bandage, wrapped around his head" (p. 217).

The novel's male characters seem to blend with each other; the "faceless man" who troubles Rennie throughout seems to be the major actor in the drama. The mosquito netting around her bed merges with her description of crawling through "the grey folds of netting" (p. 173), her response to the anaesthetic given to her in the hospital, and it also merges with the threat of suffocation she describes just before escaping to St. Antoine: "Rennie closes her eyes. Something with enormous weight comes down on them" (p. 259). Hands dominate the bodily symbols in the text as they dominate during operations. Rennie's fantasies of leaving the jail cell correspond with a patient's leaving the hospital, not necessarily alive: "Rennie will be taken to a small room, painted apple green. On the wall there will be a calendar with a picture of a sunset on it. There will be a desk with a phone and some papers on it" (p. 293). Words recur in italics — "malignant," "massive involvement," "terminal," and a statement overheard at Dr. Minnow's funeral is also italicized: "What did she die of? Cancer, praise the lord." They combine to give, through the disembodied voice of the novel, political and bodily correspondence. Blood colours the text.

Like all of Atwood's work, *Bodily Harm* is deceptive and subversive. Although the stories told by Rennie superficially follow narrative logic and give the reader a plot, that plot is profoundly misleading. A number of questions need to be answered. What, for example, does the reader gain by deciphering the clues of *Bodily Harm*, by re-reading, by stripping down the layers of the text? What is gained by the political connections between jail rooms and hospital beds, between women and texts?

The title helps our search for an answer. This novel is predominantly concerned with bodies, most notably Rennie's. It is also concerned with harm, the symbol of which, on the body, is the mark of castration. Can we discover on a woman's body the marks that will allow us to read her story? For much of the novel, Rennie reveals herself as a thoroughly manipulated writer; she repeatedly emphasizes her triviality. But her body is to be imagined as potential material for inscription. After Daniel operates on her, he says: "Think of your life as a clean page. You can write whatever you like on it" (p. 84). Later, buying postcards to send home, Rennie recalls the conversation with Daniel and reflects that "[E]mpty is not the same as clean" (p. 85). She also remembers complaining to Jake: "Sometimes I feel like a blank sheet of paper.... For you to doodle on" (p. 105). She establishes a physical difference between phallic penetration and female passivity by wondering "what it was like to be able to throw yourself into another person, another body, a darkness like that. Women could not do it. Instead they had darkness thrown into them" (pp. 235-36). For Rennie, the pen is phallic, the page the female body.[13]

The traditional powerlessness of women's writing is attacked by Hélène Cixous in "The Laugh of the Medusa" when she insists that "woman must write her self: must write about women and bring women to writing, from which they have been driven as violently as from their bodies — for the same reasons, by the same law, with the same fatal goal. Woman must put herself into the text — as into the world and into history — by her own movement."[14] Cixous also writes: "Here they are, returning, arriving over and again, because the unconscious is impregnable. They have wandered around in circles *confined to the narrow room* in which they've been given a deadly brainwashing."[15] On one level, Atwood's novel ironically illustrates the harmful inscription of the female body that results from its confinement. Bodily harm is also described in "Torture":

> But power
> like this is not abstract, it's not concerned
> with politics and free will, it's beyond slogans
> and as for passion, this
> is its intricate denial.
> the knife that cuts lovers
> out of your flesh like tumours,
> leaving you breastless
> and without a name,
> flattened, bloodless, even your voice
> cauterized by too much pain.
>
> a flayed body untangled
> string by string and hung
> to the wall, an agonized banner
> displayed for the same reason
> flags are.[16]

The metaphoric relationship between the female body and Canada connects the politics of sexual power with the politics of colonial domination; like women, Canada is only now emerging from a "deadly brainwashing." Atwood seems to suggest that the brainwashing has interfered with Canada's history and her literature.

Up to a point, the novel appears to be an intricate analysis of female history, with constant allusions to the political history of Canada. It is also a meticulous record of the dismembering of the female body. Like the split space and time of the narrative, Rennie's divided consciousness suggests both a disrupted female history and a confused sense of the self. Early in the novel, she imagines "herself from the outside, as if she was a moving target in somebody else's binoculars" (p. 40), an object of the male gaze. Inside and outside dominate the novel; so, too, do conflicts between appearance and actuality, stereotypes and realistic characters, a woman's superficial exterior and the interior text of her self. Rennie struggles with repression: "Her real fear, irrational but a fear, is that the scar will come undone in the water, split open like a faulty zipper, and she will turn inside out" (p. 80). Throughout much of the novel, Rennie is physically revolted by contact, by the necessities of touching. Hands metonymically describe such contact, its terrifying insistence. Lora's hands threaten Rennie's boundaries, and the marred fingers are another sign of harm: "She doesn't like the sight of ravage, damage, the edge between inside and outside blurred like that" (p. 86).

Rennie's operation is a complex metaphor for a split in consciousness and for the repression that results:

> There's a line between being asleep and being awake which Rennie is finding harder and harder to cross. Now she's up near the ceiling, in the corner of a white room, beside the air-conditioning unit, which is giving out a steady hum. She can see everything, clear and sharp, under glass, her body is down there on the table, covered in green cloth, there are figures around her, in masks, they're in the middle of a performance, a procedure, an incision, but it's not skin-deep, it's the heart they're after, in there somewhere, squeezing away, a fist opening and closing around a ball of blood. (pp. 172-73)

The metaphor perhaps also imaginatively describes the split female text that often results because women writers have difficulty in representing the female self in fiction. Like all writers, Rennie needs to connect with her own heart if that opening and closing fist is not to be possessed by others.

Yet *Bodily Harm* is not, finally, a negative text. Rennie begins as the sort of woman who does not want to hate men but ends by recognizing her own marking under the sign of the father, a marking that results in her physical harm. She enters the world and assumes the rule of necessity: "She's afraid of men . . . because men are frightening" (p. 290). At the same time, a new sign begins to emerge. For women, it is the sign of the mother, the sign of creativity, of freedom, of flight. The novel describes the joining of the splits that have dominated texts by women. In a passage that, on one level, is yet another view of her experiences on the operating table, Rennie also imagines joining as a moment of sexual intercourse when her body, by being touched, expands and unifies:

> Nobody lives forever, who said you could? This much will have to do, this much is enough. She's open now, she's been opened, she's being drawn back down, she enters her body again and there's a moment of pain, incarnation, this may be only the body's desperation, a flare-up, a last clutch at the world before the long slide into final illness and death; but meanwhile she's solid after all, she's still here on the earth, she's grateful, he's touching her, she can still be touched. (p. 204)

This particular joining, this moment before death is not enough. Rennie has not been fully reconstituted; she is not a unified character and has not gained control of the pen. She has to be taken farther. She must probe deeper, be opened more; she has to give birth to a new self. In a powerful doubling toward the end of the novel, Lora and Rennie become one:

> . . . she turns Lora over, her body is limp and thick, a dead weight . . . . She's holding Lora's left hand, between both of her own, perfectly still, nothing is moving, and yet she knows she is pulling on the hand, as hard as she can, there's an invisible hole in the air, Lora is on the other side of it and she has to pull her through, she's gritting her teeth with the effort." (pp. 298-99)

Hands have assumed religious connotations. Only through such laying on of hands, such joining with another woman, can the female character be represented accurately in fiction. Rennie has earned her name, has been reborn.

A three-part movement seems, then, to define the production of the female text: a recognition of the silence imposed on the female body by patriarchal rules; an illustration of the male writer's use of the female body as page; and a final enlightenment that gives birth to an independent and complete woman. When this birth occurs, the female text is ready to be written. Only then, as Cixous suggests, can women "take pleasure in jumbling the order of space, in disorienting it, in changing around the furniture, dislocating things and values, breaking them all up, emptying structures." Flying becomes "woman's gesture — flying in language and making it fly."[17] When Rennie describes flight at the end of the novel, she indicates possession of herself, a possession that also represents the reconstituted female character. Instead of superficially inscribing a character who is blank, a page, the narrator can dig deeper, reform, make whole. The character becomes a serious writer, and therefore subversive.

According to Marks and de Courtivron, the new French feminisms "poke fun at the male erection, the male preoccupation with getting it up, keeping it up, and the ways in which the life and death of the penis are projected into other aspects of culture: in the need for immortality and posterity, in the fear of death, in the centralized organization of political systems, in the impossibility of living in the here and now."[18] Atwood's text does "poke fun" at the penis, with a humour that is very black; the knowledge of the depths of its destructiveness is paramount. Throughout, the game of "Clue" implies a conjunction between play and torture, between fun and terror. Yet Rennie can imagine extricating herself from the system, even from its damage to her own writing. To pronounce herself is to deny the victimization suggested by another configuration of the game: men with the pen in the text and the victim the female character. Rennie learns to question "the centralized organization of political systems," to live in "the here and now." Luce Irigaray insists that woman's dominant pleasure is touching rather than seeing.[19] Rennie learns the importance of touching: "She can feel the shape of a hand in hers, both of hers, there but not there, like the afterglow of a match that's gone out. It will always be there now" (p. 300).

Spatial and temporal alienation certainly dominates much of Atwood's novel, and its landscape, as Rennie emphasizes, is insistently surreal. To Annis Pratt, such alienation intimates structural necessities. Pratt writes: "Since women are alienated from time and space, their plots take on cyclical, rather than linear, form and their houses and landscapes surreal properties."[20] Yet *Bodily Harm*, a moving dramatization of the female body-text, arrives somewhere. Although the time and the space of the novel are limited (a confined area, one day), the reader is shown a woman becoming her own mother, giving birth to herself. Victimized, fragmented, dismembered, the female body has regrouped and become its own subject. In a fundamental way, the title, "bodily harm," has been cancelled and the definition of femininity under patriarchy refused. Not surprisingly, "For the first time in her life," Rennie "can't think of a title" (p. 301). She and the narrator have become politically subversive; they have begun work on a new language directed towards the continuation of life on our planet.

Chapter Three

Delusion and Dream in Thomas' *Blown Figures*

At the very least half our dreams (unless I greatly err) are nothing else than myths formed by unconscious cerebration . . . . Have we not here, then, evidence that there is a real law of the human mind causing us constantly to compose ingenious fables explanatory of the phenomenon around us, — a law which only sinks into abeyance in the waking hours of persons in whom the reason has been highly cultivated, but which resumes its sway even over well-tutored brains when they sleep?

                  — FRANCES POWER COBBE
                    "Darwinism in Morals and
                    Other Essays"

Surrounded as she is by images of disease, traditions of disease, and invitations both to disease and to dis-ease, it is no wonder that the woman writer has held many mirrors up to the discomforts of her own nature.

                  — SANDRA GILBERT and SUSAN
                    GUBAR
                    "The Madwoman in the Attic"

In their coding of *Mrs. Blood* and *Bodily Harm*, Audrey Thomas and Margaret Atwood have created central characters whose split selves allow conventional female representation and subversive aggression. Such splitting suggests schizophrenia. *Blown Figures* focuses on madness compulsively, using it thematically to explode character boundaries (as, for example, it is used in *King Lear* or in *Crime and Punishment*). Like Faulkner, Thomas makes use of the liberating effects of madness on the structures of traditional narrative. Thus the fragmented text of *Blown Figures* visually and contextually mirrors the fragmented vision of its central character; the sporadic excerpts from journals, magazines and newspapers that punctuate the novel remind the reader of the madness of the outer world. Thomas uses fictional madness as subversively as did Ken Kesey in *One Flew Over the Cuckoo's Nest*, Joan Didion in *Play It as It Lays*, and John Barth in *The End of the Road*, novels that dramatize the world as a huge asylum in which, reflecting the psychological work of R.D. Laing, the writers situate characters whose apparent madness signifies their sanity. By so doing, they condemn a society that drastically restricts individual freedom.

It is specifically with this subversion of society that I am concerned, with Thomas' use of female madness as reflection and healer of cultural ills. In *Women and Madness*, Phyllis Chesler addresses the gender-specificity of woman's madness. She argues that, by bearing children, women enact "a blood sacrifice for the perpetuation of the species" and mark themselves, because of their biology, as symbols of self-sacrifice. Denied cultural supremacy, according to Chesler, "some women are driven mad," their madness apparently "an intense experience of female biological, sexual and cultural castration, and a doomed search for potency." This search "often involves 'delusions' or displays of physical aggression, grandeur, sexuality, and emotionality — all traits which would probably be more acceptable in female dominated cultures."[1] In patriarchal cultures, and in much male writing, female madness seems particularly terrifying, partly because it implies an independent female power that stimulates, in quite negative ways, masculine fantasy.

Although more concerned with the metaphoric implications of women's madness, Barbara Rigney, like Chesler, situates myths about female madness within social structures. In *Madness and Sexual Politics in the Feminist Novel*,[2] she presents a series of by-now well-known arguments about psychiatry's determinations of women's madness: that Freudian theory is largely responsible for gender limitations in studies of women; that contemporary psychiatrists and analysts still use, as the female status quo, the restrictive figure of the housewife;

that, far from being idiosyncratic, women's madness represents a psychological problem, and also a major cultural problem. Rigney claims kinship with Laing. Although Laing is not a feminist, he shares feminist concerns about the psychic damage wrought by the traditional nuclear family. Such gender-specificity is elaborated in increasingly theoretical ways in *The Madwoman in the Attic*, where the authors convincingly delineate "literary works that are in some sense palimpsestic, works whose surface designs conceal or obscure deeper, less accessible (and less socially acceptable) levels of meaning."[3] The less accessible meanings, they suggest, are contained in projections of the woman writer's own despair, projections that result in the creation of "melodramatic characters who act out the subversive impulses every woman inevitably feels when she contemplates the 'deep-rooted' evils of patriarchy."[4] In much fiction by women, the madwoman is the author's double rather than her foil; her own story rather than the culturally accepted story.

Gilbert and Gubar, then, suggest a positive as well as a negative use of madness. The authenticity and authority of women writers become closely bound up with the projected madwomen of their narratives. For Rigney, also, the peculiar ambivalence of women's split images heralds positive change. At the conclusion of her study, she emphasizes that, in many of the feminist novels she has investigated, "the doppelgänger serves an essentially positive function and is therefore a departure from the figure of the demonic double traditional in psychological works of fiction by male writers like Dostoevsky or Poe."[5] Forced to recognize her double, the female character often discovers in madness a cleansing that allows her to face the actual madness of her culture more openly, to "recognize and reject not only the pathology of social and sexual arrangements but her own participation in these arrangements as well."[6] Such doublings occur between Mrs. Thing and Mrs. Blood in *Mrs. Blood*; between Rennie and Lora in *Bodily Harm*; between Isobel and Delilah in *Blown Figures*; between Jean Price and her sister, Isa, in "Its Image on the Mirror"; between Pandora and her mother in *Pandora*; between several of the female friends of the narrators of Munro's stories; between Harriet Ross and Marshallene in *Lunatic Villas*. These doublings elaborate the healing effects as posited by Rigney and by Gilbert and Gubar. When women confront their mirror-selves, when they create characters who have the "power to reach toward the woman trapped on the other side of the mirror/text and help her to climb out,"[7] they move toward literary autonomy.

Thus, women's delusions and dreams betray failure. But interpreted from a female perspective, they also imply narrative control and power. The "moon seen from the moon / is a different thing." Freud persuasively indicates, in the study that gives its name to the title of this essay, a study about delusion and dream in Jensen's short story, "Gradiva," that the story's narrative pattern is constructed from fantasies that precede delusions, and that those delusions stand in the place of repressed memories. The delusions are allowed to enter consciousness only as distorted representations because of the untiring watchfulness of the censor. Thomas' *Blown Figures* reveals censorship, repression, and distortion. As in a dream, condensation and displacement signal a repression that the narrative presents in a returned and altered form. However where Freud ignores his writer's gender and treats the central character as representative of all humanity rather than as masculine, Thomas repeatedly draws attention to gender. And indeed, using gender as a criterion, the reader of "Gradiva" realizes that Norbert Hanhold's delusions are narratively dominated by male desire, by fetishism, while those in *Blown Figures* seem profoundly feminine. The major signifier of the male text is the phallus. But Thomas's novel instead centres the female body, the womb. From this space, the narrative emerges and elucidates female creativity.

Such an emphasis is not surprising. *Mrs. Blood* has already charted the territory and defined the limits by demonstrating the ways in which Isobel turns several months of struggle, which constitute the development and eventual miscarriage of a third child, into narrative. *Blown Figures* also concentrates on the womb, on making public what is usually silent, on conflating inner and outer. Both novels reveal the female body as an acting subject, the controller and elaborator of an experience that is idiosyncratically female. The narrator presumes that the episodes will be seen through female eyes and heard through female ears, and therefore traditional cultural assumptions are necessarily altered. For example, in *Mrs. Blood*, such alterations affect the Grail legends, the Bible, the countless masterpieces of western literature devoted to the development of male experience. Equally important, Thomas' novels also alter the psychoanalytic assumption of male experience as metaphorically central to the narrative patterns that constitute the psyche.

At the same time, the two Thomas novels psychologically complement each other. The first constructs and elaborates the death of a baby; the second illustrates a delusory return to Africa, a search for the stillborn child. The first concentrates on the physical changes of pregnancy; the second displays the psychic trauma of miscarriage. The first delineates a wasteland where the living springs dry and the flowers become parched; the second agonizingly attempts to effect a rebirth. In *Blown Figures*, Isobel struggles more intensely with guilt and retribution, with the return of the repressed and distorted memory that lies buried in both novels — the abortion that is screened by the narrative of the miscarriage. *Blown Figures* also more intensely presents female writing, painful writing, writing from silence and darkness. It elaborates a number of basic tenets in current feminist theory.

As well, the long list of women to whom this novel is dedicated establishes an increasingly female perspective. As in Monique Wittig's *Les Guérillères*, the list of female names moves toward creating a dominantly female universe. Within this universe, Isobel functions as a representative everywoman, a woman who bleeds for us all and for whom the narrator, like the analyst, attempts to forge new narrative links that will reinstate action into a traditional and emphatically static plot. A case study, this plot is constructed from fantasies that people Isobel's brain. It begins on board the HMS *Plyades*. Isobel is standing beside a woman "who held a screaming baby in her arms" (p. 12); her fixation on babies already circumscribes her experience and assigns meaning to the delusions and dreams of the text. The fictive world is carefully established. Isobel leaves her husband, Jason, and her two children, Mary and Nicholas, in Canada and embarks on a voyage to Africa, the scene of the miscarriage described in *Mrs. Blood*. The apparent object of her return journey is to find this lost child. The story is unavoidably fraught with anxiety. Even before the boat leaves shore, Isobel panics:

> "GET OFF GET OFF booms the big bass drum
> GET OFF GET OFF GET OFF
> It wasn't too late. The gangplank still connected her with the shore." (pp. 13-14)

When the boat embarks, her past threatens to rise up and engulf her. The boat's tug looks as if it were sitting in "one of her father's old rubber overshoes" (p. 40). Like Norbert Hanhold, Isobel endows the past with life. As Freud suggests about Hanhold, she becomes her own hero. This transformation begins the journey that unravels her depression and gives a certain structure to her haphazard nightmares.

The people and events on the boat give depth to Isobel's developing narrative. Like the material of dreams, they represent the phenomena of her mind. The young Dutch boy with the pink-and-white skin and the lisp reminds her of a baby. Almost immediately, she sleeps with him. The ocean crossing is filled with sexual allusions and with descriptions of erotic play, a dramatic condensation of the act and results of copulation. Various other characters also become part of the *mise en scène*, characters who wander in and out of the narrative, temporarily joining their histories with Isobel's and, symbolically, becoming representations of her own neuroses. For example, when the Dutch boy leaves the ship, she acknowledges that "each would fix in a brief memory, like a single snapshot, in the life of the other" (p. 105). The setting also reflects Isobel's anxiety. At Dakar, where the group briefly disembarks, the heat, the beggars and the souvenir sellers threaten to stifle her. When she returns to the ship, she is enclosed with a couple travelling with a four-week-old baby. The ship becomes becalmed and other episodes of escape — the dinner at the home of two members of the British Council, the visit to the beach — increase narrative suspense and illustrate the paralysis and suffocation that function as symptoms of Isobel's hysterical state.

With the same tenuous spatial and temporal connections that are employed in dreams, Isobel finds herself on a train. She is stifled and close to suffocation because "[T]he fan in the ceiling did not work and the sweat ran down her fingers" (p. 137). Trying to catch air, she leans out of the window. Baobab trees cast their ghostly reflections as the train speeds past. In the next compartment, an African man prays. The train passes into Mali, where the trees give way to "striated rock and heat and light" (p. 140). At one of the stops, Isobel is taken off the train by a uniformed soldier. This thematic concern with retribution heralds another of Isobel's psychic fixations. She has not paid enough money for the trip and her traveller's cheques will not be accepted. Finally, a stranger, an English-speaking man, inexplicably pays her fine and she is released. At midnight, she leaves the station, finds a taxi and goes to the Grand Hotel. In an evocative extension of the biblical episode, there are no rooms. Rescued once again by a man, Isobel is offered a room.

Time jumps. Isobel is now sitting in a café, *La Croix du Sud*, with a young woman, Delilah Rosenberg, and a black man, Hyacinth, both suggestively named. Her delusions gather narrative force. Delilah regales her with stories of her own various abortions and confesses that she is once again pregnant. Episodes of debt and payment become more persistent. The men who have helped her hover around; one offers further help, the other elicits sexual payment. Repeatedly, Isobel and Delilah have to wait, once for the banks to open in the morning, and then for the taxi that is to take them across the border. The waiting implies paralysis. When the taxi arrives, it moves sluggishly and erratically; it is stopped by the police and then by the driver's girlfriend. Crowded by the other passengers, Isobel again imagines suffocation. At their destination, a mission, Isobel's anxiety is compounded by news of the death of a young motorcyclist, by the sound of drums and by political references to the conflict between French and English Canada. A nun lies dying of cancer. Paranoia spreads. When Isobel and Delilah leave, they act out myth and legend as they wait for a ferry to take them across the river. The landscape, psychologically overdetermined, appears drained of colour: it "was somehow depressing, almost surreal. Tops of dead trees stuck out of the water like withered drowned arms, the flesh collapsed and wrinkled; the water, like the trees, was a strange grey color" (p. 461). Condensations and displacements multiply.

When the boat finally arrives, the women are not able to board it. Affected by the sun and her pregnancy, Delilah becomes ill. Although Isobel would like, contemptuously, to abandon Delilah to her fate, she remains with the pregnant woman through the ferry journey and onto the bus that will take them into the jungle. But their journey is again halted when Delilah miscarries. Narratively, the event frees Isobel from her connection with Delilah. But it also suggests the presence of repressed material and its increasing exposure. In a nightmarish frenzy, Isobel rushes from the hotel and hails a taxi that takes her to the border of the old town. It is a symbolic ride; she recognizes that "[D]eath is all around her" (p. 494). After walking some distance, she is picked up by a lorry, hauntingly marked by the painted words, "TWO SHADOWS." The ghostly lorry carries her into the depths of the forest. Amidst a conglomeration of bizarre and surreal images concentrated on the ritual enactment of guilt and retribution, the consecutive narrative of *Blown Figures* ends.

Because of its bizarre themes and images, and because of its spatial and chronological peculiarities, the plot of *Blown Figures* disguises and explicates Isobel's psychological condition. Its time is only superficially chronological, its episodes only superficially connected. As in dreams, the journey that moves Isobel from the new world to the heart of Africa is laden with meaning. The reader is shown an obsession. But while revealing the archaeology of delusions and dreams, *Blown Figures* connects them not with sexual fetishism but with the womb. Episodes relating to babies are repeated throughout, as are images of orality, of enclosure, of dependency. Recurring references to abortions and to miscarriages, to religious suffering and atonement and to symbolically structured landscapes illustrate the return of heavily repressed material. Like a mirror image, Isobel's journey reflects, altered, her miscarriage and abortion and employs chains of association that assist her in structuring a reasonably connected narrative. This narrative also reflects her physical condition. Throughout, she suffers from the pervasive heat, imagines suffocating in various enclosed places and becomes inured to apparently pointless waiting. Like "Gradiva," *Blown Figures* offers a fairly coherent plot and peoples its development with different characters who represent a series of delusions. However, the obsessions of the two stories' central characters differ. Hanhold is obsessed with "a complete female figure in the act of walking,"[8] Isobel with a dead baby, an "elaborate parody of birth" (p. 177). More important, her story, as Gubar suggests about Mansfield's "Prelude," is "about the move from imagining the womb as a store, a cavity, a hump, a riddle, or a bleeding wound to imagining the womb as the transformative matrix of primordial change."[9] Isobel's narrative is therapeutic; it involves the renaming of images and the altering of conventional codes.

A complicated intertextuality opens up and elaborates the central character's psychic condition. The intrusions into this novel of prior texts, specifically male texts, imply irony. Situated in a patriarchal culture, the narrator and her main character find it necessary to use known structures and forms even though they have difficulty fitting their stories to the forms. For example, the wasteland myth, which Thomas used in *Mrs. Blood*, appears in *Blown Figures*, but with a considerably different effect. In *Blown Figures*, the heroic journeyer attempts to exhaust the traditional myth in order to establish a female perspective on the story: "all the fields of millet and ground-nuts, all the lush green-ness would turn brown and cracked.... She felt that whatever she had to do she must finish it before the land dried up" (p. 217). Evil makes the crops fail and the women abort; vultures hover over decomposing corpses. As the novel nears its conclusion, Isobel comes to a grove that writhes with snakes and that nurtures rats. It also drips with rain and, as in T. S. Eliot's *The Waste Land*, the wind blows. All the trees of the forest are shaken. But in the grove, the hope for the healing of the land seems contained in the female body. The egg ceremonies that conclude Isobel's journey divert attention from the injured penis and the victorious phallus; we focus on an earlier time of female dominance.

Greek myths also reverberate throughout, carefully reconstructed to emphasize the potential of a woman's body. Isobel dreams of water "covered with spots of blood," an evocation of the river Charon where "[O]n the other bank her child held out his arms to her" (p. 169). The spots are menstrual blood, symbol of female reproduction. Homer's *Odyssey* governs many of the images and contributes to the structure. Like the *Odyssey*, the novel contains twenty-four sections; as well, variations on some of the *Odyssey*'s central incidents appear in Isobel's journey, where they are inverted to accommodate a female traveller. The Dutch boy sexually rejuvenates her, just as Calypso does Odysseus;

Miss Miller, like Athene, functions as an omniscient ear; rivers, the open sea and gardens proliferate. Once, looking into a mirror, Isobel sees "a man with one eye blind and whitely translucent" (p. 163). References to pigs recall the Circe episode. Seen through Circe's eyes, however, the focus alters, shifts into what the poet, in Atwood's Circe poems, calls "the story that counts,"[10] the story of the land, of the future, of procreation, of love. The souls of the dead, the shades, wander in and out of the narrative, reminding us of the compulsory epic journey to the underworld, although it is not to receive her father's blessing that Isobel travels. Her journey is a return, an odyssey back to a lost member of the family, the dead baby. The epic resonance that appealed to Hanhold and allowed him to imagine himself as "the greatest battle hero of antiquity,"[11] or at least as Hermes "starting out upon the journey to conduct a departed soul to Hades,"[12] embues Isobel with a different aura. She undertakes the journey to exorcise her own demons.

Other stories culturally extend the novel and encourage a dialogue of literary associations. Without these associations, the retelling of well-known stories from new perspectives lacks resonance for the reader. For example, *Alice in Wonderland* and *Through the Looking-Glass* participate in *Blown Figure*'s structure and imagery, sometimes by direct reference, sometimes by allusion. Again, the twenty-four-chapter format reverberates with meaning. So, too, does Isobel's pervasive attention to food and drink, an attention that emphasizes her introversion, her concern with the inside of her body and with the changing shapes of pregnancy. References to rabbits and cats recall Carroll's work, as do repeated allusions to decapitation. The Red Queen becomes one of the narrative's characters. Madness pervades the universe of the novel. Quotations from Carroll's work appear throughout. Sometimes Isobel imagines herself, like Alice, on the other side of the mirror, where she hears the voices of the White Queen and the playing-card soldiers. She questions her own reality. In distorted forms, eggs, serpents, lions, frogs, flowers and insects, duplicate Alice's dream universe. At the end of the novel, the sound of drums and the sudden materialization of a court repeat Alice's fantasies. The emphases on a world not seen by others, on ambiguous body boundaries and on syllogistic reasoning give superficial formal coherence to Isobel's chaotic anxieties.

So, too, do allusions to Conrad's *Heart of Darkness*. Like Kurtz's Intended, Jason (Isobel's husband) waits at home while Isobel penetrates deeper and deeper into the heart of Africa's darkness. Like Marlow, the narrator records the journey. She fears contamination: "That is the trouble now. How to rescue Isobel without touching her, without becoming oneself an Isobel" (p. 201). Allusions to cannibalism, to dismemberment (particularly decapitation), to necrophilia, to bizarre religious rites illustrate Isobel's nightmares. Even the physical symptoms of her suffering recall the stifling physical intensity of *Heart of Darkness*, the sultry jungle with its central human body: "Sometimes she felt very small inside her body, a prisoner. Ran up and down the red-hung corridors, beat at the ivory gates, peered helplessly through the round windows" (p. 32). Marlow's phrase — "we live as we dream — alone,"[13] dominates his narrative, emphasizing human isolation and indetermination. Isobel also exists in a dream state. She is alone. Horror awaits her. The involved narrator discloses a narrative of psychological stripping, a trip down a river toward some buried repression where, as Sir Thomas Browne writes, we discover that "we have all Africa and her prodigies / Within us."[14]

Such references certainly extend the meaning of *Blown Figures*, mainly because they make Isobel's idiosyncratic journey more universal. At the same time, as in "Gradiva," certain psychological needs dictate the choice of referents. On Isobel's psychic voyage to Africa, what has been repressed returns. Her voyage gains structure from the allusions to epics; the symptoms that signal her delusions are given public articulation. Her journey has been made before. At the same time, the texts Thomas has chosen function ironically. Odysseus' journey, like Marlow's and Kurtz's, is an archetypal male journey that gives rise to specific kinds of narrative patterns. In *Blown Figures*, the patterns have been cleverly translated into female patterns. For example, the battles and murders that constitute the crucial moments of male-epic narrative occasion the spilling of blood. In *Blown Figures*, blood assumes redeeming generative qualities that alter the structure of events. Isobel's journey is not marked by destructive crisis. Rather, she learns to celebrate the female cycle, the woman's ability to reconstitute life. Even Carroll's stories are translated into realistic terms. Pregnant women do change size. Eggs and holes figure prominently in women's lives, where they are perceived physically rather than fantastically. *Blown Figures* insists on certain cultural revisions that radically alter a phallocentric view of the universe.

Such claims cannot be made casually; they are as subversive as the female images that inform the various themes and that give resonance to the dreams and delusions of the text. The novel's opening shows the female body as progenitor of human life: "Cripples, one-eyed people, pregnant women: we are all the children of eggs, Miss Miller, we are all the children of eggs" (p. 11). Literal allusions to eggs — such as the plates of eggs served on the boat — at times connote female nurturing; at other times, they remind us of destruction and death: "Les oeufs éclosent dans l'intestin et y atteignent leur plein développment. La femelle se dirige ensuite, par le gros intestin, vers l'extérieur où elle pond ses oeufs et provoque de pénibles démangeaisons" (p. 224). The tension between creation and destruction is given peculiarly female significance because it focusses on birth, the difference between bearing a dead and a living child. War and physical confrontation sink into the background as life's major drama is ritualized. Ceremonies for the disposal of dead babies (to prevent their haunting the family) and for purifying the mother punctuate the text. At the end, Isobel imagines herself standing, with an egg in each hand, in the heart of the forest while a priest ceremoniously breaks an egg over her head. In *Blown Figures*, the egg (exemplified even in the shape of the female body) comes to symbolize the erotic survival of the universe: "Love is both everything and nothing, the egg, the little 'oh,' the circle, the sun, the moon, l'oeuf: all" (p. 401).

At the same time, enclosed spaces, such as an ovoid shape, constrict movement and produce anxiety. Burial, for example, occupies Isobel's mind. She recalls reading about a man so fat he had to be buried in a piano case, and she quotes an argument for burial without a coffin, "the Mohammedan way" (p. 53). The cabin of the boat is small, a tight enclosure. She remembers a conversation with an analyst; she was attempting to pinpoint her constant anxiety: "'I'm afraid all the time. Of everything.' 'Not everything surely?' Fatuous smile. 'Nearly everything. Transportation especially. And things that shut you in. Cars. Elevators. Airplanes. Especially airplanes'" (p. 20). Modes of transportation — taxis, buses, cars — evocatively emphasize Isobel's struggle between feelings of emptiness and fullness, constriction and freedom. Hotel rooms are stiflingly hot. Small containers also figure prominently. Isobel recalls that her grandfather had a "ship in a bottle, a paperweight with a picture of the Coliseum inside it" (p. 285). In a bizarre but pointed fantasy, she conjures up a man with a Gladstone bag filled with babies.

The femininity of the text is also reflected in the colours of the story. Red recurs. The opening scene suggests a specific inner space from which the vividly narrated delusions emerge. With her red hair flying, Isobel looks at the people who are waiting for the boat to leave. She sees a red-cheeked man below; a magenta streamer flies in the breeze. As the journey begins, she remembers a bright-red blanket, touched-up photos of virgins with reddened lips and cheeks; she imagines herself and the Dutch boy, scarlet from the lights, dancing together and thinks about the Red Queen in Alice in Wonderland. She also recalls a train ride she took with Jason. The seats of the train were covered with cracked red leather. Dream like, this memory blends with a moment that seems to occur in the present: soldiers enter the train on which Isobel is travelling in Africa and remove her. She clutches a red washcloth. Toward the end of the novel, she gets into a taxi. The driver wears a red cloth around his arm, a sign that someone has died. Even the earth turns red: "The borders of the avenue to the grove were planted with red lilies. The sky was blue. The priest's wives . . . were picturesquely dressed in white calico. The earth was rusty red, the colour of dried blood" (p. 523). Similar motifs are everywhere. They make up a way of seeing that informs even Isobel's dreams: a corpse clothed only in a red fez; flamingoes; red ants; a scarlet umbrella like Joseph's many-coloured coat; a cherry-coloured coat Isobel once owned; the evocative Scarlet Letter; a vermillion medicine Isobel takes to rid herself of worms; Delilah's red leotard; red traffic lights; a red butterfly that alights on Isobel's arm as she moves into the forest; red snakes hissing and hanging out of the trees; the coagulated red mud that sticks to Isobel's legs as she gets closer to the grove where she ends her journey.

The references to red clearly connote the centrality of blood in Isobel's delusions. *Blown Figures* concentrates on the blood of menstruation, the blood of childbirth, the loss of blood that signals miscarriage: women's blood. And, because they screen repression, many of the allusions are destructive. Haunted, Isobel recalls a ghastly vision of everyone she has ever known — husband, lovers, children, parents — "dangling upside down from great black meat hooks, their throats slashed, their mouths open in a silent collective scream. There was a thick, fishy smell of drying blood" (p. 29). She remembers taking her two children to the university farm, where they select a pig to be killed. The sound of the slaughter echoes in her ears. Displacing the sound, she feels "the red hot blood pour from her divided throat" (p. 139). She also recalls the miscarried baby and the doctor's voice turned into blood, liquid and arterial. Her memories of the hospital and of the nurses and doctors from her earlier life in Africa keep pushing into the chronological narrative. They slow it down, divert it, draw attention to some central wound.

Sexually charged descriptions of Isobel and the fantasized Dutch boy give psychological energy to Isobel's repressions, and allow them a dynamic return. In her role as voyeur, the narrator describes her characters' mythic love-making; she emphasizes its bloody imagery. With the casual shifts in a body's boundaries common to dreams, the Dutch boy transmogrifies into a bird whose beak Isobel attempts to disentangle from her neck. In a peculiarly vivid image, his red feathers merge with her red hair; when she looks into his face, she understands that he is blind. Then "her breasts began to bleed" (p. 338). Descriptions of perverse intercourse with the devil are marked with blood: Isobel imagines herself reaching between her thighs and wiping her menstrual blood on the devil's forehead. The nurturing maternal milk and the teeming belly are inverted; they become suggestively destructive and dangerous. Isobel's psychic agony encompasses such archetypal dilemmas. And the novel's cinematic effects emphasize Isobel's coloured experiences. Beneath recollections of the miscarriage, of the birth of her two living children, of her marriage to Jason, lies the ghost of an aborted foetus conceived with her lover, Richard. (The name repeatedly erupts from some unclear narrative space at the end of *Mrs. Blood.*) Isobel's repressed memory gives energy to the delusions and dreams that constitute the text of *Blown Figures* and returns in the fantasies of blood and violence described throughout: "The carnival was over, the child had been taken away in a silver basin, the great livery placenta thrust aside into a bucket. The woman who had killed the child lay quiet in a pool of her own life's blood" (p. 177). Isobel's attempt to repress the memory betrays itself in all the narrative levels.

Her repression results in acute physical symptoms. The novel is filled with references to disease, to female ailments and, in more bizarre extensions, to dismemberment, to decapitation, to cannibalism. The Terminal Hotel in London, mentioned at the beginning of the novel, like the repetition of the word "terminal" in *Bodily Harm*, creates foreboding. Isobel suffers from insomnia. While the rest of her family sleeps, she entertains visions of witches playing football; the balls are really heads. The wife of the mining engineer on the boat to Africa is "missing something" (p. 67), and has to carry around a little sack. In Dakar, sellers offer shrunken heads. Isobel describes an episode in which she and a friend were frightened by two grinning men in a taxi: "'where might you have ended up?' she asks herself. 'A headless torso in one of Harry's True Detective magazines? . . . . Your head and bright hair would have been buried elsewhere in a feed sack'" (pp. 146-47). Her heart aches like an abscessed tooth and her body constantly fights against the worms that infest it. Even the nursery rhymes she remembers, which constitute a kind of recitative throughout the novel, echo her obsessions: "Here comes a candle to light your bed. Here comes a chopper to chop off your head" (p. 248). A recipe for cooking a calf's head instructs the cook to "Soak the quarters about six hours in cold water to extract the blood" (p. 85). Like Atwood's Rennie, Isobel longs to be rescued from such nightmarish imaginings, to become part of a more easily interpretable narrative. She describes the same stories as Rennie does, of waiting in a dentist's chair or, strapped to the seat, in a highjacked airplane. Such stories locate and situate an anxiety that otherwise seems uncontainable.

Allusions to cannibalism combine anxiety and guilt: "I ALWAYS LIKE AN ARM WHEN SHARING" (p. 380). The reader is given information about African ants who, when they are starving, eat their own excrement. Personified animals suddenly metamorphose into food: "When done, transfer Master Piglet to a large hot platter" (p. 382). In a letter printed in an Ann Landers' type of column for the lovelorn, a young African man explains that his girlfriend's parents are cannibals. Like Conrad's Marlow, who looks at the faces of the crew taking him down the river towards Kurtz, this young man fears that these people will eat him, "particularly as I am fat and healthy" (p. 421). Toward the end of the novel, Isobel imagines herself in a courtroom similar to the one inhabited by Alice: "Isobel placed herself at the sinner's dock and confessed she was a witch. 'I ate the child in my womb,' she said. 'Since then I have never been happy'" (p. 518). Images of cannibalism multiply as the novel jerkily concludes: "I myself, Miss Miller, ate the victim's foot"; "She cooked the faeces of her sister's child"; "I shall die, Miss Miller, and you will eat me and my children"; "After we cook the flesh we sing the snakes' song . . . SHE EATS GRAND PEOPLE" (pp. 540-43).

In her study of Henry James' "The Turn of the Screw," Shoshana Felman illustrates the interpretive strategies psychoanalysis brings to narratives: "In telling at once of transference and through transference, the story acts as a repetitive border-crossing, as a constant shuttle between opposed domains: speech and silence, life and death, inside and outside, consciousness and the unconscious, sleep and wakefulness."[15] The reading of *Blown Figures* illustrates, in general ways, just such transferences as Felman describes, situating the landscape and the journey of its major character on exactly the same borders that seem to operate in "The Turn of the Screw." Thomas' text also buries the crime ("a child is being beaten")[16] and invites the reader's uncovering of its meaning.

But *Blown Figures* is more subversive than a traditional psychoanalytic reading allows it to be. The novel's various narratives are given different meanings, depending on whether they are told from Isobel's or from the narrator's point of view. Many sexual images and structures seem, from Isobel's perspective, to define and constrict the female life. But from the narrator's perspective, they assume political intensity. New narrative patterns are introduced so that events not usually included as story material dominate the novel's development. As a result, hidden parts of the female body, which seem to represent hidden or silenced stories, are persistently exposed. In *Blown Figures*, only women matter. Eggs focus attention on female generation. The novel forces us to question the primacy of masculine narrative patterns and encourages us to think of other possibilities. We are all children of eggs. And the red landscape, while it does reveal waste and loss, also suggests the life-giving propensities of women's blood. One of the narrative aims seems, then, the redemption of just that blood so often castigated as unclean. The various religious associations that coalesce around blood are consequently revised. Isobel's memories of the birth of her daughter, Mary, and of her embarrassment because of the blood-covered nightgown that betrayed her heavy bleeding, indicate a beginning re-vision. Isobel learns to question her embarrassment: "Such rich red blood, so important to the beautiful child.... The blood was a sign, an emblem" (p. 394). In the epics, in the Bible, in most of the world's literature, the shedding of blood is celebrated: the blood of battle and of destruction. In Thomas' female epic, the narrator reads blood differently. Blood is offered, not wantonly spilled.

Clearly, all the enclosed places of the novel reflect one central space, the "womb, the red-hung room which no one enters" (p. 71), although that space does not suggest Erikson's peaceful interiors.[17] Frequent reminders orient the reader to this inner perspective. Like Isobel, who sometimes observes the events of the novel through "two round tower windows" (p. 425), a trapped princess, the reader is situated inside the body. Various objects metaphorically represent the womb — eggs, balloons, footballs — while the land sometimes offers womb-like protection: "The sun beat down mercilessly on the top of Isobel's head; she submerged herself every few minutes, jelly-fish floating, suspended, safe as a baby in a bottle" (p. 110). In other places, womb and tomb archetypally join and dramatize the closeness between life and death. Throughout her dreams and delusions, Isobel's fixation merges with her obsessive fantasies about dismemberment. Memories of being scraped clean after a miscarriage and an abortion are translated, by Isobel, into deconstructed bodies. By extension, those bodies reveal themselves in a threateningly chaotic text: "A few scraps left. An embryonic finger maybe, or a toe. A little lost eye" (p. 132). The cannibalism metaphor implies a closed text, a vicious circle: "'I ate the child in my womb,' she said" (p. 518).

In various ways, the novel presents fantasies about life in the womb and therefore represents, structurally and thematically, the female body. It also assumes a female audience, Miss Miller, and presents a female narrator and a central female subject. Such inter-connections underline what Judith Gardiner claims is a notable characteristic of women's writing, that "female characters in novels by women tend to dissolve and merge into each other."[18] Like Isobel, the narrator suffers a fear of madness: "Oh god, something has been put into my head to spoil it. How difficult it is becoming to concentrate on Isobel and her new friend Delilah — they have to complicate things so" (p. 459). She suffers a more pointed fear of the dissolution and merging spoken of by Gardiner, of becoming like Isobel.

The female author's concern about being contaminated by a female character seems doubly ironic. On the one hand, it draws attention to the theoretical issue posed by Gardiner, that theorists have traditionally assumed that "stability and constancy are desirable goals for human personality."[19] But for women, more permeable ego boundaries and profoundly affective relationships make singular identity themes problematic. *Blown Figures* certainly exposes this issue. The narrator is not just constructor of the story: she is critic of it as well. Thus she can analyze traditional female characterization: "Why did you always feel as though you needed to be rescued . . . . All your life you have been as passive as a princess in a fairy tale" (p. 218). She can also criticize naïve characterization: "We cannot wait for you forever, still running behind, breathless, a tiny schoolgirl, your hand clutched to your side. Miss Miller and I have better things to do" (p. 159). But the novel also celebrates a female universe. The narrator serves the psychological function of a female dream censor and the rhetorical function of a female epic voice that extends this woman's story from the idiosyncratic to the general: "Consider Isobel, leaning over the promenade" (p. 11), or "Now that Isobel has crossed the border, now that we have introduced her to the priests and walked by her side in the northern villages, it is not too difficult to bring her to the river" (p. 409). Thomas thus forces the reader to notice certain literary conventions while the novel is subverting them. It becomes an exercise in learning to read the female text.

As well as displaying women's writing, the novel also comments on it. Disconnected words and peculiarly structured pages reflect the material of Isobel's womb, the broken baby; they also dramatically represent the traditional isolation of the female voice. Isobel has visions of "[I]nnocent words" detaching themselves from the other parts of the sentence and growing "big as signs" (p. 32). Her ability to read periodically fails: as "the letters jumped around the page like fleas" (p. 137). The body-text is persistently broken down. At the same time, the narrator situates Isobel within the structures of women's history. Isobel's mother's writing consisted of private, personal letters addressed to her daughters, private narratives of a failed life. This is women's past, and it threatens to repeat itself. Isobel suffers a terrifying aphasia. Once, she imagines that her ears and lips have been cut off, "so that speech was hardly audible" (p. 313). She also fears a loss of narrative control; she imagines herself "[S]quashed by the words, strangled by the sentences" (p. 193), and worries about her compulsion to tell tales. An old man reiterates, "A tale, a tale. Let it go and let it return" (p. 169) and the rats ask: "Do you know only one story?" (p. 313). To combat these fears, the narrator interferes; she insists on public utterance.

In all these ways, *Blown Figures* is a quintessentially female text. The delusions and dreams it describes result from idiosyncratically female experiences: a miscarriage and an abortion. The consequent condensations and displacements are female both in imagery and in organization. Eggs, blood, womb-like enclosures, bodies falling apart, people feeding on each other; all the images reflect the female body and describe a dominant female obsession. Told to a woman, by a woman, about a woman, the narrative attempts to open the hidden parts of the female body. Secrecy is transformed into confession, silence into speech, disconnected episodes into narrative.

In a statement made to the Conference of Inter-American Women Writers at the University of Ottawa, Audrey Thomas remarked:

> There are female images and female ways of looking at the world, interior or exterior. For if there is one thing that unites all the women at the conference, that needs no translator, it is our biology. For about thirty years of our lives we prepare each month for an event which generally does not take place. We ovulate, we bleed. Before this event, ages one to twelve, say, and after, in our fifties and beyond, this fact is still part of our 'Becoming' or our 'Been.' I do think it is only fairly recently that women writers have dealt overtly with this kind of experience. Where Philip Sydney's muse told him to look in his heart and write, our muse has been telling us to look a little farther down. Our visceral imagination is now coming to the fore.[20]

Freud discussed Norbert Hanhold's erotic male fantasies, unveiled their phallic meaning, established connections between the author, Jensen, and his male character. In writing *Blown Figures*, Thomas displays a perspective from which that dominating male metaphor, with its symbolic resonance, has been removed. The male voice has disappeared. Thomas has constructed a psychologically female experience. It is told through women's visceral imagination and dominated by delusions and dreams that speak the inner self. Consequently, the novel is an exercise in the reading of the female body.

Chapter Four

Sisterhood and Secrecy in "Its Image on the Mirror"

When the woman who has a sister is a writer, she leaves us a special kind of legacy, for the sister-figure is so often present in writing, not, most likely, as she was, but as the writer felt her to be. She represents a specific interaction between female Self and female Other and the conversation that a writer has with her sister in writing is often one that she could not have in her life.

— LOUISE BERNIKOW
"Among Women"

In "Feminist Criticism in the Wilderness," Elaine Showalter addresses many of the issues raised by Atwood's and Thomas' novels: issues about the female body, women's psychological development, women's language, women's cultural history and how these issues relate to women's writing. Showalter finds particularly perplexing the woman writer's relationship to a male literary tradition. I have suggested that Atwood and Thomas make use of that tradition, often ironically; they invert traditional myths, use masculine narrative structures to tell women's stories, and place in the foreground originally silenced or at least peripheral female roles. Showalter emphasizes precisely such extensions and insists that "[T]he holes in discourse, the blanks and gaps and silences, are not the spaces where female consciousness reveals itself but the blinds of a 'prison-house of language.' Women's literature is still haunted by the ghosts of repressed language, and until we have exorcised those ghosts, it ought not to be in language that we base our theory of difference."[1]

Yet blanks and gaps and silences persist. The early fiction of Mavis Gallant seems haunted by the "ghosts of repressed language," and presents to the critic a particularly bewildering façade. Her stories demonstrate female silence as it occasions male speech, the failure of women to bond with each other, the loss of the maternal voice. Metaphorically, "Its Image on the Mirror" concentrates on these themes. It is a peculiarly troubling, haunting — indeed haunted — story, filled with gaps and denials, with deceit and secrecy, with silence and suppressed speech. In the introduction to *Home Truths*, Gallant acknowledges her penchant for the hidden narrative; she argues that fiction, like painting, consists of more than meets the eye. She extends her comments to the problem of literary nationalism. Canadian readers, she states, seem particularly unnerved by narrative secrecy. They find her work difficult, or at least unsettling, to read: "I often have the feeling with Canadian readers that I am on trial. The accusation has nothing to do with style or structure or content or imagination or control of subject and form — nothing that has any connection with literature in the usual sense — but with what are taken to be my concealed intentions. I am suspected of using language to screen a deep and disobliging meaning, or to perpetrate a fraud."[2] Gallant defends herself against an inferred Canadian puritanism of the imagination and an obsessive nationalism. "Its Image on the Mirror" reflects both.

The story also tells the reader a good deal about women's silence and their secrecy. Many of Gallant's short stories and novellas display stylistic obscurity; they also privilege secrecy in the working out of the story. "Its Image on the Mirror" dramatizes obscurity by obfuscating the plot and by clouding the relationships among the various characters. It points toward a secret meaning that demands interpretive effort. In the story, secrecy characterizes narrative interpretation. Geoffrey Hartman argues that "[E]very literary narrative contains another narrative: however continuous or full the one seems to be, the other is discontinuous and lacunary"[3]. In *The Genesis of Secrecy*, Frank Kermode analyzes discontinuous and lacunary narrative as it appears in the Gospel of Mark; he discovers a persistent refusal of narrative sequence in favour of the compiling of "one crux on another, each instituting an intense thematic opposition."[4] And he argues that already obscure texts are made more inaccessible by their interpreters:

> I have spoken of deafness and forgetfulness as properties not only of texts, but of history, and of interpreters; of the preemption of sense by institutions and by theoretical presuppositions; of our readiness to submit the show of things to the desires of our minds; of the structures of explanation which come between us and the text or the facts like some wall of wavy glass. And I have suggested that interpretation, which corrupts or transforms, begins so early in the development of narrative texts that the recovery of the real right original thing is an illusory quest.[5]

Narratives invite interpretive sleuthing and sometimes become what Margaret Atwood, in *Murder in the Dark*,[6] has described as a dangerous game (sometimes the game of murder). For Atwood and for other feminist critics, silence and secrecy often assume a gender. As Atwood suggests in the essay "Simmering," gender is an issue for women writers, who pass down history "from woman to woman, usually at night, copied out by hand or memorized."[7] For women, the art of writing can become subversive, its existence a threat to an established patriarchy. Women's writing is uncanny and emphasizes a compulsion to repeat. As a result, many narratives participate in what Peter Brooks, in "Freud's Masterplot," calls a doubling back, problematic because,

> we cannot say whether this return is a return *to* or a return *of*: for instance, a return to origins or a return of the repressed. Repetition through this ambiguity appears to suspend temporal process, or rather, to subject it to an indeterminate shuttling or oscillation which binds different moments together as a middle which might turn forward or back. This inescapable middle is suggestive of the daemonic.[8]

Yet the daemonic in women-oriented texts, the hidden madwomen at their centres, carry certain political messages. "Its Image on the

Mirror" exhibits uncanny repetitions that result in a muddled and complicated text. But it also displays a cultural lacuna that forces daemonic doubling and that produces ghosts of repressed female dialogue: the conversation between sisters.

Repetition, doubling, and secrecy have structural as well as contextual meaning. Superficially, "Its Image on the Mirror" records the narrator's impressions of several episodes, not in chronological order, in the lives of her family: her mother, her father, her brother, Frank, her sister, Isa, and herself, Jean Price, now a married woman with four children. The episodes around which Jean's memory coalesces are counterpointed throughout the seven sections and repeated, like a fugue, so that Jean sometimes seems to be investigating the origins of her stories and at other times dramatizing repressions that exhibit considerable psychic tension. Her central memories are apparently historically fixed: the move from the house in Allenton during the month of June, 1955; the Labour Day weekend reunion, also in 1955, at the parents' cottage; the narrator's marriage to Tom when she is twenty-four, during the second year of World War Two; Frank's accidental death about three years later, while he is a soldier in England; a Christmas leave six weeks before his death, when the whole family is together in the Allenton house. The story is being told in 1961, when the narrator is forty-four years old and has been married for twenty years.

As this brief summary suggests, on one level the novella encourages a political reading. Many Canadian narratives do. Situated in Montreal, the story superficially traces the tensions between a WASPish young woman, Jean Price, and her glamorous, obscurely European (French) sister, Isa. The text elucidates the split consciousness that characterizes Canadian nationalism, and dramatizes the culturally charged tensions that separate the English and the French. The reader can hardly miss the implications. Jean is considered a "symbol of English Canada" (p. 143); Isa, interested in foreigners, is repeatedly described as an outsider, flamboyant. On the one hand, then, the WASP, seen through French eyes, is "flat-minded, emptily optimistic" (p. 91), "the pattern of life discarded, the route struck off the map" (p. 91). The WASP imagines Isa as romantically untidy, disorganized, mysterious. Communication between the two groups is, of course, difficult: "My mother addressed the rector in unstressed French, and he replied in their curious English. This exchange in opposing languages was the extreme limit of mutual politeness and contempt" (p. 67). The cultural, religious and linguistic separation between the French and the English echoes in all the broken connections of the novella.

Even the mother's role is part of the political allegory. Jean writes: "I don't know why our mother wanted us to steep in books so removed from Canadian life. She may have been trying to counteract the comics and the radio — the American influence" (p. 83). The mother is "English-minded" and, like the stereotyped Britisher, averse to "emotional rot" (p. 66). She keeps a stiff upper lip. Jean feels connected to her, but Isa, in a conversation with her brother, denies having a mother at all. In fact, Jean's dream in the snowbound room at the end of the story resonates with political meanings. The ambivalent fantasizing about the mother's death characteristically and nationalistically betrays yearnings for independence: "We woke from dreams of love remembered, a house recovered and lost, a climate imagined, a journey never made; we woke dreaming our mothers had died in childbirth, and heard ourselves saying, 'Then there is no one left but me!'" (p. 155). As does Atwood in *Surfacing* and *Bodily Harm* and Engel in *Sarah Bastard's Notebook* and *Lunatic Villas*, Gallant uses female characters to dramatize the cultural ambiguities that constitute the Canadian identity; she emphasizes the prolonged struggle for separation, or at least independence, that characterizes relationships between mothers and daughters.

Although a certain subversive intention can be presumed in the political allegory, this reading by no means exhausts the possibilities of the text. Its feminist polemic is much more heavily disguised; "Its Image on the Mirror" contains messages directed to women, messages that imply a discreet network of female readers. The novella foregrounds women's secrecy as a protective, political measure, often necessary for survival. The problem of narrative sequence thus becomes dominant. Encouraged by their culture to isolate themselves from each other, women often construct disrupted texts that can seem profoundly obscure to an uninitiated reader.

In an attempt to reconnect women's narratives, Annis Pratt argues that women novelists, albeit often unwittingly, have given their female readers

> maps of the patriarchal battlefield and of the landscape of our ruined culture, and they have resurrected for our use codes and symbols of our potential power . . . . They have provided us moments of epiphany, of vision . . . . In so doing, they have made of the woman's novel a pathway to the authentic self, to the roots of our selves beneath consciousness of self, and to our innermost being.[9]

Quite possibly, finding archetypal connections among Gallant's works may not clarify them. And it is unlikely that the author would want to speak of essential selves, of innermost beings. She questions such terms throughout her writing. Nonetheless, there is considerable merit in elucidating the ways in which her fiction has mapped the patriarchal battlefield and has used codes and symbols to demonstrate women's potential power.

In spite of what appears to be its clarity — a clarity that partially results from the references to actual historical events, most notably World War Two — "Its Image on the Mirror," like the Yeats play quoted in the epigraph, compulsively plays with "shadows and fantasies,"[10] with "images, analogies."[11] In the first section, which is about the sale of the Allenton house, the reader's attention is deflected from the central episode. Religious references dominate the opening paragraph and, in much the way Kermode suggests, seem to imply privileged information, hidden stories that bear hidden meanings. References to Judas conjure up secret deceit; references to Daniel allude to hieroglyphics written on the wall; references to the prodigal son allude to a desertion, an underground life, a return. The narrator emphasizes the linguistic, cultural and religious differences between the French and the English. To the English family, the tall priest who is to take over the Allenton house represents a foreign influence that extends even to the present moment of the story. The narrator will not go to look at the old house; she prefers her memories of the "pale tormented faces" (p. 58) of the seminarists behind the windows "shut tight in all seasons" (p. 58) to any later reality.

The house remains mysterious and secret, entrapped by a Virginia creeper that surrounds the windows, paralyzed like fossil-imprinted stones. The narrator insists that it was haunted by ghosts who "moved in the deserted rooms, opening drawers, tweaking curtains aside" (p. 59). She chooses to believe that "there was nothing I could change" (p. 63). The haunting extends to the bodies around her, to her sister — whose baby face was already secretive — and to her mother, who tolerates the ghosts because "she knew that her existence was a draught of air too feeble to blow them away" (p. 60). The house and the bodies that inhabit it, at first physically and later in memory, are brought together in the haunted beginning of the story. It is an uncanny doubling, an elusive return.

Like the first section, the second, Jean's description of the Labour Day reunion, is fraught with secrecy, with threatening silence, with anxiety. Just as she attempts to petrify the Allenton house, Jean tries to hold the reunion still, to see it whole. She tells the reader that she remembers experiencing contentment because everyone around her was "doing the right thing. The pattern" was whole (p. 75). But gaps in her memory and textual gaps betray a different story, a story of her sister's isolation, a negation of the harmonious design Jean is attempting to construct. Jean recalls that "[A]ll at once my gaze fell on my sister, whom I had forgotten. She sat apart from the rest of us" (p. 75). This repression of memories of her sister, the forgetting, signal one of the central problems of the narrative: the relationship between Jean and Isa. The silences and secrecies of the text reflect the problematic dialogue between the sisters. "Isobel was going, and had said nothing to me. She had not spoken at all" (p. 77). Against the noise of the speedboats and the screaming of the radio, the sisters' silence assumes symbolic significance. The section ends with an accretion of references to repressed speech: "none of that was mentioned"; "He didn't say so"; "Nothing was said, after that day"; "The less said the better" (p. 81).

Even when the sisters are physically close to each other, their conversations tend to be broken and their dialogue peculiarly circumspect. The temporal, chronological ordering of the story suffers. The space of the narrative is also problematic. The narrator constantly attempts to erase either her own or her sister's body. Projection and inversion dominate the narrative development and produce innumerable fissures. Jean simultaneously recreates and erases her sister as she describes their separate lives in Montreal. After carefully situating herself and her possessions, she sets in counter-distinction a sister shorn of commodities — empty: "She owned nothing"; "Most of her clothes looked as if they had belonged to someone else first"; "She did not keep or collect the odds and ends that seem to me, now, the symbol of women" (pp. 92-93). Having denied her sister an idiosyncratic aura, Jean also cancels her sister's physical space: "She changed apartments often" (p. 93). Jean wants to convince herself that Isa is unreal, a ghost: even "her laughter was false" (p. 92). But the empty space where her sister does not exist becomes an overwhelming presence. As she remembers clearing out the books from the family home, Jean also remembers, further back, the cancelling of her own name and its replacement by Isa's. All the books bear her sister's name, even those that belonged to Jean. The conflict between absence and presence persists. Jean remembers her past self, "glum-faced, apprehensive, barely in sight of my sister's secrets, creeping around the edge of her life" (p. 86) and describes her efforts to come into that life through the few gaps she discovers. She describes, too, her feeling of being "swollen" (p. 90) with the secret of Isa's love for a married man, a man as mysterious as Isa, a conspirator in silence. The sexual images are potent.

Jean's voyeurism is repeated in the act of writing. The writing illustrates the active-passive duality that is again and again played out between the sisters. While attempting to deny her passivity by authoring the story, Jean embues Isa with mystery, as if Isa were the heroine of a romance and Jean the outcast, the listener, the reader. Indeed, Isa threatens to stifle her; she remembers herself, as if the moment existed in the present tense, arriving from the cold and frozen Montreal streets, putting on Isa's "scuffed moccasins which are dirty and too big" (p. 95), entering a dimly lit apartment where her conversation, achingly flat, is out of place and where the other people pay her only the most cursory attention. She cannot imagine herself as part of the story she has written. Then Jean recalls Isobel and her lover walking toward her on the dark Montreal streets, the very stuff of narrative. But in the cold, the snow, the dark, the emptiness, Isa's face alters: first it is an open flower, then it is closed and dying. Isa shuts off the flow of narrative and refuses permission for her sister-author to characterize her. Jean remains the watcher on the street, a figure "historically permitted, morally correct" (p. 100), a young woman who sleeps with the help of sleeping pills. She is repressed.

Other memories also assume considerable psychic intensity and operate as traumatized stops in the life of the narrator. Her meeting with her future husband, Tom, is one of these moments, an apparent inversion of the voyeuristic pattern that dominates Jean's relationship with Isa. But Jean's description of the event again betrays her desire to assume her sister's life: Tom had proposed to Isa and been rejected. Twenty years later, at the moment of writing, Jean confesses that she is still dominated by secrecy and silence. She admits that "[T]here are questions I could ask . . . if I thought I was safe. It was a long time ago, his having wanted Isobel, but the wrong question might still pull down the house. You can never be certain of that house, even if it has been standing twenty years" (p. 104). Once again, the sisters have failed to nurture each other. They play out an apparently preordained separation that infects the narrator's ability to construct a coherent narrative, and that becomes the pattern for her relationships with other women. The silence between Jean and her Montreal roommate, Alma, demonstrates the unforged connections that result, ironically, because they had nothing in common "except that we were women" (p. 108). Since this particular bond signifies secrecy — the living room is kept dark; Jean is not able to "say what I thought" (p. 107); Alma lives on sleeping pills — the relationship interferes with, rather than supports, narrative clarity.

When Jean remembers receiving news of her brother's death she focusses not on her brother but on Isa. She tries to capture through language the environment of her sister's life: Isa works in a dirty, dark apartment, once the maid's quarters in a more elegant house; her boss, in some unspecified way, seems to be a thief. Her life is shrouded in secrecy. Failed connections are metaphorically emphasized when Jean cannot reach a female cousin she phones. The Montreal streets through which the sisters wander assume labyrinthine proportions and refuse to disclose their centre. Jean also recalls episodes from a visit with Frank six weeks before his death, a visit that seems dominated by understandings between Frank and Isa, secrets Jean vaguely overhears but is unable to interpret. The three of them attend a party where everyone "represented something other than himself" (p. 143), a signal (as it was in *Mrs. Blood*, *Bodily Harm*, and *Blown Figures*) that deceit and disguise have assumed psychic intensity.

The atmosphere of the whole country is secretive. In many of Jean's memories it is wartime, and she recalls the newspapers silenced certain stories. The streets of Montreal are as empty and forsaken as Jean is; she confesses that her major response to intense feeling is blankness. Detectives and spies inexplicably wander in and out of the stories of other people's lives, keeping the sense of foreboding powerful throughout the novella. Most important, masculinity has been erased from the country. Jean's father is mentioned only superficially. He is a significant absence: "We had lost my father miles back" (p. 69); "My father, who has become too deaf to listen to reason, bores us" (p. 112); "He sat physically shrunken" (p. 131). Suzanne is married to a soldier who exists in some "sham landscape" (p. 128) like a ghost. These figures haunt the text. Yet neither the father nor Suzanne's husband nor Frank nor even Tom, Jean's husband, seem potent enough to be the story's central ghosts. Jean ponders the problem and decides that "[T]he ghost in the Allenton house cannot be Frank's. If Frank had left part of himself there I would have felt him then, that night. He left no trace; nothing of him came back" (p. 131). Jean's narrative is not addressed to men, nor is it about men; her séance lies elsewhere.

Indeed, it is with other women that her narrative links need to be forged. Yet such links are exceedingly difficult to create. In Gallant's novel *A Fairly Good Time*, the main character, Shirley, describes her letter-writing relationship with her mother back in Canada as "an uninterrupted dialogue of the deaf."[12] The dialogues that exist between the female characters in a Gallant text frequently seem stilted and unnatural, filled with gaps and fissures, failed communications. In the final section of "Its Image on the Mirror," the narrator describes a scene that characterizes the predominating silence and secrecy between Isa and the narrator — the representative women of this novella. Throughout, Isa's room, no matter where it is, has represented herself, her body. Jean's efforts to see into these various rooms metaphorically suggest her desire to understand her sister, to share her life. In the novella's last reported scene, Isa comes into Jean's room in the old house at Allenton. It is the weekend the sisters receive the news of Frank's death. The fictional Isa, like a nineteenth-century heroine of romance, is unapproachable, a golden girl, a projection that separates women from each other, a pretense. Her friend has labelled her, *"Personnage aux Plumes."* Such characterizations of women do not encourage communication; instead, they make women remote from each other. In writing of her sister, Jean finally attempts another perspective, an alteration of the romantic genre into the realistic. She fails. But the effort to see Isa not as lavish and extravagant but as simply a "tall, slouching, untidy girl" (p. 148) is a significant interpretive strategy. It emphasizes the necessary stripping of the heroine before she can become a sister.

"Its Image on the Mirror" concentrates on showing how doubling and repression merge, particularly in the anxiety-fraught relationship between sisters; the story also reveals the ways in which such narratives function as a return of the repressed. The sense of the uncanny permeates other relationships. Although the inscribed secrecy between the sisters accounts for much of the unsettled structure of the text, another figure comes into focus spatially and temporally, a figure biologically responsible for the story's other doublings and reflections — the mother.

Jean emphasizes her mother's physical proximity at the beginning of the story. The two of them sit close together in the car on the day in June when the Allenton house is sold. Jean's physical awareness of her mother persists throughout and often assumes ghostly overtones. Like the "expiring" (p. 59) Allenton house, the mother's body seems effervescent, shadowy, spectral. Psychologically, her boundaries are far from clear. Jean merges with her: "As I grow older I see that our gestures are alike. It touches me to notice a movement of hands repeated — a manner of folding a newspaper, or laying down a comb. I glance sharply behind me and I know I am reproducing my mother's quick turn of head. Our voices are alike . . . I am pleased to be like her. There is no one I admire more" (p. 65). Repetition significantly influences the narrative. But Jean's reflection of her mother also illustrates certain narrative difficulties. Like a small child, Jean, herself the mother of four children, describes her mother as a symbol of authority, without a "sandgrain of weakness or compassion or pity" (pp. 65-66). She admits her own fear of assuming authority, in text or in life, by insisting that she is less able than her mother to control her own children. Her desire to merge with her mother and her simultaneous vision of her mother as unattainable and remote create a classic ambivalence that seems often to structure narratives by women. Jean attempts separation and criticizes an impossible physical symbiosis that "would have been wrong: it would have been an attempt to put myself in her place, think for her, sense what she ought to feel" (p. 66). But immediately she imagines herself still at home, creeping in her mother's "small shadow, welcomed as companion and errand girl" (p. 66). Such ambivalence makes it difficult for Jean to construct the narrative links she hopes to forge between herself and her mother. The voice of that "old madwoman" (p. 70) is essential to the projected and desired dialogue between sisters.

The structure of the story also reflects the maternal figure. In each of the seven sections of the novella, Jean returns to her mother, centring her, trying to reveal her, and come to terms with her. She acknowledges that her marriage to Tom was engineered by her mother, who "instantly saw in Tom a man who would do" (p. 101) and who, knowing that Tom had first proposed to Isobel, nonetheless put "her moral strength, her contempt for men and her knowledge of their weaknesses" (p. 102) on Jean's side. The mother insists on Frank's Christmas visit to the girls in Montreal; when she hears of his death, the mother brings the family together. She appears to be "full of silent answers" (p. 112), the controller of the story. Partially, then, the various episodes Jean describes are meant to situate her in a relationship with her mother, a relationship that will help her analyze her own authority as a writer. Because she wants to repeat her mother's life, specific narrative links occur, such as her insistence that she "was part of my mother and father, and my children were part of me. I had succeeded in that, and Isa had failed" (p. 77). For women writers, the connection with the mother apparently remains crucial: "[m]y husband said, 'Your mother ought to leave you alone. She's always after you for something.' I answered meekly, 'I know, but she has only one daughter now. There's only me.' He could not know that her bothering me was a victory. I was the only daughter: I had won" (p. 64).

Sisters and mothers, broken connections, secrecy: "Its Image on the Mirror" reflects all these subjects from a peculiarly Canadian perspective. And, like *Bodily Harm*, *Mrs. Blood*, and *Blown Figures*, it significantly documents female creativity, the stories that emerge from women's experience. Its narrator, Jean Price, rivets our attention. More self-consciously than Isobel or Rennie, Jean undertakes a subtle interpretation of the female body, which is central, and also of the social and cultural meanings of women's lives. She elucidates the problems of female existence as she experiences them. In *A Reader's Guide to the Canadian Novel*, John Moss remarks that Jean Price is "ironically conscious of her own voice."[13] She is. But her self-consciousness is of a peculiar kind. Frequently, instead of clarifying the reader's understanding, Jean's voice interferes, misinterprets, confuses. As if echoing the central issues of the stories she tells, she experiments with secrecy; she often disguises her own voice so the reader is left with no reliable witness.

She presents herself "like any other woman of my age and my condition" (p. 77), an affirmation that suggests her representative function. Even in her secrecy, she is everywoman. She also tells us that she has carefully taught her children that there is no special country and "no magic solutions" (p. 84); that she represents the "historically permitted, morally correct" (p. 100); that she is part of "an ordinary family" (p. 130); and that she and Isobel are very "ordinary" (p. 153). Her assertions emphasize her efforts to elicit the reader's trust and to pass off her story as straightforward. But in spite of her apparently objective accounts of herself, her "normal" role as a character in the various stories she tells and as the main interpreter of these stories, Jean fails to convince us of her guilelessness. Throughout, she undercuts statements, denies the accuracy of descriptions, is unreliable. For example, in the opening paragraphs, she sets up a picture with religious overtones that seems meant to establish specific narrative themes. By holding still life's panorama, she purports to see it whole. But after framing her memory of leaving the house in Allenton on a July day in 1955, she immediately undercuts it: "My mother says I saw nothing of the kind" (p. 58). Her memory is unstable, her interpretation questionable.

Her narrative vagueness persists throughout the text. Statements like "One night I saw, or thought I saw, or may have dreamed" (p. 147) draw attention to the narrator's refusal to take responsibility for her memories. The reader is made uneasy: Jean's contradictions paralyze interpretation. Systematically, she constructs a framed memory: "I felt, that afternoon, the closest feeling I have to happiness. It is a sensation of contentment because everyone around me is doing the right thing. The pattern is whole.... The Sunday papers lay on the grass. There was the slightly sad atmosphere that hangs in the air between summer and autumn" (p. 75). But within her asserted wholeness, other memories return. As we have seen, her sister sits apart, "straggly," "unkempt," "washed-out," "isolated and lost" (pp. 75-76); the sounds of a Shostakovich symphony shatter the air; Poppy, Frank's daughter, remains foreign and obscure. Like the opening picture contradicted by her mother, this picture, too, carefully structured, is immediately contradicted by the narrator herself. Indeed, every story of the novella follows the same pattern: a concise summary of a scene and of the characters who populate it followed by a backtracking, a contradiction of the stability and therefore of the accuracy of the carefully rendered setting.

In spite of the apparent correctness of description — the careful detail, the sensual vividness, the Wordsworthian wholeness of memory — "Its Image on the Mirror" fails in exactly the specificity it claims. Memories that initially seem singular are revealed to be iterative. Remembering the night of her twenty-seventh birthday, Jean vaguely asks: "Was it that night or another I knew that news of my husband's death would be a release?" (p. 89). Serial actions dominate the text: "my mother liked to say"; "she had always said." Fact and imagination perversely cancel each other out: "She may not have said 'blotting out the light,' and I may distort the remembered scene if I say she put up her hand, flat, to indicate the kind of shutting out" (p. 151). Ambiguous expressions such as "I wish I could say," "say that it happened once," "if she had been challenged about it, she would have said," "must have felt," "what my mother did not say aloud," "might have spent" are repeated throughout. Specific denials — "I am afraid I have given two misleading impressions" — increase distrust of the narrative voice. Jean often gives a long, carefully interpreted description as if a thing had really happened, only to end with statements acknowledging the event as a wish, a fancy, something that might have happened that way but clearly did not. " 'Ears too,' said Frank, but I must have dreamed that Frank said this" (p. 141). Ellipses structurally emphasize the textual gaps: " 'All the same, you'd think they would . . . .' Either Frank often forgot to finish his sentences, or I forgot to listen to the end" (p. 136).

The secrecy that contextually dominates the relationship between Jean and Isa and that characterizes general relationships among women has a structural basis. The stories describe secrecy and also effect secrecy because of the way they are told. Indeed, "Its Image on the Mirror" is also about language. As many twentieth-century narratives do, the novella dramatizes an unsettling failure of verbal correspondence by attempting to release imaginative language from specific reference. In another Gallant story, "The Moslem Wife," Jack is a man who is "closed to ghosts, deaf to their voices."[14] Frank, in "Its Image on the Mirror," represents narrative failure precisely because he believes that words can circumscribe the perceived world. But this typical Gallant theme also foregrounds the paralyzing difficulties of meaningful communication, particularly (as Jean repeatedly illustrates) between sisters: "I wanted her to say, You and I are alike, and we are not like any other person in this room. But, of course, she never did" (p. 91); "When I am there Isobel will not speak. Into this social vacuum (I shall not go) I make conversation" (p. 96).

In *Among Women*, Louise Bernikow describes the psychologically necessary narrative elaboration of the secrecy between sisters: "The conversation among sisters proceeds subliminally. They speak to each other in dreams, implant one another in their novels, make gestures whose meaning is buried to the outside eye."[15] Narrative merges with dream, projection with self-discovery. Bernikow also says the apparent silence between sisters speaks as loudly as their clamour, "silence on the subject of sensuality, silence about those longings, so much like the silence between mothers and daughters. But there is silence, too, on those matters that would remove one sister from the other, the throwing off of repression being but one form that longing takes. Abandonment lurks behind the realization of these female longings — in the eyes of the sister."[16] Bernikow's poetic description parallels the events in Gallant's novella, the problematic relationship with the mother, a life-long search for union, a life-long search for separation and, all the time, like a *leitmotif*, the agonizing struggle between sisters.

Finally, then, Gallant's narrative serves multiple political functions: women's lives and Canada's are interwoven. Showalter suggests reasons for the merging of national and gender issues in the work of women writers in countries like Canada: "From a political perspective, there are interesting parallels between the feminist problems of a women's language and the recurring 'language issue' in the general history of decolonization. After a revolution, a new state must decide which language to make official."[17] The female narrative insists on links that may not appear to exist in the culture. The writer gives them back. Although the narrative gaps, the hauntings, the constant allusions to secrecy suggest a failure at the level of the sisters' communication that results in a more radical narrative failure, there are also new links in the sub-text that can be deciphered by feminist readings. Jean gives her sister a voice by writing about her; she gives Canada a unity by linking its disparate halves.

"Its Image on the Mirror" tells the reader a good deal about women writing about women in Canada. The world of the novella is misty, just as misty, for example, as the world of Conrad's *Under Western Eyes*, which is, according to Kermode, "only by trickery and collusion got into a square, well-lighted box."[18] Jean insists that her narrative "is a small memory, of no importance: one sister visits another. Words are omitted, and the wrong things said — wounding, hopeless, inevitable" (p. 94). The cultural and personal boundaries revealed in the text are imprecise and the face of the narrator is vague, projected in constant desiring: "It was Isobel I imagined as the eternal heroine — never myself. I substituted her feelings for my own, and her face for any face described" (p. 84). In this manner, woman's narrative space is usurped and ghosts take over. The immediate retraction of descriptions of the perceived world, and the extensive use of iterative structures emphasize the failure of narrative (and national) authority. The narrator also parodies female characterization by using the stereotyped splitting and doubling that have often constituted such characterization. One sister is plain, one beautiful; one straight-laced, the other wild; one tidy, the other messy. If sisters cannot connect, female characters will remain split.

In the final section of the story, when the sisters temporarily come together, the narrator attempts to erase her mother as the major narrative link. When Isa comes to her room and admits that she is pregnant, Jean immediately cautions her: "'Don't tell Mother'" (p. 149). Jean wants to replace her link with her mother by linking herself with Isa. And Isa, at this moment, needs Jean to buffer her, to protect her from everyone else. Yet the mother remains. Both sisters feel that the mother can read their minds, can see through walls, though neither apparently feels capable of reading the mother accurately. The text demonstrates an anxiety of influence. Sisters ought to be able to connect without murdering their mother. But although Jean asks the reader to leave Jean and Isa enclosed in the room at the end of the novella, sitting together on the bed "with our childhoods between us going on to the horizon without a break" (p. 153), she cannot leave the story there. She returns to her mother, she recalls a dream of mothers who die in childbirth, leaving the baby solitary and alone. Apart from the colonial implications of this dream of the dead mother, its psychology resonates with parallels to Freud's cultural interpretation of the death of the father in *Totem and Tabu*.

At the end of the novella, Jean describes a letter she remembers writing to her husband on the weekend of her brother's death. Her sister has just confided in her and Jean imagines her own voyeurism to be over. The door has been opened and she has "moved into the bright rooms" (p. 149) of her sister's life, a plot no longer without horizon, a plot with squarely marked boundaries. Isa communicates with Jean because she needs something, this time someone to help her because she is pregnant. As Jean thinks back on the events of that night, she wonders if any connection at all had been made, whether she was altered or reached a plateau from which she would never retreat. Older, she doubts the revelation of that long-ago night. This memory also proves to be false, "a flaw in the story" that reflects the flaw some people saw in Isa's face. Jean recalls that Isa spoke as if she were a person who has lost her language, in "faulty English" (p. 152). The letter written on that night betrays the flaws and omissions, the hesitancies and incompleteness that characterize the novella itself. The plot is not rational. Sequence falters.

In a number of ways, Jean's letter is a metonym for "Its Image on the Mirror." In it, Jean refuses the final word that would circumscribe the image on the mirror, give it fullness and character, make it clear: "The story could wait. It would always be there to tell. I might never tell it, but there is something in waiting for the final word" (p. 154). But no final word comes. Like the distant letter, the narrator's story is another accretion of images, of flaws, of gaps, of lost language. If, as Spacks claims, "to progress from contemplation of mirrors to vision through windows . . . marks an advance in human possibility,"[19] Gallant's novella illustrates a failure to make the progression. Only in later Gallant stories, where the mothering of texts becomes a more privileged subject, will the ghosts be made vital and the silenced voice articulate. This early novella refuses its female characters closure. It opens the story to innumerable problems about women writers and the material they use. Indeed, because it struggles to exorcise the ghosts of repressed language, to "return to life" (p. 155), it shares in the project of bringing into the text and into narrative development real connections among female characters.

Chapter Five

Women's Desire/Women's Power:
The Moons of Jupiter

When one begins with the study of women and derives developmental constructs from their lives, the outline of a moral conception different from that described by Freud, Piaget, or Kohlberg begins to emerge and informs a different description of development. In this conception, the moral problem arises from conflicting responsibilities rather than from competing rights and requires for its resolution a mode of thinking that is contextual and narrative rather than formal and abstract. This conception of morality as concerned with the activity of care centers moral development around the understanding of responsibility and relationships, just as the conception of morality as fairness ties moral development to the understanding of rights and rules.

— CAROL GILLIGAN
"In a Different Voice"

Rather 'sublimation' involves giving up an infantile, unmediated relation to jouissance and operating in the register of metaphor and mediation, operating effectively in an adult order.

— JANE GALLOP
"The Daughter's Seduction"

Women's writing reveals complicated patterns that are as sexually specific as the psychical delusions that occur from a miscarriage or the uncanny connections between a woman and her sister and mother. Women's narratives also structurally substantiate psychological concerns. Various writers use gaps in narrative coherence to point to female repression, or emphasize beginnings while demoting endings, or retell myths so that the organization and emphasis are altered. Women writers also question a dominant bias, both in the narratives and in the critical theory that accompanies them, by positing a desiring female subject, conscious of her gender, who acts in response to her own needs. Women's novels and short stories suggest different paradigms for female characters; the reader is asked to interpret these characters against the new paradigms.

In many of the stories in *The Moons of Jupiter*, Alice Munro creates central female characters who struggle to open new spaces in the text and, occasionally, try to live within them. For these characters, the Wife of Bath's question, "What do women want?" with its Freudian extensions, seems central. Munro focusses on female desire, which she illustrates through patterns that emphasize the objects of the desire and women's creation of narratives about their desires. Her female characters are not new women: they represent past and present and dramatically act out old plots of female desire, masochistic and apparently victimized. At the same time, they consciously consider their positions in such plots. Sometimes that consideration results from the splitting of narrator and major character; distance effects irony. But a number of these stories are first-person confessions in which the narrator, a writer, uses her own experience of love as exemplum. Frequently, Munro's first-person narrators attempt to demonstrate the dissidence between conventional love stories and desiring female subjects-writers.

"Female" desire is, nonetheless, a suspect term, even if used metaphorically. Freud speaks of only one libido, a masculine, aggressive one. Today, feminist theorists are analyzing the dynamics of desire in an effort to determine how it is represented culturally in sexually specific ways. Cixous translates the term as "*jouissance*" and argues that women's "libidinal economy is neither identifiable by a man nor referable to the masculine economy."[1] She admits that a patriarchal society has made "female desire a meaningless term by situating women objectively. As we have seen, Atwood describes such objectification by using John Berger's *Ways of Seeing* as a central reference and by dramatizing, in *Bodily Harm*, the degree to which women, as the objects of male gaze, have been denied subjectivity. Most often, culture answers the question of female desire by insisting that women want what men want, and see themselves as men see them.

Cixous recognizes that a woman has few satisfactory precedents to lead her toward acting out her desire, that "no longer knowing where to put it, or if she has any," a woman "conceals the most immediate and the most urgent question: 'How do I experience sexual pleasure?' What is feminine *sexual pleasure*, where does it take place, how is it inscribed at the level of [the] . . . body, of [the] . . . unconscious?" Most important, in terms of narrative theory, "How is it put into writing?"[2] Other theorists also attempt to locate women's sexual pleasure. Luce Irigaray insists that it does not speak the same language as men's desire, but has been "covered over by the logic that has dominated the West since the Greeks."[3] She posits its specificity. It "diverts the linearity of a project, undermines the target-object of a desire, explodes the polarization of desire on only one pleasure, and disconcerts fidelity to only one discourse"[4] Women, Irigaray argues, can enjoy total sexuality because they are not obsessed with the penis. Their economy is not phallic. Indeed, in *Lives of Girls and Women*, Del, the narrator, in her attempt to understand female desire, discovers man's obsession. To her, the penis is funny: "Raw and blunt, ugly-colored as a wound, it looked to me vulnerable, playful and naïve, like some strong-snouted animal whose grotesque simple looks are some sort of guarantee of good will. (The opposite of what beauty usually is.) It did not bring back any of my excitement, though. It did not seem to have anything to do with me."[5] When she later discovers its power to control women, she is appalled: "It seemed to me impossible that he should not understand that all the powers I granted him were in play."[6]

In *The Daughter's Seduction*, Jane Gallop also investigates the "feminist's place . . . as *desirer*."[7] She emphasizes the work of Montrelay, who argues, like Irigaray, that "Feminine sexuality, the alternative, the rival to (always masculine) desire is characterized by contiguity. . . . No longer parallel with a phallocentric economy, 'contiguity' is more radically other. 'Contiguous' means 'touching, nearby, adjacent.' Feminine sexuality, unlike the mediation of the visible which sustains phallic desire, is of the register of touching, nearness, presence, immediacy, contact."[8] Gallop stresses Montrelay's extension of female desire. Because *jouissance* is "enveloped in its own contiguity," it does not wait simply for closure, but can be ignited at any point along the line. Extended culturally, such desire alters production and makes of praxis an immediate pleasure.

According to Gallop, the male economy is impatient for products, "theses, conclusions, definitive statements,"[9] and cannot easily be used by female writers. In Munro's short story "Material," the narrator recognizes her need for a closeness that, while she desires it, also places her "at the mercy" of others' whims. Men, she believes, do not suffer this stultifying conjunction of desire and powerlessness: "Both of them have decided what to do about everything they run across in this world, what attitudes to take, how to ignore or use things. In their limited and precarious ways they both have authority. They are not *at the mercy.* Or think they are not."[10] As a result, how to combine desire with power becomes a major question for women; it is a problem in terms of the authority of their narrative techniques.

Munro is intrigued with the ways in which such physical problems metaphorically reflect in the text. Throughout her work, individual female characters display permeable body boundaries, and in cultural terms, reflect a changing social position in which their roles shift constantly. In *Lives of Girls and Women*, Del confesses to having "ambiguous" natural boundaries and claims to soak up "protective coloration wherever it might be found."[11] Theorists Chodorow and Gilligan say that such mergings are typically female. About Munro's feminine perspective, Beverly Rasporich argues: "the shifting perspectives of her feminine voice may undermine a logical or consistent philosophy, but in a historical sense they are an evocative and instinctive articulation of society in transition, and of women in search of themselves."[12] As Del's mother claims: "There is a change coming I think in the lives of girls and women."[13] In story after story, Munro dramatizes these changes, keeping her narratives fluid and open. Common themes — the sense of living underground in a subtext, the discrepancy between "outer" and "inner," vaguely defined ego boundaries, the need to merge with others — create narrative patterns that structurally indicate women's perceptions of themselves. Her stories shed light on the dark places of women's existence. By turning women's lives into narrative, Munro denies women the secrecy that has traditionally kept them mysterious and articulates the problems they encounter as desiring subjects.

In the twelve stories of *The Moons of Jupiter*, Munro concentrates on women's perspectives in ways that allow old and new narratives to exist together. In the opening story, "Connection," the limits of the text are established by the female body, which is represented by four maiden ladies, cousins of the narrator's mother, who is also part of the structure of the story. The narrator focusses on the cultural meaning of their bodies: "In those days it seemed to be the thing for women's bodies to swell and ripen to a good size twenty, if they were getting anything out of life at all; then, according to class and aspirations, they would either sag and loosen, go wobbly as custard under pale print dresses and damp aprons, or be girded into shapes whose firm curves and proud slopes had nothing to do with sex, everything to do with rights and power" (p. 1). Like fruit, a frequent female metaphor in the visual arts, these bodies obey certain natural functions. But their class also is marked, reflected in their clothing, the pale-print dresses and aprons worn by the women of the lower classes, the heavily girdled bodies, armour-plated, of higher-class women.

Michel Foucault writes of the cultural bonds between desire and power. He argues that "pleasure and power do not cancel or turn back against one another; they seek out, overlap, and reinforce one another. They are linked together by complex mechanisms and devices of excitation and incitement."[14] The narrator of "Connection" links desire and power, and the subject comes up in other Munro stories. But for women, the "complex mechanisms . . . of excitation and incitement" seem enormously problematic. For women, and for female characters in literature, power and sexuality can be mutually exclusive. The woman who chooses certain kinds of power — the independence of earning her own living, for example — may well have to live alone. In fact, a major triangle in women's stories is lover, work, self, a structure that Munro uses often. Many of her female characters have chosen to live alone. "Connection" establishes the direction of the collection; it illustrates the political reasons for the existence of spinsters and their solitary path to independence. The story also describes the sexual dynamics that, for women involved with men, separate power from desire.

An early anecdote in this first story illustrates such separation. About bulls and women, the story introduces the theme of rape and suggests that one of the silences in female texts involves sexual violence against women. The discussion is curtailed, actually suppressed, when the women realize that the young narrator is listening. Older women do not discuss sex with younger women. All the narrator understands is that the word "rape" "meant something dirty" (p. 3). Her mother misleads her by telling her that "rape" is another word for "purse," that in fact "rape" means to have your "'[P]urse stolen'" (p. 3). Sexual camaraderie does not connect women, as it seems to connect fathers and sons. Separated, desire and power prove incompatible. Woman's own desiring is irrelevant in the sexual marketplace. To have her purse stolen, to be raped, can lower a woman's value as the desired object and, furthermore, rape controls women by emphasizing their powerlessness. Women's understanding of their sexuality must deal with powerlessness as opposed to power, with passivity as opposed to activity, with following as opposed to leading. For women, the activity of desiring frequently becomes the passivity of being desired.

Contrary to custom, the cousins in "Connection" are sensual in spite of their single status. The narrator remembers their cigarettes, their chocolates, their fondness for American coffee and for liquor. Their sensuality depends on their independence. They make fun of love, jokingly singing "The Indian Love Call" and "Women Are Fickle," songs that underline their rejection of marriage. Without men, they have pleasure and maintain their own voices.

This opening story also emphasizes social class. Certain desired connections illustrate vividly how women who want power use their sexuality. The narrator critically analyzes her own marriage, a socially better marriage than her mother's. The man she marries despises her background. Years after the marriage, one of the cousins comes to visit and a cruel game is played out between the narrator and her husband: the cousin is made to appear vulgar and ridiculous, an old maid. The narrator knows she is siding with power, that what she has sold herself for is "a pleasant recognition" (p. 12) of her own value. But she also knows that her value is precisely the value of her husband. She is no longer a desiring subject. When the cousin leaves, Richard's statement condenses class and sexuality in terms of power: "'What a pathetic old tart'" (p. 17). Richard is a conservative man misreading the independent woman who is full of "movement, noise, change, flashiness, hilarity and courage" (p. 16).

Because of her marriage, the narrator is in an ambiguous position. Culturally conditioned, she admits that she used to love to look at "advertisements showing ladies in chiffon dresses with capes and floating panels." The advertisements were a window into a world that resulted from an upper-class marriage. At the same time, she insists that "the cousins' flowery dresses used to remind me of them [the advertisements], though the cousins were so much stouter, and not pretty" (p. 17). Desire and power once more connect. Like her cousins, the narrator learns that her marriage is keeping her powerless. She begins to understand the limitations of Richard's vision and the impositions of his speech. Her own voice has been drowned out. Metaphorically, this revelation occurs in many stories by women; only when the male voice is silenced do women begin to hear their own voices and connect with the world of women to discover a power independent of men's desire.

Not all the single women in *The Moons of Jupiter* possess an enviable independence. In "The Stone in the Field," the complementary story to "Connection," the narrator describes her father's side of the family: six unmarried sisters as repressed and silent as the mother's cousins are articulate and outgoing. Unlike the prosperous bodies of the mother's cousins, these women have bodies that are bent and thin and tight. They all look alike, "their faces were pale, eyebrows thick and furry, eyes deep-set" (p. 25). They do not travel; they remain stationary and enclosed, like women who "belonged in another generation" (p. 22), their endless toil — cleaning, ironing, and cooking — the only marking of their lives. They have remained as simple and naïve as children. Unlike the mother's cousins, who seem to be windows into some wider, more glamorous world, these aunts contract the dimensions of experience and make it appear infinitely small. The landscape, with its ruts and rows of plantain and dandelion, reflects the shrinkage. So does the yellowing and peeling house, isolated, without even a telephone wire to connect the family with the outside world. When the narrator and her family arrive at the farm, the greeting is silent; physical contact is absent, the world dry. The lives of the sisters are encompassed by the limits of their farm; and their activity by their endless cleaning, cooking and ironing.

The narrator's mother can scarcely comprehend their lives. She imagines that "they would yearn for things, not only material things but conditions, abilities" (p. 29). But their desire seems drained away. The grown narrator acknowledges a certain narrative defeat in the face of such silence and obscurity, particularly in comparison to the boisterous noise of her mother's cousins. She writes about her father's cousins but when she wants to translate the central object of the story, the stone in the field, into a metaphor for the desire of one of these dessicated women, she fails. Silence seems absolute. In terms of narrative, she admits that she no longer believes "people's secrets are defined and communicable, or their feelings full-blown and easy to recognize" (p. 35).

Between them, these two stories introduce the major themes explored in the rest of the stories in the collection. On the one hand, female characters are presented as independent, powerful, able to act out certain desires, self-contained. Typically, such characters need to operate in plots that exclude men. When they are judged by male characters — and they often are — they are dismissed for being too loud, too vulgar to be taken seriously. On the other hand, the silent female character makes narrative plotting extremely difficult. Repressed, she remains within the confines of the home, a narrow setting, and fears all physical contact. Dramatic structure fails. Faced with this female dilemma, several of the characters of Munro's stories attempt a middle course. For example, in the first two stories, the narrator's mother seems to steer this middle course. She attempts independence, is married, has children. But in a Munro story, the balance is always precarious. Questions proliferate. If women give in to sexual desire, do they become powerless characters? Are the plots of their stories retributive? Can powerless women create stories? When women are related to lovers, whose voice does the reader hear? What is the language of female desire?

These questions are pursued throughout the collection, most notably in four stories devoted to precarious love affairs. The most immediate of these stories, "Labour Day Dinner," describes an affair that is about to end. It is also a dramatic analysis of female masochism. The central character, Roberta, is presented by a narrative voice that is bemused, slightly irritated, marginally tolerant. The narrator indicates that Roberta's independent life as an illustrator is superficial, and speaks as if she were a mother chiding a lazy child: "Roberta meant to keep busy illustrating books. Why hasn't she done this? No time, nowhere to work: no room, no light, no table. No clear moments of authority, now that life has got this new kind of grip on her" (p. 141). The reader is also invited to criticize. And Roberta leaves herself open for criticism. In the plot of her lover George's life, Roberta has less and less space. Like the traditional heroine in a hero's story, she "can feel her own claims shrinking" (p. 142). So sensitive to all her lover's moods and gestures that she has virtually ceased to exist independently, she responds like a cipher. When George criticizes women who wear long skirts, Roberta stops wearing them. When he refuses to speak to her on the way to a dinner party, she "feels herself curling up like a jaundiced leaf," an image that even she herself recognizes as "hysterical" (p. 136). Because she is unable to tell her own story, the narrator takes over Roberta's space, objectifies the character, makes it difficult for the reader to hear Roberta at all. Interferences like "This is what Roberta is saying to herself" (p. 154) remind the reader constantly of this distancing.

Not surprisingly, Roberta believes that "love is not kind or honest and does not contribute to happiness in any reliable way" (p. 140). Her desire drains her of energy and leaves her weak and powerless. Her condition is reflected in the eyes of her daughters, whom she no longer seems capable of controlling or directing. Her older daughter writes in her journal that if what her mother is experiencing is "love I want no part of it. He wants to enslave her and us all and she walks a tightrope trying to keep him from getting mad. She doesn't enjoy anything and if you gave her the choice she would like best to lie down in a dark room with a cloth over her eyes and not see anybody or do anything" (p. 147). Desire has turned an "'intelligent woman who used to believe in freedom'" (p. 147) into a sufferer. Yet the central dinner that gives the story its title — like the dinner in Virginia Woolf's *Mrs. Dalloway* — brings order to the chaos of Roberta's life and imposes apparent narrative coherence. When she has pinned down the various people around the table, Roberta discovers that she feels "competent, relieved. Indifference has rescued her." More important, she extends this competence to her relationship with George by admitting that "[T]he main thing is to be indifferent to George — that's the great boon" (p. 156). If involvement increases women's powerlessness, Roberta can see the point of struggling toward distance: "She has to go all the way, to where she doesn't care. Then he feels how light and distant she is and his love revives. She has power. But the minute she begins to value it it will begin to leave her. So she is thinking, as she yawns and wavers on the edge of caring and not caring. She'd stay on this edge if she could" (p. 158).

The car accident that ends the story illustrates Roberta's partial epiphany. As they drive away from the dinner, Roberta, George and the two daughters are almost hit by an oncoming car. The brush with disaster, both titillating and terrifying, briefly allows them that uninvolvement earlier recognized by Roberta: "What they feel is strangeness. They feel as strange, as flattened out and borne aloft, as unconnected with previous and future events as the ghost car was" (p. 159). This correlation emphasizes the sense of timelessness that is often the aftermath of pressure and illustrates a release from desire. It shows relief from immediate choice and allows the suspension of power struggles. But it also focusses attention on the act of writing for women. If women are more affective than men and have, as Chodorow suggests, a sense of self "continuous with others,"[15] and a definition of themselves that is relational, how do they achieve the distance from their material that writers seem to need? Is it possible for women writers to release themselves from their bodies? In Munro's story, Roberta's body, with its "flabby armpits" (p. 137), its wrinkles and spots, its "haggard look" (p. 137) dominates the narrative. Yet the narrator separates from the character she writes about, thereby achieving distance. The story is an illustration of the very problem it dramatizes.

The other three stories in *The Moons of Jupiter* also function as literary theory, mainly because the central character in each is a writer. Lydia of "Dulse" is a forty-five-year old poet who suffers an identity crisis that, within the narrative's development, becomes a partial rite of passage. She has achieved the state Roberta attempts: Lydia feels emptied of desire. Her condition results from a recently ended love affair. She has been depressed, has been unable to "make the connection between herself and things outside herself" (p. 41), has been unable to keep herself together. She describes herself as a hollowed-out egg carton. This acknowledgement of emptiness is not unusual for abandoned women; in terms of narrative plots, it often ends in the ravings of madness or the silence of suicide. But Munro is not interested in such endings; instead, she probes the condition itself.

The story seems to ask how women and men can survive together if women give over power in order to be loved. It also questions the structuring of narrative plots that posit women as desiring subjects. Lydia's experiences seem cautionary and prophetic. The old masochistic plot dominates part of the story. Lydia recalls her visits to a psychiatrist who asks her, at one point, "why are you with somebody who can always pull the rug out?" (p. 55). Her lover, Duncan, maintains power over her by repeatedly comparing her to other women he has loved, a method of deflating her and of estranging her from other women. He keeps his own territorial rights, the dominant space in the plot. Within that space, Lydia learns "pathways around the apartment" (p. 54), finds places where she is allowed to sit, discourages her friends from visiting, sacrifices her sexual desires to Duncan's and allows him to control the tone of the conversation. Indeed, she erases her identity, hoping by such an abdication to bind her lover more closely to her. Yet although this information retrospectively functions as a conventional female narrative, the story itself investigates its legitimacy. Why women should give men such power over them, why they should allow their voices to be controlled and their boundaries defined, are the therapeutic concerns of the text. The plot of seduction and betrayal is opened to interpretation. Questioning it, Lydia asks: "what gave him his power? She knows who did. But she asks what, and when — when did the transfer take place, when was the abdication of all pride and sense?" (p. 50). She recognizes that she has allowed the desire to be loved to dominate her sexual life.

 The story emerges from a kind of hiatus, a tempting time of Lydia's freedom from desire. Various relationships occur in the present moments of the story. In the dining room of the guest-house in the Maritimes where she spends one night, Lydia meets an old, effete gentleman, an American who has spent a lifetime idolizing the writer Willa Cather. Staying there also are three working men at different life stages. Because she is a writer, Lydia tries to imagine what an affair with each of the working men would mean. How would the story constitute itself? She realizes that two of the men would use their power against her, and the story would be much the same as the one she has just finished, the one she has painfully analyzed with the help of the psychiatrist. The third man becomes a narrative possibility. With him, a more pleasant story would evolve. He is the man women ought to fall in love with and marry, "the sort of man she has known when she was a child living on a farm not so different from his, the sort of man who must have been in her family for hundreds of years" (p. 52). With him, the landscape would be known, real, although absent of desire and therefore of invention: "should she have stayed in the place where love is managed for you, not gone where you have to invent it, and reinvent it?" (p. 52). Should she have allowed herself to be a character in a story already written for her?

 If she is to be the author of her own story, if she is to have power of her own, she must invent and reinvent love. None of the relationships she imagines allows her such freedom. Her final conversation with the old man exposes her dilemma of power and desire. The conversation is about Cather; the plot of *The Lost Lady* drifts in the air. The old man insists that the homosexual Cather intimately understood male-female relationships. His belief in the artist's creative knowledge shelters him. But Lydia questions an artist's ability to know things she has not experienced, to write unmotivated by desire. She finds no answers. At the moment, "muffled up, wrapped in layers and layers of dull knowledge" (p. 50), a situation that leaves her mind unclouded, but remembering vividly the confusion and near madness of being "driven by desire" (p. 50), Lydia seems emotionally paralyzed. In fact, the narrator uses Lydia's dilemma to describe the aesthetic tension between creativity and experience, between living in an ivory tower and living in the actual world; the narrator also dramatizes certain idiosyncratic difficulties in the creating of a female voice. Desire takes away Lydia's authority. Although "[S]he has plenty to say about it, given the chance, because explanation is her habit," "'she doesn't trust what she says, even to herself; it doesn't help her. She might just as well cover her head and sit wailing on the ground'" (p. 50). Yet, emptied of desire, will she be able to write at all?

In "Bardon Bus," Munro uses a first-person narrator. Unlike the central characters of "Labour Day Dinner" and "Dulse," the narrator of "Bardon Bus" has discovered a voice and is therefore in control of her own story. More subjectively than Lydia, she reveals her feelings about a finished love affair. Bemused by the differences between loneliness and independence, between isolation and affiliation, she, like Munro, chooses the traditional figure of the old maid to represent women's problems with connection. Constructing her idea of the old maid as she would a character in a novel, the narrator, who is also a writer, describes the old maid as a woman who can tenaciously hold to a solitary idea, a solitary man, a solitary desire; a person who can maintain a "life-long dream life" (p. 110) and who can hold to desire in secrecy. The narrator imagines imitating the old maid. Like a writer, the old maid becomes a dealer in secrecy and fantasy. However, for this narrator, old maids also suggest masochism. Like Lydia, this female character has brought herself round to the central problem of desire and power for women, pleasure in suffering; she links masochism to the woman writer's imagined muse. For a moment, herself the old maid, she describes a recurrent fantasy, "the moment when you give yourself up, give yourself over, to the assault which is guaranteed to finish off everything you've been before. A stubborn virgin's belief, this belief in perfect mastery; any broken-down wife could tell you there is no such thing"(p. 111).

In a more complicated way than in "Dulse," this sexual and aesthetic fantasy implies the woman writer's problem with the authoritative voice. Longing to be mastered, the narrator has trouble developing independence or mastery. To give in to a man, to give in to the Muse, patterns behaviour so that women writers sometimes connect composition with suffering. Thus, for this narrator, writing caters to masochism: "Those detailed, repetitive scenes . . . had become a plague. All they did was stir up desire, and longing, and hopelessness, a trio of miserable caged wildcats that had been installed in me without my permission" (p. 123). More generally, for her, desire seems triggered by evil. Even when she goes to look for clothes, she admits that the dress she wants is "displayed against the black paper in a way that makes it look sinister, and desirable" (p. 125). Like the "assault which is guaranteed to finish off everything you've been before," the linking of the sinister and the desirable glorifies rape.

The story analyzes women's creativity. It becomes a demonstration of the elements that go into the female text. The narrator distances herself from her characters, referring to the man she is in love with as "x," "as if he were a character in an old-fashioned novel" (p. 112). Desire, power, and masochism narratively cross through each other. The affair (the story's central incident) seems both distant and immediate, vague and clear. The narrator admits that she does not understand the man's story and is not able to read his text: "I dreamed that x wrote me a letter. It was all done in clumsy block printing and I thought, that's to disguise his handwriting, that's clever. But I had great trouble reading it" (p. 114). Her dream, a kind of metaphor for the story itself, indicates the narrator's freedom from desire to be an illusion. Anxiety pervades it. The letter is delayed; the telephone doesn't work. Most significantly, in the dream, the narrator finds herself burdened with a baby, the classic literary punishment for a female character's misplaced desire.

This story makes use of other devices that demonstrate the simultaneous involvement and distancing attempted by the writer-narrator. For example, she is living with another woman, Kay, whose affairs overtly become material for her narrative development. As an observer of Kay's love affairs, the narrator can assume that objectivity attempted by Roberta and Lydia; she separates herself from the desiring subject. She describes in detail affairs in which Kay falls in love violently and frequently, each time taking "up a man and his story wholeheartedly" (p. 116). Kay's loss of her own voice disguises the narrator's similar, although not absolute, loss. The narrator represents Kay as an exempluum of modern women: "She does what women do" (p. 116). In the rise and fall of Kay's fortunes, the narrator sees literary possibilities: "When love is fresh and on the rise she grows mystical, tentative; in the time of love's decline, and past the worst of it, she is brisk and entertaining, straightforward, analytical" (p. 117). In other words, she is a text that demonstrates the learning of man's language, "figuratively or literally" (p. 116), the fact that love is "'the desire to see yourself reflected'" (p. 117).

Other material comes from a lunch the narrator has with a man she met during her affair with x, a man "tall, slight, stiff" who has an "elaborately courteous and didactic style" (p. 118). From him the narrator gets a lecture on gender, on male and female sexual power: "'Think of the way your life would be, if you were a man. The choices you would have. I mean sexual choices.... Men can get younger women'" (p. 121). He interprets men's ability to attract younger women as a stimulus to men's greater involvement with life, their constant renewal, their freshened vitality. For women, however, such competition seems to him disastrous. Women, unlike men, are forced "'to live in the world of loss and death!... The uterus dries up. The vagina dries up'" (p. 122). Women are removed from life. His moral is the same as many of the represented affairs in the various stories. It is also masochistic: "'It's only by natural renunciation and by accepting deprivation, that we prepare for death and therefore that we get any happiness'" (p. 122). For women, then, denial of the body becomes the answer. These stories question such drying up, such distancing. They also question such a loss of power.

The scenes the narrator dredges up repeatedly illustrate a loss of power, a masochistic abandonment to passion. The female character she creates in one fantasy seems almost unconscious, the epitome of passivity. She is also on display, spread out on the bed, her legs open, her arms flung out "as if she had been struck down in the course of some natural disaster" (p. 123). The narrator worries about her own appearance and is partly convinced that "more dramatic clothes might have made me less discardable" (pp. 124-25). She sees herself as discarded, as empty. Separated from her lover, she feels that she does not exist and announces that "I can't continue to move my body along the streets unless I exist in his mind and in his eyes" (p. 126). Sitting in a bakery, she looks out to the streets, hoping he will suddenly appear. She flirts with the possibility of letting herself go, with allowing the "lick of pain" (p. 127) to take over, to achieve the "queer kind of pleasure" that goes along with it, to dwell on "everything that is contradictory and persistent and unaccommodating about life" (pp. 127-28).

At the same time, she sees the necessity of displacement, although she has trouble defining it. One of her dreams helps. The dream, she says, is "far away" from her waking life. In it, "x and I ... were wearing innocent athletic underwear outfits, which changed at some point into gauzy bright white clothes, and these turned out to be not just clothes but our substances, our flesh and bones and in a sense our souls." The dream seems a dramatization of the metamorphosis of carnal into spiritual love, erotic desire into more distanced agape: "Embraces took place which started out with the usual urgency but were transformed, by the lightness and sweetness of our substance, into a rare state of content" (p. 127). When she tries to analyze this dream, she finds that she has not the proper words, that the dream, as she constructs it, sounds banal, movie-like. But the dream reveals that separation from desire experienced by Roberta at the dinner table and by Lydia after the end of her love affair. It allows the narrator a certain power, most obviously because the figures in it are not like those of waking life: they have equality. They are also removed from their bodies. It shows caring — but not too much. As a writer, the narrator recognizes that "misplacement is the clue." Like Stephen Dedalus's God, she could then remain "within or behind or beyond or above . . . refined out of existence, indifferent."[16]

In the last of these interpretations of desire and power, "Hard-Luck Stories," the telling of stories becomes the central theme. Structured as a retrospective triangle, it is briefly introduced by a conversation in the present between two women, a conversation that, as the other three stories in this group have done, connects women's desire with the stories they compose. The "ironical-twist-at-the-end sort of stories" (p. 181) that the narrator's friend Julie admires represent the three stories the women recall telling in the past, and also the story that contains them all, Munro's story. Thus, commentary overlaps dramatization and the dynamics of story-telling are laid bare. Again, but more emphatically, the questions posed have to do with the issues that seem most apparent in women's fiction: the achieving of distance; textual and bodily boundaries; endings; voice; the secrecy of hidden texts. It is a story about "the complaints many women make" (p. 183), but the personal context of this theme extends to social structures. It becomes political and the problem of distance that has informed each of the stories is a major problem in perception. The power struggles that permeate the hard-luck stories the women tell, although personal, seem also metaphors for broader tensions.

These tensions become apparent in the retrospective account of a dinner the three central characters shared in the past. Conventionally structured, the story of that dinner is a triangle in which two women — the narrator and her friend Julie — entertain a third person, Douglas, the narrator's lover in the present. Apart from revealing the kinds of stories women tell, the stories also emphasize a male audience. Douglas, like Duncan of "Dulse," George of "Labour Day Dinner" and x of "Bardon Bus," is represented as able to distance himself from the trivialities of daily life; he gains power from such distancing. He is a collector, an archivist who deals with "old diaries, letters, records" (p. 184), personal memorabilia that allow him insight into human dramas without his participating in them. Consequently, he remains "preserved," a "boyish-looking man" who reminds the narrator of the "jaunty grim looks you often see in photographs of servicemen in the Second World War" (p. 185). Compared with the susceptibility to aging that the female characters of these various stories endure, the "attempted transformation" of Lydia of "Dulse," when her lover criticizes her, the disgust George evinces towards Roberta's "aging body" (p. 137), the collapse of splendour into absurdity that the narrator of "Bardon Bus" believes to be catching up with her, Douglas, like the other male characters of these stories, seems removed from the process of aging. Even with the slight bulge over his belt and his greying hair, he controls his body, distances himself from "the world of loss and death" (p. 122).

His attitude to love also contrasts with the narrator's and Julie's. As she does with his appearance, the narrator generalizes his relationship with women, describing the swiftness and privacy of love's onset with the speed of his recovery. For men of his type, the narrative seems characteristic, the plot "predictable" (p. 182). Just as Douglas's business of old books and papers seems to him alive, vivid, active (books, like "bold rogues with the instincts of gamblers and confidence men" [p. 185], fascinate him), so does a love that involves the prospect of money with its "intrigues and lies and hoodwinking and bullying around" (p. 185). If he were to tell stories, they would not be about hard luck.

But the stories told are hard-luck stories, and they are told by the female characters. Julie's two stories, like the narrator's, meticulously annotate painful desire. She tells of eating gluttonously, of suffering bulimia and its merging, as women's physical suffering in these stories tends to do, with passionate desire. Julie's desire was for a young man who claimed to be a psychology student at the local university but who turned out to be a mental patient. Her second story involves a psychologist, an American man who led an encounter group she had belonged to some years before. The man claims to fall in love with Julie and writes her constant letters, "'confessions of self doubt'" (p. 190); he praises her for being "'aloof and wise'" (p. 190). She admits that she got to depend on his adoration even though she never took it seriously. But, like the psychology student, he has been duplicitous; he has collected women from all his encounter groups. When he is exposed, Julie feels she has been the "victim of witchcraft" (p. 190). During the telling of these stories, the narrator confesses her worry about Julie's effect on Douglas. She believes that women worry about introducing their female friends to men, anticipating the man's being "bored or put off" (p. 189). But the male audience of these stories is not bored. Like a voyeur, Douglas sings: "Back and side lay bare, lay bare" (p. 191).

The narrator also decides to risk exposure. The story she tells seems simple, a weekend visit paid, a discovery that her lover is still in love with their effete hostess, the dawning knowledge that the other male guest is also an old lover of the hostess, the awareness that the two men are being pitted against each other, "just to stir things up" (p. 195). Nothing like an epiphany emerges from the series of vignettes she presents. Yet they constitute a peculiarly political story. The central female character, the hostess, is so rich that her money seems physical, like "long lashes or a bosom" (p. 192). The narrator sees that "[I]nherited money can make a woman seem like a treasure" (p. 192). One of the themes of this hard-luck story establishes women as commodities and demonstrates the possessiveness of masculine desire. The hostess's position in the triangle is profoundly destructive, as the narrator realizes. "To be a femme fatale you don't have to be slinky and sensuous and disastrously beautiful, you just have to have the will to disturb" (p. 195). As an explanation of her understanding of love, the narrator's story isn't particularly helpful; but as a political statement, it confirms her own belief that love is not "rational, or in one's best interests, it doesn't have anything to do with normal preferences" (p. 195), and proves, once again, that the love that everyone values is not the marrying kind, but a passion that is "like a possession" (p. 195).

In this story-within-a-story, the narrator sees herself as having been her lover's "sensible choice" (p. 195). This choice excludes blinding passion. It allows her, as well as the man, narrative distance, and connects with the framing story. The graveyard the three characters walk through at the end of the story serves as the objective correlative of this lesson. The narrator thinks about the crudity of desire in the face of death. She hears "the silly sound" of her own voice "against the truth of the lives laid down here. Lives pressed down, like layers of rotting fabric, disintegrating dark leaves. The old pain and privation. How strange, indulged, and culpable they would find us — three middle-aged people still stirred up about love, or sex" (p. 196). The graveyard represents the opposite to possessed love. Disintegrating, rotting, the bodies there have no more connection with fetishism, with desire. But death is not a solution. The trillium, on the other hand, is. As she looks at the footstools in the old church in the graveyard, the narrator recognizes various elegant insignia in the needlepoint: the crosses of Saint George and Saint Andrew, the dove with the olive branch in its mouth. What first appears to be a lily turns out to be a "homely emblem," a trillium, Ontario's flower. This sign comforts her. Like the trillium, the narrator is not exotic, but immediate, homely and finally sensible. In spite of the fact that Douglas is indeed the lover of her story, she feels obscurely justified.

The final and title story, "The Moons of Jupiter," seems a summary commentary on the struggles between desire and power that have complicated the narration of the various stories. It is the story of a daughter's relationship with her father. In Munro's fiction, it balances an earlier story, "The Ottawa Valley," from *Something I've Been Meaning To Tell You*, where the daughter struggles to relate her writing to a mother whose indistinct edges and refusal to fall away present her with the persistent problems of narrative distance.[17] In "The Moons of Jupiter," the problems are somewhat different. In *The Daughter's Seduction*, Gallop insists that "[I]t may be historically necessary to be momentarily blind to father-love; it may be politically effective to defend — tightly, unlucidly — against its inducements, in order for a 'relation between the sexes,' in order to rediscover some feminine desire, some desire for a masculine body that does not respect the Father's law."[18] The daughter in "The Moons of Jupiter" acknowledges the difficulty of the father's law, his "bleak and dangerous" childhood (p. 219), his criticisms of articles about her, his puritanism.

She also attempts a balanced perspective. Her father's heart becomes the central topic. In the hospital, it is a text: "On the screen a bright jagged line was continually being written. The writing was accompanied by a nervous electronic beeping. The behavior of his heart was on display" (p. 217). Narrative, fathers, and daughters thus merge. The difficulty, even the presumption, of "dramatizing what ought to be a most secret activity" (p. 217) presents the narrator with problems of voice, of stance, of contact. It also foregrounds the problem of desire.

The landscape reflects the emotional life of the writer-narrator. She recalls the early years of a now-defunct marriage, her small, demanding children, the boring environment, the men returning from work, identical, the blur of "the West Coast rain falling. Dark dripping cedars, shiny dripping laurel" (p. 223). As correlatives of a repressed emotional state, the dripping trees suggest a subterranean sexuality that seems both terrifying and appealing. By the father's law, women's desire has no clear locus, is contradictory and ambiguous. Like all the stories in this collection, this story dissects the problem. Repression, the tidy suburban home, the safe love, the sleepiness are what the narrator has rejected. In the words of the narrator of "Hard-Luck Stories," she has "taken the risk" (p. 184). At the same time, she is now attempting separation from her children. Without such separation, she fears that she will be unable to write, will be as drained of creativity as Roberta is. The narrative thus emerges from a hard-won space between a dying father and two almost grown daughters, a suspended space where the narrator struggles for her own physical and textual boundaries.

The story also concretely dramatizes another crucial problem for the woman writer: her closeness to the narratives she creates, the ambiguous mingling of desire and powerlessness. Unlimited desire threatens formlessness. For this narrator, two experiences become the foci for the formal structuring of narrative. She recalls an episode from her older daughter's infancy when the baby was being tested for what her mother feared might be leukemia. Because of her terror, the narrator underwent a slight pulling away from her baby daughter: "There was a care — not a withdrawal exactly but a care — not to feel anything much" (p. 229). That partial withdrawing, the distancing of the self from experience, also implies control, a control her daughter now struggles to achieve as she distances herself from her mother, remains "[I]ncommunicado" (p. 230). The other episode occurs in the story's present. As she sits in a planetarium, time and space alter dramatically around her. Realism is abandoned for "familiar artifice" (p. 231). That artifice she courts in the Chinese gardens. As she sits on a stone bench and remembers the show at the planetarium, she experiences a removal from the body described in *Bodily Harm* as being "up near the ceiling."[19] She remembers that she "felt like one of those people who have floated up to the ceiling, enjoying a brief death. A relief, while it lasts" (p. 233). In such images, the writer achieves distance.

Other stories in the collection investigate extremes: on the one hand, caring too much; on the other, not caring enough. For women, the problem proves intransigent. Culturally and psychologically conditioned to be nurturant, affective, even dependent, women have often traded independence and power for love. Even the power of loving has often escaped them. When asked by the analyst what she wants, Lydia tentatively answers: "For him to love me?" But the analyst answers her with another question: "Not for you to love him?" (p. 53). In narrative terms, distance becomes a major problem for the woman writer who chooses to write from the female perspective and to situate her stories specifically within women's lives. In *Toward a New Psychology of Women*, Jean Baker Miller writes that "[E]ventually, for many women the threat of disruption of an affiliation is perceived not as just a loss of relationship but as something closer to a total loss of self.'"[20] Because women tend to stress relationship over autonomy, webs rather than hierarchies, women writers are faced with establishing satisfactory ways of distancing themselves from the events of the story, of giving the narrative voice authority, of separating the creating self from the characters in the text.

Munro dramatizes the problem. Important technical devices emerge. In the stories with third-person narration, the invisible narrator achieves a cool, slightly condescending tone. The reader is obliged to contemplate women characters who are having trouble controlling passion. By manipulating her characters, the narrator can establish irony. Abruptly opposing points of view collide with each other, as in the alternating involvement and separation experienced by Roberta or Lydia. The first-person stories are quite different in tone. They solve the problem of distance by using a narrator who is a writer and who therefore appears able to structure experience aesthetically, rather than personally. These narrators are also able to offer technical commentary on their predicament. In "The Stone in the Field," the narrator draws the reader's attention to silence and secrecy, to the impossibility of complete communication; the narrator of "Labour Day Dinner" points to the rights of choice. Although both first- and third-person stories display irony, the separation between the narrative voice and character in the third-person stories gives didactic rather than dramatic support to experience. Displayed in this way, female masochism becomes absurd, a warning. In the first-person stories, on the other hand, the survival of the narrator to structure the story demonstrates a contravened powerlessness. Indeed, as Cixous suggests, "[B]y writing her self, woman will return to the body which has been more than confiscated from her, which has been turned into the uncanny stranger on display."[21]

Finally, the correlatives that conclude many of the stories — the stone in the field, the dulse, the trillium, the planetarium — demonstrate a transformation of immediate experience into narrative. Metaphor creates distance. It also gives the writer power over her material. These stories demonstrate female lives at their most vulnerable, women's conditioned powerlessness in passion, their sexual masochism. As a result, the male voice is necessarily dampened. Although the stories explore sexual relationships, the woman's role as sufferer dominates the narrative development. Munro's characters realize the fear of autonomy that appears in the stories women tell. Subversive writers analyze that fear rather than accept it. Masochism is demystified, and the way is opened for female characters to unite desire and power. Because metaphor and mediation allow participation in "an adult order,"[22] desire becomes a political problem: it pushes the boundaries of private suffering into wider cultural contexts.

Chapter Six

Pandora and the State

No myth is more familiar than that of Pandora, none perhaps has been so completely misunderstood. Pandora is the first woman, the beautiful mischief; she opens a forbidden box, out comes every evil that flesh is heir to; hope only remains. The box of Pandora is proverbial, and that is the more remarkable as she never had a box at all.

> — JANE HARRISON
> "Pandora's Box"

Novels that depict female apprenticeship and awakening not only alter the developmental process, but also frequently change its position in the text. The tensions that shape female development may lead to a disjunction between a surface plot, which affirms social conventions, and a submerged plot, which encodes rebellion; between a plot governed by age-old female story patterns, such as myths and fairy tales, and a plot that reconceives these limiting possibilities; between a plot that charts development and a plot that unravels it.

> — ELIZABETH ABEL, MARIANNE HIRSCH, and ELIZABETH LANGLAND
> Introduction to "The Voyage In"

In women's stories, the articulation of the female self and the demonstration of connections with other women reflect cultural conditions that, in traditional narrative, have seemed peripheral to women's lives. Placed within history, the lives of the female characters in these stories stretch narrative possibilities and insinuate cultural alternatives that, even when they are imaginary, imply future enactment. One of these alternatives postulates control of male violence. In *A Room of One's Own,* Virginia Woolf argues that without women to serve as looking-glasses, to reflect man's image, "all our wars would be unknown . . . mirrors are essential to all heroic action."[1] In novels written by women, female characters often refuse that function; some seem remarkably opaque. Sometimes male characters virtually disappear from the fictional world, as if their existence were entirely dependent on reflection.

In Atwood's *Bodily Harm,* as Rennie becomes involved in politics and therefore in history, traditional assumptions about violence become gender distinctions and the conventionally predestined working out of political tensions — that is, through war — becomes questionable. When Paul tells Rennie that he is involved in revolutionary gun play, Rennie recognizes her sexual titillation, a titillation that has historically pandered to male violence; but she also recognizes its terrifying immaturity: "'Who's shooting at you?' says Rennie, who is trying very hard not to find any of this romantic. Boys playing with guns, that's all it is. Even telling her about this is showing off, isn't it?" (p. 244). Before the end of the novel, she comes more fully to understand the important lesson of women's novels: female support of male violence increases it, and increased violence leads to war. Women's masochism becomes politically dangerous, as many of Munro's characters realize. In "Its Image on the Mirror," a war plays in the background, politicizing private lives, surfacing to kill the brother and to separate the sisters from their husbands, to alter the stability of their world. The otherwise almost silent father contemplates the possibility of massive destruction: "We have lost the sense of seasons; our climate has been degenerating since the first nuclear explosion in Nevada a generation ago. He remembers that radioactive clouds traveled from Nevada to upstate New York" (p. 112). Apocalypse shadows the narrative.

In Sylvia Fraser's *Pandora,* war resonates within the dynamics of family relationships. The book's genre, the *bildungsroman,* focusses on cultural conditioning as it reflects itself in individual development. The myth of Pandora serves the author well. Represented as the first woman, Pandora was, like Eve, created by man to explain the presence of worldly evil. By opening the forbidden box, Pandora alters the face of the earth. She is also a sexual temptress who distracts man from duty and honour. The myth condenses culture and psychology, specifically around sexuality. For girls to grow up with the conviction of innate perversity (and uncontrollable and therefore threatening curiosity) reflects ideological conditioning. However, as Juliet Mitchell argues, "[U]nderstanding the laws of the unconscious . . . amounts to a start in understanding how ideology functions, how we acquire and live the ideas and laws within which we must exist."[2] Fraser's novel undertakes a full-scale attack on modes of production and woman's contemporary role in the family, as well as on the whole cultural history of the west, where women have been held accountable for a large portion of mankind's suffering.

The connections between cultural conditioning and psychological development have been the focus of considerable investigation in the past decade. From a sociological perspective, Chodorow's work has been extremely helpful in documenting the various ways in which society helps structure individual psychology. By investigating an individual's internalization of culture and analyzing such psychological functions as "fantasy, introjection and projection, ambivalence, conflict, substitution, reversal, distortion, splitting, association, compromise, denial and repression,"[3] all functions highlighted in *Pandora*, Chodorow undertakes to "advance the sociological understanding of the organization of gender."[4]

The political connections among class, colonial oppression and sexual oppression also need psychological and sociological grounding. In her 1972 book *Women, Resistance and Revolution*, Sheila Rowbotham argues that "if the revolutionary movement is to involve women, not as supporters or attendants only, but as equals, then the scope of production must be seen in a wider sense and cover also the production undertaken by women in the family and the production of self through sexuality."[5] Theoretical determinants for such "seeing," as I suggested in the introduction, are hard to come by. Various scholars are currently attempting to lay the groundwork for political interpretations of gender that will throw light on the relationship between women and modes of production. For example, in *Feminism and Materialism*, Annette Kuhn and AnnMarie Wolpe have concentrated attention on problems as wide-ranging as feminism's connections with materialism, with the sexual division of labour, with the state's involvement in the oppression of women and with education's support of such oppression. In the essay "Structures of Patriarchy and Capital in the Family," Annette Kuhn connects psychoanalytic and Marxist theory to indicate how sexual and political ideology is passed down through the family structures of western civilization. She argues that "the notion of patriarchy does indeed unite property relations and psychic relations. Patriarchy — the rule of the father — is a structure written into particular expressions of the sexual division of labour."[6]

Catherine MacKinnon also confronts theoretically familial and political structures. Positing that "sexuality is to feminism what work is to Marxism,"[7] she argues that "[T]he substantive principle governing the authentic politics of women's personal lives is pervasive powerlessness to men, expressed and reconstituted daily *as* sexuality. To say that the personal is political means that gender as a division of power is discoverable and verifiable through women's intimate experience of sexual objectification, which is definitive of and synonymous with women's lives as gender female. Thus, to feminism, the personal is epistemologically the political, and its epistemology is its politics."[8]

MacKinnon insists that the dynamics of consciousness-raising that marks the women's movement and that results in feminist theory becomes, like the dialectical materialism that powers Marxism, "the collective critical reconstitution of the meaning of women's social experience, as women live through it."[9] She also argues that the private sphere, which confines and separates us, is

> . . . a political sphere, a common ground of our inequality. In feminist translation, the private is a sphere of battery, marital rape, and women's exploited labour; of the central social institutions whereby women are deprived of (as men are granted) identity, autonomy, control, and self-determination; and of the primary activity through which male supremacy is expressed and enforced. Rather than transcending the private as a predicate to politics, feminism politicizes it. For women, the private necessarily transcends the private. If the most private also most 'affects society as a whole,' the separation between public and private collapses as anything other than potent ideology.[10]

MacKinnon opens to wider investigations the problematic connections between psychoanalytic and cultural approaches to femininity.

How does Sylvia Fraser's novel demonstrate the politicizing of the private? Suggesting the sexual politics of the family as the training ground for full-scale destruction, Fraser presents — beneath a series of metaphoric games, for example Monopoly — a radical criticism of sexual dichotomies. At the text's centre is the young Pandora, and the world in which she moves toward maturity is a fairly rigid, sexually differentiated one. Mothers and fathers are perceived as different kinds of people, not merely different persons. That the message given the reader concerns sexual ideology is not surprising. Although all the children of the novel sometimes behave in calculating and cruel ways, the encouraged cruelty of young boys who grow up to be men dominates the action. Indeed, *Pandora* methodically anatomizes social structures that foster the development of such philosophies as Nazism, a philosophy filtered through the world during the historical period of Pandora's growing up.

Fraser's attempt to revise the myth of Pandora has powerful politicized gender implications. In an interview with Alan Twigg, Fraser emphasizes her feminism: "There was a time when it was considered an insult to be labelled a woman novelist, but now I almost would consider it flattering, because I think women today are miles ahead of men in terms of emotional health and awareness. Essentially, it's the result of the women's movement."[11] Thus, while a number of the female characters described in this novel lead obviously unsatisfactory lives, the representative character, Pandora, is most certainly a revision of the myth of womanhood. Based on material that has traditionally been devalued — the female body — and told in a language that has traditionally been silenced — female language — *Pandora* recognizes "another sort of life."

In the representative family of the novel, the Gothics, the struggle between a father's rage and a mother's forbearance dominates the early action and suggests ways in which gender patterns are reproduced. Nancy Chodorow highlights such reproduction: "In an industrial late-capitalist society, 'socialization' is a particularly psychological affair, since it must lead to the assimilation and internal organization of generalized capacities for participation in a hierarchical and differentiated social world, rather than to training for a specific role."[12] Like the families described by Lillian Rubin in her study of working-class America, *Worlds of Pain*,[13] the Gothic family reveals particular economic tensions that make more absolute the division of labour within the family and that insist on the father's apparent dominance. Yet the novel also reflects a more universal familial organization. The passive, quiet twins, Ada and Adel, obey authority and, because they are female, emulate their mother's secondary role in the hierarchical patriarchal structure where the father's authority, no matter how bizarre, is accepted. *Pandora* dramatizes the family as the ground in which certain sexual tensions first blossom, the place where civilization establishes and develops its discontents. Pandora's father's rage defines him; her mother's hymn-singing defines her. Metonymies multiply as sexual dichotomies assume increasingly complicated meanings. Lyle Gothic's steel hook replaces one of his arms. His hook and his "steel-rimmed" eyes (p. 11), interpreted by Pandora as narrow windows of rage, suggest machine-like impersonality. Against him, Adelaide's incorporeality is no fit adversary. Pandora imagines her mother leaving her body behind and floating off on the notes of the hymns she constantly sings.

Marital tension fills the house. Lyle Gothic sits in the living room, shouting for his wife to bring him a drink, while the wife slavishly sifts ashes in the basement. Pandora watches. She sees her mother run to her father, observes her sisters as they flatter him with quiet attention. She watches and she learns, for she knows something about plagues. With Nietzschean insight, she recognizes in this patriarchal family the presence of barely controlled violence. Her father belligerently asks: "'*When* have I ever struck *any*one in this house? When have I ever done *any*thing to *any* of you, but work my ass off for you?'" (pp. 21-22). Lyle Gothic's bewilderment is real; overwhelmed by his mother and by the houseful of women he has to support, he does not know why he is constantly furious, or why he is unable to discuss his feelings. Caught in the gender battle, he seems doomed to play out a foreordained part. When Pandora questions male authority, she infuriates him. He threatens to throw her naked into the street, stripped of all the signs of his protection and his name, a father's response to a daughter's subversion.

Why does Pandora rebel? Partly, her narrative function is to question the daughter's role in a father-dominated family. But Fraser has also provided us with several psychological determinants. Pandora is intelligent, periodically reckless, questioning. As the youngest member of the family, she benefits from the chance to observe her sisters' and mother's status. Like her author, she seems more interested in women than in men — for example, her maternal grandmother and her teacher, Miss Macintosh. Her birth suggests a female creation of the world, in "flesh-heave, mountain-burst, joy-throe, pain-spasm, silt, seaweed, dinosaur dung, lost continents, blood, mucus" (p. 9). Against this female genesis, the religion of the fathers seems stultifying, even deadly. Pandora angrily defies that religion: "'*In the Beginning God made this lovely world. God who is Good, and who Always was.*' . . . It was my father. He laid the World, and he killed the Easter Bunny, and he *choked* Baby Victor!'" (p. 136). Her perverse catechism haunts the novel. Men and boys use aggression in their efforts to make the world fit their desires so that the *mise en scène* of the family is precisely the one posited by Freud in *Beyond the Pleasure Principle*, the cosmic battle between life and death. Because the tensions evoked are universal and increasingly deadly, the intelligent and wilful Pandora — the new woman — needs to find a new space and new rules.

Sexual perversion becomes a social metaphor. The contracted Eden that is the neighbourhood Paradise Park harbours a male snake who exposes himself to Pandora and her girlfriend. The breadman, thought by Pandora to be her friend, sexually accosts her. The experience frightens her and creates a physical revulsion that extends to all the men and boys she knows. It extends, too, to her own body, which embarrasses her, so that "Fear and shame gorge like buzzards on her burden of guilty knowledge, leaving only a few twisted bones" (p. 72). The narrator critiques Freud's seduction fantasy, finally interpreted by Freud as not actual, but an hysterical symptom, an "expression of the typical Oedipus complex in women."[14] In *Pandora*, real occurrences structure the female psyche in ways that lead to subversion, not hysteria. By presenting a profoundly alienating sexual experience that is inevitably associated with the aggressive father, the narrator suggests a less phallocentric interpretation of female development. Pandora learns to value her own femininity precisely because she finds the masculine world unappealing. Freudian theory narrates male, not female, desire. In the novel, much of society reflects a perverted masculinity. At St. Cecilia's Home for Cripples and Incurables, the priests in their black robes intimidate Pandora; when an old man forces her to eat one of his candies, her disgust almost chokes her. The phallic implications are obvious: "Pandora thinks about Job's hooked thumbs. She thinks about her father's steel hook" (p. 161). The extra thumb she imagines to be growing on her hand seems, like a small penis, to conflate masculinity and disease.

Class struggle combines with sexual struggle. Pandora's family dramatizes the original division of labour, expressed in current sexual dichotomies. Lyle Gothic, the butcher, metaphorically demonstrates the providing male, the original hunter. He literally brings home the bacon. The hymn-singer, Adelaide Gothic, metaphorically demonstrates motherhood. She is responsible for the moral growth of the children; she is long-suffering and patient. Enclosed within the patriarchal home, she sings: "Chained to the World, to Sin ty'd down / In darkness shall I lie" (p. 19). Other families in the novel also exhibit class and sexual struggle. When Pandora goes to Ruth-Anne Baltimore's birthday party, she observes a capitalist family portrait, a Gainsborough: "Gilbert Baltimore positions himself behind Ruth-Anne and her mother, on their Hepplewhite loveseat. The bowl of his pipe rests against the lapel of his smoking-jacket" (p. 188). This reification of the patriarchal family, one of the mainstays of a capitalist economy, structures the novel. Indeed, the novel's space is a Monopoly board and its class divisions function according to Monopoly properties; Oriental Avenue, for example, is one of the cheaper properties on the board. The acquisitive impulse that dictates the rules of the game dominates the whole of Pandora's world. Specific references to American patriotism also stress capitalist structures. When the magician performs at Ruth Anne's party, "[T]he Union Jack rises on a flag-pole from his left pocket. The Stars and Stripes rises on a flagpole from his right pocket" (pp. 189-90). Between these powerful forces exists Canada, a little like Pandora herself.

The conventions of the *bildungsroman* allow Fraser's narrator to establish the family as basic to class and sexual conflict. Through them, the reader can connect the family's dynamics with those of the wider world, which the central character gradually enters. When Pandora moves outward, she discovers that male aggression dominates society. Bigotry controls the very institutions that might be expected to escape it — church and school. Class dictates many of the school's practices. Ruth-Anne carries with her, like a banner, her upper-class home, which is the envy and the scourge of Pandora. *Ressentiment* festers: "Pandora buries her fists in her green eyes. One more drawer in that bloody pencilbox and she would have become a socialist" (p. 200). Racial, religious and sexual strife controls the politics of the schoolyard. Against a forming female society, the boys sadistically effect disruption. Their sadism is also practiced against members of their own sex, who draw attention to themselves by their powerlessness or their difference. Dirty Danny is cruelly beaten because he is a "Wop." Japanese children are unmercifully teased. The newspaper, with its repeated atrocities, seems to lend authority to the boys' actions. Jessie Christie and other boys get pleasure out of tormenting girls not necessarily by physical prowess (Jessie wears glasses), but by using belittling sexual innuendo, which humiliates them. A young Jewish boy, the same boy Pandora's Christian mother has labelled "an Hebrew" (p. 172), someone who "doesn't accept Jesus Christ" (p. 173) and who would be an unsuitable husband for Pandora, becomes the butt of pranks that rapidly turn into acts of war. When the community makes Jason the scapegoat for allegedly tampering with the church's sacrament, the town participates in the Fascist philosophy that dominates Europe during Pandora's growing years. Canada is not immune. The male voices of the school principal, of the policeman and of the priest pronounce the rules.

Yet the patriarchal law that is evoked during this episode proves wrong. When the police come to Laura Secord school, to check up on a crime so *"awful only a BOY could think of it!"* (p. 215), Pandora feels suffocated. Like her father, the policemen fill up all her space. When they unite with the principal and the priest to condemn Jason, they connect themselves with the boys' unholy trinity of father, son and holy ghost: Godfrey Trumps, Jessie Christie and Horace Ghostie. Against their Fascism only Pandora's favourite teacher, Miss Macintosh, stands out, and loses her job. Pandora has received a pragmatic lesson in subversion: *"Can school, church and state* ALL *be wrong?"* (p. 222). Fittingly, the lesson comes from a woman: "'People *do* make mistakes. Even people with titles and uniforms. *Especially* people with titles and uniforms because sometimes they think they can't go wrong'" (p. 220). Pandora and her friends go to a movie, a dramatization of war that turns out to be a sado-masochistic fantasy, an exhibition of dismemberment, of torture. It ends by totally denying life: *"The camera plays over a bombed-out school. It focuses on a dead child, cradling a doll with the head blown off.... A fluffy kitten lies crumpled against a garbage-can, its silent white fur splattered with blood"* (pp. 202-03). The movie episode conflates with a confrontation Pandora has with her father; he has had her cat exterminated. In this way, the narrative suggests that world violence is an extension of the patriarchal home. Like Rennie Wilford's conclusion in *Bodily Harm* — "she's afraid of men because men are frightening" (p. 290) — the words *"War is Hell"* reflect, in *Pandora*, a dominantly masculine pursuit.

Pandora's introduction to the law is not a step on the road to maturity, but rather a cautionary lesson about the fallibility of the patriarchy. She also learns that women have a moral responsibility to object to injustice. Pandora's final confrontation with Jessie Christie dramatizes her knowledge, her new morality. When Jessie proves to be the culprit in the murder of an old woman's cat, Pandora isolates herself from the family and assumes the role of avenger. Her attack on Jessie's clubhouse represents a different dealing with men: not subservience but subversion. It releases her. Even when Jessie taunts her with sexual insults, Pandora ignores him: "The sun dances madly in his glasses. His tongue wags like the red crossing-signal. He puffs up his brass-buttoned chest, juts out his chin, ruffles and rattles his feathers. Pandora passes the unshriven Jessie Christie without seeming to notice . . . *Jessie Christie is dead"* (p. 234). She needs a new religion and a new law.

Pandora appears to be a fairly radical novel, one that strikes at patriarchal establishments and practices. Its style contributes to its subversive perspective. Specific rhetorical devices insist on the reader's constant attention and reflect the narrator's interest in the tensions she describes. For example, hyphenated words ("flesh-heave, mountain-burst, joy-throe, pain-spasm") illustrate a split and doubled narration, which is also emphasized in the reader's conflicting views of what is happening. Such ambiguity needs a fluid language, one that is not reified. The notion of a specifically female language is certainly a controversial one. Nonetheless, as Jane Gallop points out, many current French feminist critics "see 'neutral language' as itself an 'area of oppression,'" and want "to use the fluid, the inconsistent, the unfinished to undermine the oppressive 'phallic seriousness of meaning.'"[15] Fraser does not attempt a radical linguistic exposé, the way French-Canadian writer Nicole Brossard does; nor does she use fragments of the culture as text, like Audrey Thomas, who emphasizes woman's peripheral position while dramatically resituating woman within it. But the style of *Pandora* encourages the reader to question traditional grammatical forms and traditional meaning.

Pandora's narrator wants the reader to laugh at language, and the text is filled with puns that often undermine rigid meanings. The narrator has fun with words; she doesn't take them quite seriously and refuses them authority. At the same time, she never loses sight of the atrocities committed through language: "The Nasty Vowels grab Pandora's golden curls. The Nazi Vowels shave her head. The Vowel Nazis drag her *bump! bump! bump!* down the attic steps, and *hup! hup! hup!* out into the snow. The Foul Nazis strip off her nightie, with their black germ-hands" (p. 101). Alliteration, assonance, and onomatopoeia privilege sound. In Pandora's early world, sound dominates sense. (Pandora cannot read.) The narrator's playing with sound reminds us of language's oral roots. Echoes of northern sagas appear here and there, recalling societies where old and powerful women like Grannie Cragg exercised power. When Pandora tries to teach her grandmother to read, Grannie Cragg assures her that the vowels, those "Nazi Vowels," "'wouldn'ta helped me where I been, Chickee, and they aren't going to help me where I'm going'" (p. 80). Language becomes Pandora's, and the narrator's, tool for rebellion, a direct extension of the psyche: "Room 3 ripples with silent hysteria: Fear, embarrassment, shame, mingle with the high-tension pitchpipe notes *quivering, quivering, quivering*, against the windows like supersonic sound trapped in crystal, leaping from nerve-ending to nerve-ending, tightening, twisting, tuning the cords of each nervous system into an instrument of unbearable sensitivity" (p. 88). The emphasis on sound finally draws attention to Pandora's voice. She will not become a silent woman, or a cowed one. We hear her voice throughout.

Other stylistic devices emphasize the sexual dualism that is the novel's major concern. Throughout, italicized type alternates with ordinary type, overtly splitting inward and outward narration. Many of the passages in italics present Pandora's often unacceptable private thoughts, residue of the unconscious, and contrast them with a socially sanctioned outward expression. As might be expected, the intruding unconscious reveals sexual tensions, just those dichotomies that inevitably, although not always obviously, structure society's institutions — home, school, church, and court. Cultural development and personal development intersect. Because she moves back and forth throughout, Pandora, both idiosyncratically and mythically, represents a history of femininity and an individual female *bildung*. She thinks about her parents:

> *I wish I could get out of my skin. My mother gets out through her mouth. She slides out on her treble clef when nobody is looking. My father explodes his skin. He splatters everyone with hot skin, and then he grows another. My father sucks in all the air in the room, and everyone else has to squash themselves against the wall, and rub off their noses so as not to prick him.* (p. 91)

The description is certainly personal; the metaphors are homely and the interpretation of Adelaide and Lyle Gothic characteristic. At the same time, however, Pandora contrasts femininity and masculinity and stresses the ways in which fathers oppress and mothers escape. Pandora's subterranean life seems a narrative of rebellion that periodically surfaces to mingle with the outer narrative of her life. Even her hair metonymically represents these shifts: "Her braids, replaited by Arlene, are a testament to determined amateurism. One of her elastics is broken. Pitch-forks stud the reinstated halo like a cockeyed crown of thorns" (p. 117).

One of the major questions raised by the stylistic peculiarities of the novel has to do with the control of language and the control of fictional forms. Virginia Woolf began the discussion of the influence of gender on language and form by arguing that, because tradition has been male, women writers have difficulty relying on it. The sentence as well as the shape of the work, Woolf claimed, "has been made by men out of their own needs for their own uses."[16] In *Mrs. Blood* and in *Blown Figures*, Isobel and the narrator undertake to revise the language of the myths that have for generations privileged male metaphors. Simplistically put, the womb replaces the penis. Formally, Thomas' novels reflect the change by drawing attention to broken connections — for example, with excessive use of dashes or by disrupted chronology or by peculiar pagination. In *Bodily Harm*, the subversion of language is a major theme: when Rennie discovers that her body is being written in a foreign tongue, she recognizes the importance of taking back the ownership of her own body and therefore controlling her language. Pierre Macherey insists that critics can discover a text's ideology only in "the silences, the denials, and the resistance of the object," so that the effort to enunciate the text's "silent significance," its "determinate otherness"¹⁷ produces new knowledge. Textual fissures — as, for example, in the silences and gaps of "Its Image on the Mirror" — present ideology and dramatize the secret lives of women, their otherness. But from them, new knowledge emerges. For Pandora, that new knowledge assumes a specifically female voice.

Stylistically, the construct of an outspoken narrator emphasizes the political nature of the text. In *Pandora*, the narrator prescribes, so that the novel's combination of narrative and analysis, of fiction and sociology, connects it with contemporary feminist writing — such as *In a Different Voice*, where Gilligan punctuates case studies with critiques of fictional characters, or *Of Woman Born*, where Rich mingles events from her own life with literary and cultural analysis. Like these women writers, *Pandora*'s narrator implies significant connections between fictional characters and the actual world. Such connections, feminist critics emphasize, question masculine tradition as exemplified in literary form. They insist on the intrusion of the personal voice into public utterances and present the isolated case study as representative. Although *Pandora* is fiction, the narrator dominates our reading by inserting long passages of behavioural analysis into the text, underlining the presence of a judging observer, not unlike the observer-narrator of *Blown Figures* who, apart from dictating to the fictional character ("How silly you are Isobel, I could rub you out like a chalkboard," [p. 227]), also manipulates our reading by speaking directly to us ("The three people who concern us are sitting in padded vinyl armchairs" [p. 151]).

In *Pandora*, politics results from the narrator's frequently subversive interferences. For example, by not allowing a traditional reading of the Pandora myth or the myth of Canada's passivity in terms of world politics, the narrator undercuts conservative ideology. The patriarchal family is questioned; so are the school, the church, the law. Biblical narrative assumes a female, rather than a male, resonance. The novel's introductory revision of Genesis is notable for its exclusion of masculine creation and its dramatization of female production. The "lost continents" (p. 9) are made from the blood and mucus of the female body and the long geological history evoked by references to the bursting forth of mountains and to the residue of "dinosaur dung" (p. 9) condense the female "flesh-heave" of birth and the traditional mythology of patriarchal history. From the beginning, *Pandora*'s narrator has codified female and male, implying the former's creativity and the latter's destructiveness. The father squints at the world "through the narrow window of his rage" (p. 9).

When directly retelling myth, the narrator's voice usually sinks into the background. But at other points in the novel, that voice assumes a didactic and obtrusive tone, and fictional, dramatized events receive instant interpretation. Pandora looks around her, senses, feels, observes. Simultaneously, the narrator categorizes Pandora's idiosyncratic development and makes it more general. Under headings like "Standards of Social Congress and Exchange," "Standards of Dress," "Standards of Street Deportment," "Standards of Difference," "Standards of Competition," and "Standards of Decency," the narrator objectifies the social codes that dominate the lives of the people on Oriental Avenue and, by extension, those of the middle-class WASPS whose lives seem to be judged. As in the opening of the novel, sexual dichotomies are placed in the foreground. We are told that Oriental is a "street of women," that "Saturday is a male day, Sunday a female one" (pp. 33-34). Although both men and women live on Oriental Avenue, women are responsible for almost all the direct conversation, and the reader hears most of what is said through women's ears.

The novel seems reported and commented on from a female perspective. Although the gender of the narrator is not announced, it seems fair to say that the narrator is female. This theoretical problem has been discussed by Susan Lanser in *The Narrative Act*, where Lanser argues for its political significance. According to her, the insistent critical use of the generic "he" to refer to unspecified fictional narrators is not ideologically neutral; instead, it carries the assumption that gender is irrelevant to the ways in which we perceive texts. Yet, Lanser says, "contemporary research has amply demonstrated that gender is one of the strongest determinants of social, linguistic, and literary behavior in patriarchal societies . . . . Gender-based distinctions have been influential in the writing and reading of literature and, I believe, also permeate the structures of narrative; in an andocentric culture male and female voices are not heard in the same way."[18] Lanser returns to the problem of the narrator's gender. Because "white heterosexual males of a certain socioeconomic position constitute the dominant class in Western society," readers most often assume the unmarked narrative voice — and unmarked writing in general — to be male. "The presence of a female extrafictional voice . . . thus presents an interesting problem in narrative convention. If the extrafictional voice appears to be female (i.e., if a woman's name appears on the title page) will the unmarked narrator be assumed to be female as well? . . . I will suggest that the *noted* presence of a female name on the title page signals a female narrative voice in the absence of markings to the contrary."[19] Lanser's argument appears to apply to *Pandora*; although the narrator's remarks are presented with apparent text-book objectivity, the reader, I believe, assumes the narrator's femininity.

Furthermore, language and event gain irony because gender matters to the text. For example, what could have been a straightforward attack on religious bigotry, or on capitalism, or on the ways adults make life unbearable for children, becomes, in the whole episode that takes place in Paradise Park, sexually pointed. Like the Garden of Eden, the park is spacious, a "magnificent ten-acre greensward" (p. 45). Its God, the aristocrat Sir Edward Arley stands "granite-jawed," prepared to "smite the earth, with his gold-knobbed cane" (p. 48). References to Nazis creep in. A "panzer division" (p. 46) of gardeners keeps the grass groomed. Gender-distinct descriptions occur throughout. The two fountains, the one in memory of a daughter (*"Flow gently, Sweet Afton"*), the other in memory of a son (*"Fight the Good Fight"*), ironically underline stereotyped attitudes toward femininity and masculinity. Only on "Wilde Corner," with its reference to Oscar Wilde, do Pandora and Arlene feel free to relax. Finally, the serpent in Paradise Park turns out to be a sexually perverted man who exposes himself to the girls; earlier, he was described as looking like a soldier or a German spy.

The narrator also comments on Pandora's development, allowing her voice to sound like a teacher's. She informs the reader that the seats in the miniature world of the classroom are equivalent to houses (we are never far from the game of Monopoly, the novel's metaphor for capitalism), that "[I]deally, a girl's bestfriend will reflect her status or improve it," that, among the couples now being established, "[T]here will be divorces, there will be separations, there will be partner swaps, but these will be handled within the group in an orderly fashion. No girl who is 'in' will dare risk a general reshuffling that may leave her 'out'" (p. 149). These remarks are certainly economic; references to commodity fetishism and the class struggle dominate them. At the same time, the remarks are also sexual. The narrator separates male and female development, stressing girls' relatively dependent behaviour, a behaviour that, in terms of the novel being discussed, necessarily affects the kind of *bildungsroman* that will reflect female lives.

The narrator also insists that the reader analyze the various characters of the novel from a qualified sexual perspective. To this end, she makes statements that generalize the specific:

> The boys — unlike the girls — are learning to define themselves as individuals, by what they can do, rather than as group members, by how others react to them. Their teams are, to a considerable extent, chosen across grade and classroom lines on the basis of skill and dominance. Most of them are more concerned with what they play, than with whom they play. Rules and rituals are used to define the game, not who plays it. When material wealth changes hands,

it does so as the spoils of victory, not as tokens of friendship." (p. 157)

Gilligan observes that "the stories that delineate women's fantasies of power . . . convey a different sense of its social reality. In their portrayal of relationships, women replace the bias of men toward separation with a representation of the interdependence of self and other."[20] *Pandora*'s narrator emphasizes, through the language she uses, the different *bildung* of girls and boys. Most tellingly, she makes a moral judgement. Although words like "skill," "dominance," "rules," and "rituals" are relatively neutral, when attached to the expression "the spoils of victory," they assume moral overtones. The macrocosm, for which the boys' schoolyard society proves to be a microcosm, is, in the novel, Hitler's Germany. Female passivity proves harmful, an outgrowth of traditional sex roles that deny power to girls and women. But the narrator does not advocate female imitation of male social behaviour. Rather, she advocates a "different sort of life," a life in which Gilligan's web dominates, where the configuration in and out takes precedence over up and down.

The narrator never misses a chance to emphasize the negative results of a dominantly patriarchal system. She interprets aggression as ultimately destructive, particularly to the degree that it is encouraged by fathers. When the police come to the school looking for the boys who have desecrated a church, no one imagines that the culprit might be a girl. Ironically, at first the girls feel that their virtue, their passivity, is valued. Yet as the proceedings continue, another message, impressed on the reader by the narrator, seeps through. It is the message that is finally understood by Rennie Wilford and that ultimately makes her subversive. Pandora realizes "a shift in the balance of power: The girls, once superior in their innocence, are now inferior through lack of participation. The boys, once impotent in the face of authority, are now initiates in a secret society bonded by risk" (p. 218). This camaraderie, celebrated by writers like Lionel Tiger as "male bonding," comes to mean fascism in many novels by women writers.

I would argue that the didactic narrative voice in *Pandora* obliges us to take the sexuality of its content seriously, to acknowledge that the gender of the writer makes a difference and to be aware that the sex of the central character determines the ways in which the reader weighs that character's experience. I suggest that the narrator sets herself up as a female speaker and also as an ideal female reader; she refuses to allow a misogynist interpretation of the myth of Pandora. Certain apparently casual remarks — like Ruth-Anne's comment that her mother says "'boys are rough, but if they like you they'll do what you want, but you have to tell them without them knowing, because girls are more ci-vil-ized'" (p. 175), or the description of Pandora as "Cinderella entering the ball, with pumpkins on her feet and rats in her hair, and no Fairy Godmother in sight" (p. 186) — assume a political slant. The narrator directs us toward a radical reading that will structure cultural violence differently, that will question male dominance. She therefore functions somewhat like a metaphor for the kind of readings that seem appropriate for much women's fiction.

Fraser's attack on the patriarchy continues to the end of the novel, and it implies increasingly terrifying cultural catastrophes. Men are associated with war throughout the book. When Lyle Gothic prophesies the future as the novel draws to a close, he sees the second of the wars to end all war smoothly shifting its focus. The nuclear age dawns: he "sits on the porch in his wicker chair, reading about the collapse of The War on one continent, and its intensification on another; erasing the Union Jack from the boats and planes of his loyalty, and replacing it with the Stars and Stripes; shrinking the enemy from blond giants to black-haired dwarfs, raising their voices from gutteral to super-sing-song-sonic; moving from the trenches to the jungle trees; keeping his airpower; amassing his fleets, and then, of course, preparing to make that switch in psychology from The Rocket to The Bomb" (p. 253). That psychological switch means the possible annihilation of the human race. It reflects Freud's "fateful question" at the conclusion of *Civilization and Its Discontents*: "whether and to what extent" human beings "will succeed in mastering the disturbance of their communal life by the human instinct of aggression and self-destruction . . . . Men have gained control over the forces of nature to such an extent that with their help they would have no difficulty in exterminating one another to the last man."[21] Even the Monopoly game Lyle Gothic plays against imagined opponents — Howard Hughes, J. Paul Getty — becomes an economic correlative for the violence he sees all around him.

Yet the myth of Pandora should balance possible destruction with a more hopeful prophecy. And it does. It, too, calls upon "eternal Eros,"[22] a new myth. In the novel's final section, Pandora tentatively becomes the inheritor of her grandmother's money and therefore of a "different sort of life." Her "different" life suggests her removal from the economic restrictions of Oriental Avenue. Pandora knows that her father and mother have agreed to give up their share of the grandmother's legacy to invest in their daughter's future, a gesture that helps to release her from some of her fear of her father's power: "Lyle looks up, once, from under war, inflation and the bristling denial of his own inadequacies with a fierce expression which, if examined carefully, would not seem angry" (p. 254). And, because it is concerned with the construction of the new woman, the novel symbolically offers a positive conclusion to the female *bildungsroman*, a conclusion traditionally perceived in more negative terms.

The ending functions as a metaphor for contemporary women's extrication of themselves from hampering social structures, an alternative destiny. In the novel, the world creatively opens up and hope dominates. Female sexuality at last blossoms. The matrons of Oriental Avenue are subsumed in a different vision of femininity. Pandora and her friend Arlene "haul themselves onto their island. They sink back into its poachy contours. They embrace, trailing strands of albumen. They feel each other's beating hearts. They press their bodies in mutual exploration . . . Lips, their juice and flexibility. Cheeks, their comfort and contour. Chests, their budded mystery. Bellies, their warmth. Hands, their infinite variety. Thighs, their power. Genitals, their vulnerability" (pp. 246-47). After Pandora's squalid baptism in the mud in her father's ruined victory garden where she makes "angels in the *uck-guck* iodine muck" and feels "the rats fall out of her ears" (p. 233), her rebirth seems remarkably positive. Remaking history, she and Arlene become the first women, "wallowing in primordial stew" (p. 246).

Pandora's lot does seem more hopeful than the lot of the old Eve. One old Eve is Aunt Rosie, whose attempted suicide results from a social system she cannot defeat. Emotionally dependent on men, an imitator of Ginger Rogers, Veronica Lake and Rita Hayworth, Rosie compensates for the fact that she cannot fight by getting herself voted "The Girl I'd Most Like to Be Torpedoed With" (p. 60). Symbolically, after she jumps from a window, her reconstructed face is *"a mosaic of broken mirror bits"* (p. 251). Pandora's inability to see her own reflection in the mirror and her smashing of that mirror emphasize its symbolic significance, its traditional reflexive function, its connection with a stultifying rather than a positive narcissism. That connection, this novel shows us, can be changed. The inheritance given to Pandora will allow her to live another sort of life, a life different from her martyred mother's, from her silent and reproducible twin sisters', a life different from her irascible father's.

Ironically, as Erwin and Dora Panofsky point out, the two major twentieth-century representations of the myth of Pandora, Paul Klee's and Max Beckmann's, characterize her box as the ultimate symbol of horror and despair. Beckmann's "gouache . . . first anticipated and then recorded the horrors of the atomic bomb: his 'Pandora's Box' is a small, square object charged with an incalculable amount of energy and exploding into a chaos of shattered form and color."[23] Fraser rejects such a reading. Instead, in spite of the very real threat of total destruction, she insists that a new kind of woman has a chance to change the world: "Pandora steals downstairs, outside, into the balmy night. She runs barefoot, through the squishy-grass. She drinks rain-splash from the throat of a lily. She dances, white nightie, under the rain-splayed stars, following the fireflies as they make fire-love, in checkmarks, to her mother's mimosa; seeing them illumine her father's cabbages to at least the status of pumpkins" (p. 254). Such positive images of transformation illuminate the darker world of war and destruction; love, generation, even a certain freedom seem possible. In this novel, Pandora becomes the symbol of hope; the plagues of the myth are consigned to a dominantly male destructiveness. In the face of sadism, rage and despair, in the face of Jessie Christie as she turns from him, Pandora becomes a "real landscape" (p. 245), one that promises future growth, even a new Eden.

At the end of *The Reproduction of Mothering*, Chodorow reviews her various confrontations with social psychologists, most of whom believe that "there is nothing inherently *wrong* with a sexual division of functions or roles — with the sexual division of labour."[24] Certainly, theorists agree that men's and women's work should not be valued differently, that work done in the home and work done in the marketplace are both essential. But as Chodorow points out, "historically and cross-culturally we cannot separate the sexual division of labor from sexual inequality."[25] Women's child-rearing roles seem frequently to generate male dominance. The patriarchal family reflects such dominance. In *Pandora*, Lyle Gothic worries about his masculinity; his need to be superior to the women of his family results in aggressive acts. Socially and politically, such a family structure has proved to be dangerous. *Pandora* dramatizes this danger and shows, in the most intricate detail, the interplay between male dominance and Fascist ideology. At the same time, it also shifts attention to "female identity, as defined by doing rather than being" (p. 158). Imagining herself as Medusa or the more contemporary Wonder Woman, Pandora will learn to control her own life and will become a subversive new woman. With her appearance, this novel seems to suggest, the structures of the traditional family may begin to collapse.

Chapter Seven

Maternal Vitality in Gallant's Fiction

Looking at the complex and fascinating web of the spider and following its thread, Spinsters can spin ideas about such interconnected symbols as the maze, the labyrinth, the spiral, the hole as mystic center, and the Soul Journey itself. In order to think of these interlacing themes, Hags must be able to weave and unweave, discovering hidden threads of connectedness.

— MARY DALY
"Gyn/Ecology"

And when you are in power, Women of the Earth, when you share this power with Men of the Earth, here is one little suggestion: why not create a ministry of Gigantic Ears whose most important task would be to listen to the Discourse of the People. Gigantic ears mindful of the people, can you imagine?

— LOUKY BERSIANIK
"The Euguélionne"

Fraser situated women in a threatening familial structure, in a culture that assumes a number of Fascist characteristics. Mavis Gallant places her characters in reactionary political locations at moments of historical crisis. In Gallant's work, numerous connections appear between racism and sexism. The title story of *The Pegnitz Junction* and the six Linnet Muir stories in *Home Truths* resonate with references to World War Two; "The Pegnitz Junction" refers to the war as it touched Europe since its conclusion; the Linnet Muir stories refer to war as it was reflected in Canada during its occurrence. Although Gallant experiments with the ideological and aesthetic possibilities of silence, the voices of the more openly political fictions seem to possess greater authority than Jean Price's in "Its Image on the Mirror." The author also overtly experiments with literary creativity, specifically with the idiosyncrasies of female creativity. Inevitably, Gallant's theories of literary production merge with her politics, a politics that includes gender. She joins with many women writers in focussing subversively on war. Through truncated narrative patterns, she demonstrates violence's dead end while balancing destruction with an alternative narrative, one that stresses creative production. Her female characters establish a game plan that revises traditional western culture. This is art at its most engaged.

Her fiction has not always appeared in such a light. An early reviewer of *The Pegnitz Junction* wrote that its stories evoke a "stagnant woman-crowded world that is hinged on ritual, where the figures display a recurrent impotence in rebelling against a conservative code of feminine behaviour which is serving only to destroy them."[1] Ritual there certainly is, and women characters dominate much of the action. But instead of demonstrating female passivity in the face of recurrent violence, Gallant's stories celebrate the activity of the female imagination. For example, in the lost, baffled world of "The Pegnitz Junction," only Christine, the central female character, makes connections. Similar dynamics operate in the Linnet Muir stories, where the female artist, by the strength of her imagination, holds together a world attacked by masculine violence (war, repressive political ideologies) and maintained by decaying old men who, although unable to fight, are nonetheless life-denying.

To some extent, "The Pegnitz Junction" prepares the way for the later *künstlerroman*, the Linnet Muir stories, by dramatizing creativity in the process of developing. Christine is immediately involved in translating experience into stories. The novella also seems to be a narrative advance, in terms of defining creativity, over the earlier "Its Image on the Mirror." In the earlier story, the narrator holds back information, attempts to make connections that fail, remains obsessed with her image and seems unable to articulate reliably the hauntings and secrecies of the events she describes. "The Pegnitz Junction" exhibits a more extroverted imagination. Where Jean Price is a reflector, Christine is a conductor. A creator, Linnet Muir, comes even later. For Mavis Gallant, the female imagination is a complex mechanism. It develops, in relation to culture, intricate devices for exhibiting degrees of authority. The social and cultural milieus she invokes interact with women's stories, dramatizing not the traditional literary view of women's outsidedness or their concern with the petty and the small, but exhibiting their profound connection with human survival. Neither utopian nor escapist, these narratives function as guides toward rethinking the whole human experiment.

The effects of World War Two dramatically permeate the lives of the people in "The Pegnitz Junction." Personal problems partially blinded the narrator of "Its Image On The Mirror" to catastrophe (indeed, Dr. Minnow of *Bodily Harm* suggests Canada is blind). In this novella, Fascism is more immediate and more terrifying. It weaves through all the stories told on the metaphoric train journey the characters take from Paris to West Germany. On the train are Christine, a young woman of twenty-one; her lover, Herbert, who is ten years older; and Herbert's small son. As George Woodcock suggests, among other things, the journey emphasizes a certain historical and cultural aimlessness, "the wanderings, without an as yet assured destination, of a Germany which has not yet recovered a sense of its role in history and, indeed, fears what that role might be if it were discovered."[2] The train is stopped, then rerouted, and so on.

Christine, the major female character, symbolically dominates the action. In an article in *Atlantis*, Ronald Hatch analyzes the symbolism: "In some ways Christine is the *exemplum* of modern woman, in that, while engaged to a theology student, she is also the lover of Herbert, the engineer. She cannot make up her mind whether to embrace religion, with its metaphysical solace, or applied science, with its manipulation of present-day reality."[3] Although Hatch's remarks seem to apply to all modern people, not specifically to women, the story does emphasize the tension between the religious and the secular life, between the metaphysical and the factual, even between the active and the passive. Nonetheless, the content of the story, with its borders and its barbed wire, suggests a Fascist structure that, accompanied by sexual harassment, implies a political reading that places gender differences in the foreground. Certainly, as in all of Gallant's fiction, conflicts between imprisonment and freedom illustrate general dilemmas of the imagination. Yet Herbert, who "was scrupulous about providing correct information but did not feel obliged to answer for pictures raised in the imagination" (p. 23), is compared with Christine, who thinks "that Herbert's information left out a great deal" (p. 9). Herbert seems stiff and controlled. Fascist régimes, the story reveals, disastrously constrict the imagination. At the same time, in the novella's political conflicts, and in the conflicts of the Linnet Muir stories, imagination seems sexually specific. Indeed, Gallant's work illustrates Patricia Spacks' conviction that "imagination has been for many women the seed of grace, and often the subject as well as the impetus of their writing."[4] From a variety of perspectives, Gallant's female characters attempt to define imagination against the patriarchal structures that threaten to silence them.

Both in structure and in content, "The Pegnitz Junction" establishes some of the criteria for Linnet Muir's later illustration of the development of the female writer. Presented as a series of radio broadcasts, the stories that make up the novella wander, like the train, from one plot to another. But their apparent aimlessness is misleading. As the central antenna of the novella, a metaphor that operates throughout, Christine picks up the static and chaotic interferences of post-war Europe. She tunes them into coherent narrative that, because it leaps back and forth between Europe and the United States, implies a methodical, worldwide Fascism. Although Christine's passivity as a conductor of information suggests female sensitivity and intuition at the expense of rational composition, the metaphor additionally implies organization and control. And Christine also creates stories. In structure and in theme, the main consciousness of the novella is female.

Christine's story situates the reader. She comes from a small German city that has been rebuilt after it was bombed in the war. Ironically, it now looks "as pink and golden as a pretty child" (p. 3). Like the town, Christine appears simple, even naïve. Her appearance is as deceptive as the fictions she hears and constructs: "She had a striking density of expression in photographs, though she seemed unchanging and passive in life, and had caught sight of her own face looking totally empty-minded when, in fact, her thoughts and feelings were pushing her in some wild direction" (p. 4). Such splitting has various meanings. Like many major female literary characters, Christine is filled with hidden stories that, culturally and politically, have remained unrecognized because they have not been articulated. Her apparent acquiescence to the *status quo* is misleading; her vacuous expression signifies subversive tendencies, not empty-mindedness. Suggestions of suffocation and disguise symbolically reveal Christine's situation, as they reveal central Europe's situation following World War Two. Christine's femininity is made significant because the man with whom she travels describes his past as a history of unfaithful women. The model for such women is his lost mother, whom he remembers as a "bloated sick woman eating sugar and telling bitter stories" (p. 13), but he also connects loss with a wife who has *"streaked off like a hare"* (p. 84), leaving him with a young son. He longs for female nurturing.

Several other characters contribute to the sexually decadent atmosphere of the novella and to its presentation of various forms of Fascism. A Norwegian man shares the train compartment with Christine and Herbert; his comments on German repatriation serve as a kind of *leitmotif*, pointing to the virulent persistence of Fascist ideologies. Like all the characters of the story, he acknowledges the striking discrepancy between appearance and experience, particularly in cultural terms. Just before he leaves the train, he sees a detachment of rather unruly military conscripts lounging about the station at Pegnitz, young men who seem to be caricatures of the Hitler youth. Christine comments on their apparent youth and poverty. But the Norwegian understands Fascism: "'They always looked that way . . . . They were always very little and very ugly, but they frightened us'" (p. 75). The story's themes revolve around the persistent threat of Fascism. Toward the end, references to art, marriage and women condense in a single episode that emphasizes Fascism's insidious control. The local newspaper has just run a series of articles attacking a display of abstract photography at the town's museum. The series of photographs is entitled "Marriage." Christine tunes into the thoughts of the museum's curator. He is incensed by the town's apparent low-brow misinterpretations and resultant condemnations. The newspaper sarcastically published a picture of the photographer as a baboon, his subjects as naked graces represented as three stout German matrons. The caption reads: "ARE GERMAN WOMEN BABOONS AND MUST THEY ALWAYS EXHIBIT THEIR BACKSIDES?" (p. 65). As the curator understands, art in Fascist régimes can only be defended "as far as the first row of barbed wire" (p. 67). The episode also points to an interpretation of the female body as the property of the state.

The incident extends in another direction when a group of women taking an instructional opera tour becomes stranded at one of the train stations. The group's male leader begins to chant loudly the names of famous German writers and composers, all of them male. The ritual chant climaxes with references to the "Adolf-time," the apparently inevitable result of dominantly masculine ideology. Not encouraged to participate in making culture, women are excluded from the list; they are seen as property of the state. Christine transmits the irony of the situation. The opera-tour leader recalls a distinguished foreigner pointing to a new opera house and saying: "'If only you Germans had thought more about *that*.'" But as the tour leader tells the story he points, apparently by mistake, at "a gap between two women sitting with their knees clenched" (p. 71). His gesture symbolizes one of the novella's central themes — the gaps and silences in women's narrative.

The gap is high-lighted by another male character, the conductor. Toward the end of the story, he aggressively confronts the women on the opera tour, shouting at them until they look "positively ill with terror" (p. 81). But, characteristically, they respond to his hostility with silence; they counter his aggression with passivity. Obviously, neither silence nor passivity leads to narrative construction. Christine's metaphoric role as an antenna is quite complex. Like the writer, she watches; more important, she listens. She becomes like Louky Bersianik's ministry of *Gigantic Ears* in *The Euguélionne*, whose "unique function would be to be *democratic*."[5] By listening, Christine discovers that the stranded women possess tremendous magnet-like sensitivity, which seems to attract "everything to themselves" without their being conscious of it (p. 87).

The women accumulate the disparate bits of information that need narrative structuring and interpretation if they are to be turned into stories. Metaphorically, they seem to represent the raw materials out of which the female imagination forms. Christine's function assumes another dimension. Her job is to collect and store information that can become narrative under the proper conditions. Like Christine, interpreters of women's stories must be on the same wave length, must, to use Kolodny's words, be familiar with the "contexts of judgement"[6] within which women's stories are written. Only when these contexts cohere can secret texts be deciphered and the gap between women closed.

One story illustrates precisely Christine's storing of female narrative. An old woman shares the train compartment with Christine, Herbert, and the Norwegian, and Christine picks up her thoughts. The woman's thoughts link Fascist attitudes to women with the structuring of stories. With her "sparse orange-blond hair," her "printed dress," her "black shoes" (p. 17), the old woman represents all the ordinary women of the novella, particularly the sad-faced and silent group taking the opera tour. She is also the clearest of the "stations" Christine receives, a point that is emphasized by setting her story in italics. Her story demonstrates the uncelebrated nurturing and perseverance that constitute many silent female lives. As a subtext, it is a dramatic example of women's conventional and unacknowledged space.

The whole of the text is punctuated by the old woman's thoughts. The people who populate her memory as Christine transmits the messages become the characters in a fully developed narrative: two first cousins, male and female, who are married to two other first cousins. It is a peculiarly introverted group. The old woman is one of the four people. Together, the four leave Germany to go to the United States. The story is inevitably political. The men's careers advance in the capitalistic American working world. (They make kitchen equipment that, during the war years, is used on submarines.) Nurturance and destruction are paired, and the old woman's concentrated remembrance of past meals assumes metaphoric relevance. Her thoughts become a culinary history of the United States: "During the depression . . . we ate beans, sardines, peanut butter, macaroni" (p. 38); or "one whole winter she would not eat anything but bottled sandwich spread on ready-sliced bread, said only Jews and krauts and squareheads ate the dark" (p. 35); or "I fed them all through the war, stood at the electric stove, making oxtail soup on the one hand, baked squash on the other, bread and milk when my cousin had his ulcer" (p. 38). The old woman sees life in a peculiarly female way.

Her story, a history of daily events silently lived, is paralleled by Christine's story, and is therefore understood by her. Because she is so attuned to the woman's mind, Christine begins to formulate a literary theory. That theory emphasizes beginnings from a quite different perspective from the one suggested by Edward Said's paternal-fraternal origins. Christine understands that it is "from the woman that the silvery crystals took their substance; she was the source. *It started this way*, Christine understood. She looked carefully at the woman who was creating information . . . . *This was the beginning*" (p. 23). The novella describes and illustrates beginnings. Christine, who constantly creates stories for little Bert, asks him: "'What do you want as a beginning this time?'" (p. 86) and, when Christine is picking up the story of the disguised American army wife, the narrator assures us that she "understood all this from the beginning" (p. 77). Indeed, narrative beginnings and endings assume political as well as narrative importance. For the civilian with the scarred hairline who "was prepared for the end, perhaps the end of everything living, and he knew that endings were in blood" (p. 58), Fascism has created devastating endings. Only an apocalyptic imagination can interpret the barbed wire, the obliterating bombings of the war. For him, violence structures stories. That violence is often directed at women. The pantomime of the conductor who transforms himself into a tyrant to frighten the women merges with Christine's somewhat shocked awareness that, at one point in the story, the three men she sees — the conductor, Herbert and the Norwegian — are simultaneously thinking of rape.

These signs of violent endings, which are associated with Fascism, are superimposed with narrative beginnings that imply creativity. The suggested political allegory allows women, who are responsible for the nurturing and preservation of life, a major part. Women seem more committed to beginnings than to endings, more concerned with narrative continuance than with abrupt conclusions. In an interview with Geoff Hancock, Gallant has discussed some of the political problems that concerned her when she was writing the novella. Referring specifically to an assignment given to her when she was a journalist in Montreal — to describe some of the concentration-camp victims of Nazi atrocities — she insists that "[W]hat we absolutely had to find out was what has happened in a civilized country, why the barriers of culture, of religion, hadn't held, what had broken down and why."[7] "The Pegnitz Junction" demonstrates relationships between racism and sexism by connecting, objectively and subjectively, women and narrative structure.

The novella establishes connections between Fascist ideology and truncated narrative patterns. The six Linnet Muir stories also make political connections that underline the importance of ideology in shaping the ways in which stories are told. Because they are *künstlerroman*, they make particularly clear the relationship between culture and the formation of the artist. Linnet Muir, the writer, reflects her experience of Canada during the years of World War Two, and her developing ability to write about that experience. She is able, retrospectively, to write her autobiography. In the novella, Christine seems to have been an earlier representation of the creative process, the stage at which material is filtered and organized. Occasionally, she also undertakes the beginnings of stories. Linnet is concerned with structuring stories and with the uses of journal material, the connections between drama and fiction, poetry, all the various genres that suggest her apprenticeship and that reveal some of the ways in which experience dictates form. Linnet is a representative writer, particularly sensitive to the female voice.

Although not told in chronological order, the six stories seem to annotate Linnet's creative development. Various events focus that development: the escape from her mother, who is in the United States; her return to Montreal, where she lived as a child; her search for her dead father; her first job; her interest in a married man; her recollections of visits taken with each parent; her rediscovery of her godmother. The stories that result from these apparently traumatic happenings record, in structure and content, Linnet's experiments with writing. But, less obviously, they also show the development of a specifically female creativity.

That development is a slow process. The stories begin with Linnet's words — "My father died" (p. 218) — and continue by juxtaposing, with her artistic development, his death and her consequent wanderings. For George Woodcock, that juxtaposition seems culturally and aesthetically significant. He writes: "The search for her father is significant in view of Gallant's own theory that perhaps the distinctive Canadian theme is to be found in the role of the father, who in our literature seems always more important than the mother.... The search for the father is, in a very real sense, the beginning of Linnet's search for truth."[8] Many Canadian novels by women concentrate attention on the mother, and they contradict Woodcock's thesis, but these stories about Linnet manifestly concentrate on the father. Linnet assures the reader that "his death turned my life into a helpless migration" (p. 219) and announces that she "kept waiting for him to send for me" (p. 228). At the same time, the stories also dramatically reveal the incongruity and ultimate failure of such a mythic model for women. For Linnet, the claim that "every narrative (every unveiling of the truth) is a staging of the (absent, hidden, or hypostatized) father'"[9] is simply not true.

Linnet's stories seem to subvert the paternal narrative. As she learns to be a writer, Linnet discovers that the male narrative is not hers. Signs of a gradual rejection occur throughout the stories. When she visits a painter friend of her father's and asks him for a memento of her father, he has "nothing" (p. 230) to give her; indeed, the images of his own painting remind Linnet of bubbles that "floated off the page" (p. 231). Her father's absence does not propel her into art. Certain material seems to be missing. For example, she does not remember where he spent his waking life, just that he spent it "elsewhere" (p. 285). Her women friends have similar difficulties. One woman, in her struggle to tell her father's story, becomes entangled in a series of contradictory endings. As in "The Pegnitz Junction," in *Pandora* and in *Bodily Harm*, the imagined endings connect fathers with destruction and Fascism. Linnet describes a women "whose father died.... She invents different deaths. Her inventions have become her conversation at dinner parties. She takes on a child's voice and says, 'My father died at Buchenwald.' She chooses and rejects elements of the last act; one avoids mentioning death, shooting, capital punishment, cremation, deportation, even fathers. Her inventions are not thought neurotic or exhibitionist but something sanctioned by history" (p. 234). Although apparently historically accurate, the paternal narrative proves to be fictional.

Unlike her friend, however, Linnet does not remain a child. She acknowledges the narrative of the father as a dead end for women writers. She rejects a culture of death and destruction. For the daughter, the father's physical absence becomes a textual absence; even his voice is lost, not only because of his taciturnity, but also because Linnet is unable to reproduce it. She associates his death, which was kept from her, with silence. Her dream of the missed train, with its frequent temporal interferences and its plummeting downhill passage, signals Linnet's rejection. For her, it is a dream of the impossibility of creatively using the myth of the father. In her recollections, the major step in her artistic development is her understanding from the "reading of myths and legends that this journey was a pursuit of darkness, its terminal point a sunless underworld" (p. 284). With this understanding, the dream vanishes. By rejecting the journey to the underworld, the classical rite of passage that assures the son's inheritance from and continuation of his father, Linnet reveals the impossibility of a woman using it as a major narrative construct. She even rejects "inherited property" (p. 232). The old-boy network that dominates the office where she first finds a job attracts her scorn. It is an office filled with men "rotting quietly" (p. 244). Later, she describes a newspaper office where she learns, ironically, that "women's autonomy is like a small inheritance paid out a penny at a time" (p. 318).

But the rejected narrative of the father is imaged most strikingly in Linnet's construction of the drama of the remittance man. Conflating the contents of all six of the Linnet Muir stories in content and style, this central story is also a political allegory. Like "Its Image on the Mirror," it tells the reader about Canada as it is perceived through female eyes. The "romance" (p. 266) of the remittance man is a father-engendered narrative; the central theme is an erring son's exile. Politically, the remittance man seems to represent one side of Canada's relationship with Great Britain — the male side. The erring son is exiled to Canada for displeasing his father economically or sexually or both; he spends the rest of his life looking back toward a homeland represented, in his imagination, by the patriarch, the voice of the law. Because he cannot break with the old world, he is unable to settle in the new. It is a common Canadian story, and it emotionally illustrates the conviction of inferiority that permeates the Canadian identity. It is also a masculine story.

It is a drama in which, "[L]ike all superfluous and marginal persons, remittance men were characters in a plot" (p. 266). According to Linnet, however, a woman would be unable to write it ("no son was ever sent into exile by his mother" [p. 267]), nor would any daughter be its subject ("no one has ever heard of a remittance *woman*" [p. 267]). It is a weak story, and it generates even weaker ones, for the exiled sons carry everywhere their disgrace, offering it, as their patrimony, to their own sons if they have any, or to the empty ground if they do not reproduce. The remittance-man story emerges as a dramatic castigation of patriarchal structures that affect the artist's nationality as well as her creativity: "It was the father's Father, never met, never heard, who made Heaven and earth and Eve and Adam. The father in Canada seemed no more than an apostle transmitting a paternal message from the Father in England — the Father of us all" (p. 269).

Like Christine, however, Linnet is much less interested in endings than in beginnings. She interprets what appears to be the story's fatalism as a "load of codswallop" (p. 267) and insists that "[E]ven at nineteen the plot was a story I wouldn't buy" (p. 267). She knows that, for her, the paternal narrative is a dead end, truly a "pursuit of darkness," not conducive to good fiction. Like the secrecy of "Its Image on the Mirror," the silences that Linnet experiences throughout her apprenticeship suggest deceit. They seem narratively empty. As a result, just as Linnet's father disintegrates into insubstantial myths, his "sickness for England" (p. 235) finally killing him, so the story of the remittance man proves to be a cultural and sexual dead end, an impotent narrative. In terms of Linnet's art, it is superfluous and marginal. Dominated by class and sexual snobbery, the narrative amounts to nothing more than a "ghost story" (p. 271).

Her search must be undertaken from a different perspective. Like the young Stephen Dedalus, Linnet attempts to establish the influences of family and country on her artistic development. But she discovers that she must also understand the significance of gender on her development. Her story — her flight from her mother, her rejection of the United States, her return to Canada — seems quite different from the classical male narrative. For one thing, she gradually begins to understand the significance of the mothering of stories. In terms of the remittance man, that ghostly narrative, she asserts that "[A] mother's vitality would be needed to create ectoplasm, to make the ghost offspring visible" (p. 271), that "even an erratic and alarming maternal vitality could turn out to be better than none" (p. 271). Her remarks elucidate her development as a writer. To use the metaphor from "The Pegnitz Junction" — the "gap between two women" (p. 71) — Linnet gradually learns that women are vital and can create rather than destroy; they need to connect with each other. Instead of dramatizing the supposedly quintessential Canadian search for the father, Linnet's stories demonstrate another quintessential search, that of the daughter for her mother. To find her mother's story and to reproduce her mother's voice is the female artist's major narrative enterprise.

Linnet's search begins with a narrative separation. Linnet introduces her series of vignettes by pronouncing her mother abandoned: "all at once I lost interest. I was fifteen when this happened. I would forget to answer her letters and even to open them. It was not rejection or anything so violent as dislike but a simple indifference I cannot account for" (p. 218). However, the remaining stories poignantly and ironically show that Linnet has by no means left her mother behind; instead, she has brought her every step of the way. As she struggles to become a writer, her mother's voice, not lost in the snow, echoes in her words; her mother's stories return in Linnet's new fictions. Her father's ghostly presence becomes a cover for the more psychologically ambivalent but more fruitful connection.

The struggle to separate from the mother propels the narrative adventure. As the first maker, the creator, the mother threatens to stifle her progeny, to dominate the stories the daughter wants to create for herself. Linnet recognizes and articulates the difficulty: "From time to time she attempted to alter the form, the outward shape at least, of the creature she thought she was modelling" (p. 218). At the same time, to find her own voice, the daughter needs to find her mother's. Linnet's description of her mother begins a simultaneous distancing from and incorporating of the mother. She announces that her "mother was highly visible; she had no secrets" (p. 229), but her insistence on her mother's visibility shifts when she attempts to back away from description by announcing that "I won't begin to describe her, it would never end" (p. 230). This contradiction (the mother's apparent clarity, Linnet's inability to describe her) informs each of the stories. Like an underground stream, Linnet's mother flows beneath all her daughter's memories. Sometimes the mother dominates them, as, for example, when "[S]he made herself the central figure in loud, spectacular dramas which she played with the houselights on" (p. 230). Her loudness suggests the daughter's fear of being silenced by her mother's voice, or of sounding like her. Other female voices echo the mother's. In "Between Zero and One," Mrs. Ireland describes the battle between the sexes. She represents the terrifying possibility of marriage as "a watershed that transformed sweet, cheerful, affectionate girls into, well, their own mothers" (p. 259). Initially, Linnet imagines all married women as Red Queens.

Yet Linnet comes to understand that, to give vitality to her work, she must come to terms with her mother. She cannot shed her. The "crippling irony" and the "calm review of events" (p. 277) that Linnet assumes to be necessary qualities of good prose fail her when she tries to write of her mother. She needs a different approach. It is the fourth story, "Voices Lost in Snow," that marks a shift in her attention from her father to her mother. Although ostensibly about her father, the story reveals his failure to listen and, finally, to communicate. But in the space left, her mother begins to figure prominently. Through her, Linnet is able to reach back to her female ancestors, to her grandmother; she learns how to locate herself. Writing of the grandmother, Linnet can empathize with her and recognizes that this tough old woman "would have preferred a life of solitude and independence" (p. 286), a life impossible for a woman of her time.

Her repetitions of her mother become marked. For example, her mother's penchant for Russian novels recurs in Linnet's fascination with Russia. Once, Linnet even admits a bond with her mother. Describing their response to the lonely whistle of the steam train, she admits that "[f]rom our separate rooms my mother and I heard the unrivalled summons, the long, urgent, uniquely North American beckoning. She would follow and so would I, but separately, years and desires and destinations apart. I think that women once pledged in such a manner are more steadfast than men" (p. 289). She remembers, too, a childhood visit to her godmother. It is apparent to her that Georgie was in love with her father and, on this visit with him, she admits "that my guileless-seeming needling of my godmother was a close adaptation of how my mother could be, and I attribute it to a child's instinctive loyalty to the absent one" (p. 291). And she repeats her mother's need to rewrite "other people's lives, providing them with suitable and harmonious endings" (p. 287). Although not particularly interested in endings, Linnet does need to rewrite her mother's life. Indeed, as her writing changes, she discovers how to give her mother a voice and a personality, to create for the reader "her comparative youth, her quickness, her somewhat giddy intelligence" (p. 307). As her father's voice becomes increasingly silent, her mother's becomes more noticeable.

Part of Linnet's growing literary sophistication involves her in coming to terms with her position as a woman writer. Although each of the stories sets up certain gender dichotomies, the last story presents cultural assumptions and political barriers that interfere with the woman writer and, ultimately, with the production of the female text. Looking back at her beginnings as a journalist, Linnet recognizes that then, as well as now, "[B]ehind frosted glass doors lurk male fears of female mischief" (p. 321). That mischief, Pandora's mischief, what Karen Horney calls "the dread of women,"[10] relates to male loss of power and to fears of castration. Men distrust women, and it becomes difficult for them to read women's stories. Linnet assumes that the male journalists she worked with believed women to have "no inborn sense of history" and therefore to be inventors of "absurd stories" (p. 321). At one point, Linnet admits that the pervasive male fear of women makes them invisible even to themselves. It situates Linnet in an unknown space, somewhere between zero and one, and links her with an ahistoricism that suggests a female inability to get the facts right or to understand major world issues. As Linnet comes to learn, stories quoted as "women's stories" are usually male stories, "[C]elebrated newspaper hoaxes" (p. 321). But she also knows that "[T]he umpires of ground rules" (p. 321) will not give women's stories a chance; "Wartime security hangs heavy" (p. 321) and the umpires prefer to use war correspondents who will write masculine stories instead of women's stories, men who will punctuate "their accounts of Hunnish atrocities perceived at Claridges and the Savoy with 'Roger!' and 'Jolly-oh!' and 'Over to you!'" (p. 322).

In comparison to the mentality that creates the atrocious war stories that have been "sanctioned by history" (p. 234), the female imagination assumes a political dimension. It suggests another story, another sort of life. History narratives, Linnet sees, leave out too much and are dominated by male aggression, by war, by Fascism, by the terrifying spectre of Nazism. Linnet discovers what that narrative has done to women when she is sent to interview her godmother, the woman who had once loved her father and whom, for her mother's sake, she had rejected. Between them, "a deserted continent" (p. 327) still stretches. In her interview with the godmother, Linnet remains "seamless, and as smooth as brass" (p. 329). The separation between women dominates them both; neither can give the other any opening at all. Unlike her mother, whose differences she has acknowledged and whose similarities she has lived, Linnet sees in her godmother the old, unvital woman, who has "adopted the principle of the absent, endangered male" (p. 327). That principle involves the support of male fiction and the consequent dominance of masculine narrative. As she writes of that godmother, Linnet achieves greater understanding through narrative extension. But the life that seemed "silent and slow and choked with wrack" (p. 329) had once interfered with Linnet's own vitality; it was a barrier to her writing. From the godmother, Linnet inherits nothing. Georgie even erases the relationship: "All my godchildren were boys. I never liked girls" (p. 328). Yet Linnet, by the time she "could hear the past" (p. 329), is able to tell stories about her godmother. She is, as Bernikow suggests, learning to "find or make foremothers."[11]

Together "The Pegnitz Junction" and the Linnet Muir stories are narrations that place women in central positions as narrators and as subjects. At the same time, they emphasize the emergence of women's stories from the gaps and fissures of texts. "The Pegnitz Junction" creates a metaphor that draws attention to this female space. The dominated women sitting in the station assume their own meaning because they attract others' stories to themselves. At the same time, individual male voices are weakened, although masculine political structures remain powerful. The men described by Linnet either die (the father, the doctor) or are crippled and impotent, their voices altered and their authority absurd: "Mr. Tracy had been snow-blinded . . . . He had recovered part of his sight but had to wear mauve glasses even by electric light. He was nice but strange, infirm. Mr. Curran, reputed to have one kidney, one lung, and one testicle . . . had not wanted a girl in the office" (p. 239). Narratively impotent in women's stories, the male characters are pulled back, silenced, so the female writer can present a "faithful record of the true survivor" who, through her fiction, can construct "a superior civilization" (p. 233).

In the novella and in the short stories, men are associated with endings, often violent endings, whereas women are metaphorically associated with creative beginnings. Christine's persistent attempts to tell little Bert a story result in a series of beginnings that punctuate the other stories of the novella and that end it, ironically, with yet another beginning. Linnet also focusses on beginnings: each section of her autobiography is presented as a new short story. She repeatedly announces her rebirth: her escape from her mother; her new job; her marriage. Against this persistent beginning again, endings become associated with male characters. Christine believes that "nothing is ever finished" (p. 84); the hotel porter screams "[I]t is too late" (p. 7). Uncle Ludwig and Jurgen embrace apocalyptic horror. Terrified by visions of "ties consumed, flakes of fire on the compartment ceilings, sparks burned black on the first-class velvet" (p. 36), Christine longs for the open air.

Bersianik calls the kind of stories that interest Christine and Linnet "the Discourse of the People."[12] Gallant's work draws attention even to the silent speaking of women. It also weaves unusual narrative connections among women's stories, connections that offer alternative readings of contemporary life. Like Fraser's, that reading is shadowed by a global fascination with annihilation. Connected with characters such as Mr. Gothic, who sits on his Canadian porch making "that switch in psychology from The Rocket to The Bomb" (p. 253), Gallant's male characters seem more concentrated on death than on life. Even Herbert of "The Pegnitz Junction," who prides himself on being "a pacifist and anti-state" (p. 16), has little patience with other people and expects "a great deal in the way of behavior from civil servants" (p. 16). More important, he does not understand women's stories. He protects his son from "the shock of female nakedness" (p. 6) and announces that little Bert has never seen a pomegranate. Political allusions connect public and private life, situating often forgotten women characters in a space of their own. Finally, Gallant insists on a female imagination that celebrates creation rather than destruction. Like *Pandora*, her stories politicize the private. They are neither escapist nor utopian, but seem to be alternatives to total destruction. The "hidden threads of connectedness" that Daly mostly relates to women's age-old magic have here been translated into the contemporary world where, after long silence, women writers are beginning to structure narratives in ways that produce new, tentative visions of a world no longer dominated by destructive plots. This is indeed "creative weaving."[13]

Chapter Eight

Colonial Metaphors:
The Honeyman Festival and *Lunatic Villas*

Mother was us, and underneath all she believed in — love, mercy, magic — she had a toughness and a fear. She had feared her father; the mother was distant, invalid. Perhaps the British are right to separate the child early from its mother, hoping to escape the seven generations' transfer of the consciousness of sin. But what shall we pass on if not what we are?

— MARIAN ENGEL
Sarah Bastard's Notebook

*This is my place here This is in my skin
Let me in Get out of here
But nobody hears me
They give a deaf ear with my own ears
The words of strangers continue to lodge in my mouth
I no longer live in me I am colonized from all sides
Chilled with unknowns I am haunted from top to bottom.*

— FRANCE VEZINA
Les Journées d'une
anthropophage

In work by women writers, significant literary themes result from a developing female literary tradition. Female characters are repeatedly used as epic voices to define Canada. The narrator of *Surfacing* undertakes a quintessential Canadian cultural journey into the forests of Quebec; Rennie, in *Bodily Harm*, enacts a Canadian political allegory. She appears as a unique literary character and as a dramatization of the naïve, apolitical stance sometimes assumed by Canadians abroad. In "Its Image on the Mirror," Jean Price and her sister, Ida, allegorically enact some of the tensions between French and English Canada; in *Home Truths*, Linnet Muir needs to travel from the United States back to her home in Canada before she can write about the development of her artistic life. Most of these contemporary novels and short stories by women assume Canadian settings. Even *Mrs. Blood*, which takes place in Africa, and *Blown Figures*, which is imaginatively set there, refer frequently to the Canadian landscape. These writers offer a map of their country in ways that stress the necessity of sharing their sense of place, their "here."

But apart from Canadian content and setting, the sense of country also results from metaphors. Because the reader sees life through the eyes of female characters, attitudes and experiences appropriate to women's lives structure the narratives and dominate the tone. Mother-daughter patterns represent generational flow; creativity and maternity metaphorically connect; sisters enact narrative secrecy; plot development results from female desire; as a life force, femininity counteracts excessive masculine aggression. By becoming feminized, Canada gains real significance. Historian William Kilbourn points to Canada's conservative past using metaphors that, in terms of gender, contrast Canada's development with that of the United States. For example, he writes that "in a masculine world of the assertive will and the cutting edge of the intellect, a certain Canadian tendency to the amorphous permissive feminine principle of openness and tolerance and acceptance offers the possibility of healing."[1] Kilbourn states the case too politely. When Canadian nationalism and feminism intertwine, the results are radical. Openness and tolerance and acceptance disappear. They are replaced by political and social questions that, while they definitely point toward healing, involve tremendous upheaval before new forms can evolve.

Female writers tend to present ironically political, cultural, even economic structures that interfere with generation. In an early Engel novel, Sarah Bastard struggles with her country and connects that struggle with the literature she studies:

> those of us who operate from bastard territory, disinherited coun-

tries and traditions, long always for our nonexistent mothers. For this reason, I delved five years . . . in the literature of Australians and Canadians, hoping to be the one to track her down. In the nineteenth century there were unashamed Colonials. In the twentieth a few geniuses, and a host of Sarahs looking for themselves; too late finding their modes and models.[2]

But the host of Sarahs has not been too late. Since Bastard's historical overview, the field of Canadian literature has opened up. Connecting with and overcoming some of the problems of colonialism, women writers have incorporated Canada's struggle into aesthetic constructs.

The intensity with which Canada's women writers pursue Canadian themes reveals an aesthetic commitment to their country. Such is the case in both *The Honeyman Festival* and *Lunatic Villas*, where Marian Engel creates fictional worlds dominated by women who, in a variety of sometimes direct, sometimes oblique ways, represent Canada herself. Like the earlier *Sarah Bastard's Notebook* and in fictions such as *Bear* and a number of the short stories of *Inside the Easter Egg*, these novels present female sexuality and Canadian identity, often allegorically, as problems of a similar and related magnitude. Both novels illustrate Canada's contemporary political and cultural tensions. In *The Honeyman Festival*, the tensions seem psychologically similar to those experienced by a woman who analyzes her female identity. In *Lunatic Villas*, they have become more culturally focussed. The characters in *Lunatic Villas* have assumed roles that define conflicts inherent in formerly colonized countries. The narrator attempts to demonstrate Canada's relationship to the mother country, and makes passing observations about a threatened economic and political domination by the United States. Both novels are nationalistic and imply rituals that allow cultural differentiation, particularly from more powerful countries such as Great Britain and the United States. These rituals are predominantly female and have to do with conservation, with mothers who bear and look after children, with the female imagination — in other words, with female creativity.

For example, on one level, *The Honeyman Festival* moves in mythic, pregnant timelessness; Minn is not "dependent on days, on structured time" (p. 10). But on another level, the narrator persistently evokes Canadian history. The central metaphor of the house, "less a house than an obstacle-maze" (p. 12), resurrects the Victorian age. It is rented and therefore it is, like Canada, colonial. American influence appears throughout. Honeyman, the American who befriends Minn in Paris, is a caricature, a Hollywood man older than Minn: "A head on a grand scale, big-planed; and a body to match, bellyless, loose-jointed,

Western and mythic in walk" (p. 14). The novel concentrates on stories about him and demonstrates, as Canadians of the 1970s realized, that the American personality dominates Canada.

The Honeyman Festival also focusses on the female body. As it opens, Minn is pregnant; "[T]he globe of her belly" rises above the "waterline to meet the spotted ceiling" (p. 1). So dominant is that pregnant body throughout the novel that it seems to encompass the earth. It is celebrated: "it was her own flesh, the whey-colour of the moon, livid Cranach-flesh, very delicate to look upon, the skin so stretched it divided itself into cells so that at last she believed in cells" (p. 1). That very celebration marks the female text. In *Woman and Nature*,[3] Susan Griffin begins by tracing the harmful associations that have been culturally created between women and nature, the female body and the earth; the concluding section of her study assumes a female perspective similar to Minn's. In the sections on "Our Nature" and "This Earth," Griffin celebrates the close connection between women and the soil and articulates women's knowledge in a powerful diatribe against the destruction of the earth. It is a diatribe that Minn pronounces, as well. In a female genesis similar to the one described in the opening of *Pandora*, Minn emphasizes the female capacity to produce life. Time ticks around her; she can hear it expand. As she lies in the bath contemplating her stomach, hieroglyphics of the creation of the world and the slow march of developing human life are illustrated there. In her pregnant body, history becomes real: "Blue fingers of stretch-marks held up her belly. Later, they would fade to pale striations, silver tracks of glaciers or snails" (p. 3).

This invention of the world carries with it "something primaeval and sinister" (p. 3), something subversive. Like *Mrs. Blood*, this novel also seems suspended, operating in a hiatus that represents the waiting for a birth. Minn comments that "[T]here's no action for me, no direction. Everything is confused and flaccid . . . . Where are my hard, dry surfaces?" (p. 47). The peculiar sensation of shifting boundaries, which is strikingly imitated in the structure of both novels, suggests the pregnant female body. The spaces of the novels — hospital room and bedroom in Thomas's novel, house in Engel's — become extensions of that body. The women look out from inside these spaces as they look out from inside their own bodies. They imagine themselves, ironically, as latter-day Rapunzels. Their definitions of reality are specifically female. As Minn says: "I am . . . valuably connected — by this foetus I so desire to spew — to a kind of reality" (p. 53). Marked by the solidity of the flesh, by the insistent temporal demands of the developing baby, the narrative time and space become the female body.

Female mysteries join with colonial metaphors. As in many works by women, *The Honeyman Festival* includes fairly traditional female characters who draw attention to subversions of the female role. Minn is visited by a social worker, called Jane-Regina, who has difficulty understanding Minn's casual approach to motherhood. In Canadian novels, characters like Jane-Regina also serve an allegorical function: they are connected with Great Britain. As her name suggests, Jane-Regina runs her own home like a queen, "as if it were an empire" (p. 20). She thinks hierarchically and separates human beings into "ladies" and "gentlemen." Simultaneously, Jane-Regina represents the failure of the sound of the woman's voice in much fiction. Such characters, immaculate, cold, profoundly silent about what their womanhood means to them, fail to connect with other female characters. When she and Minn meet, "[T]here were icebergs in the seas between them"(p. 19).

Jane-Regina is perfectly appointed and perfectly British. Against her, the narrator sets up a distinctively Canadian woman. Representing the new country, Minn exercises her right to make independent decisions. She becomes a subversive character, notably imperfect, complex yet quite recognizable to the female reader. For example, when she looks at a recent book devoted to raising children, a book written by a man, she admits: "Child-raising manuals continually destroyed her, pushed her against monoliths: the perfect housekeeper, the perfect disciplinarian, the perfect mother. There was no way of raising herself to a decent level of achievement" (pp. 27-28). Male judgement frustrates her. She will not present herself as the perfect Madonna.

American cultural influence also exasperates her. Minn remembers admiring "How Young America Lives." She and a girlfriend envied the elaborate homes, the emphasis on family togetherness, the clothes, "their pert gingham shirts and everyday Yankee blue-jeans" (p. 28). But she also remembers this typical Canadian pastime as one her own family eschewed by refusing American magazines. Canadian history is further illustrated in some of Minn's references to her mother, Gertrude. As she recalls her mother's life, Minn gives an encapsulated women's history of Canada: "Gertrude, in pince-nez at her desk in Victoria College in 1909, the first girl in the district to go to the university" (p. 42). Later, when times get hard, Minn describes her mother "marrying the new lawyer in town, Willie Williams, beginning to round on him. Having Annie, losing little Alan. Alice left alone on the farm, pinched and thin in the Depression, looking after her grim father. The night he died hunting till dawn for big George V pennies to close his eyes"(p. 43).

In *Bodily Harm*, Dr. Minnow warns Canadians about their naïveté in thinking they can escape political commitments in the modern world. In *The Honeyman Festival*, Canada's conservatism is also attacked. As she thinks about her home town, Minn sees that "[I]f you don't know how to make a new world, you fall back on the glow of the old one" (p. 41). The influence of Great Britain is marked. As well, the church still dominates the town of Godwin, although its cultural importance has markedly faltered: "The old people enter shuffling, singly or in pairs, not many of them. They walk softly and choose their seats modestly in the middle, never too forward and self important, at their own and the minister's focal length, and sit silently" (p. 41). Minn fights such conservatism. Yet, a true Canadian, she does not choose to break with her background. When she returns to Godwin, she discovers that her mother and her aunt have mellowed; Minn recognizes her need to have her "children's reality verified" by her mother's acknowledgement (p. 71). Certainly, she knows the "hopelessness of reinventing" (p. 79) the dying world of her mother's generation. Yet the proffered salvation of the United States is no solution either. Honeyman's son, with his American personality and accent, does not suit the Canadian temperament.

Language plays a major role in the education of the daughter, who learns to speak correctly, and in Great Britain's class hierarchy. In the novel, the main female character rejects the language that culture deems most appropriate for women. Minn's powerful mother attempts to teach her daughter proper speaking. But Minn ironically rejects it, choosing instead a language that issues from the female body. Her mother has taught her that "[W]e don't say pee, Minn, we say tinkle." But Minn parodies the lesson: "That's what we teach our respectable daughters . . . . The earth-mother sits cycladic on the toilet, the great gush of bladder weighted by foetus follows. She tinkles. The inundation of the world from the fearful mother-cunt, the rain of fertility, the brooding of the goddess: that is called tinkle" (p. 44). Just as Canada has struggled to reject the mother country's class system, so women are casting off systems that have tried to keep them silent, separated from their bodies. Minn's insistence on speaking her own language in her own voice is also Canada's.

Certain gender issues are also moral issues. For example, personal affairs — that is, the lives of women — appear in conflict with culture, particularly with culture's major artifacts. The film director, Sam, and the housewife, Minn, act out a dramatic dialogue: Sam quotes passages from *Paradise Lost* while Minn keeps up a steady commentary, in

French, on the housewife's concerns. As Sam quotes descriptions of Eve subservient to Adam, Minn outlines the proper order in which to clean a house and wash the dishes. The bilingual dialogue draws attention to literary history and demonstrates the cultural importance of Milton's masterpiece and the cultural exclusion of trivial female experience. Because Minn is unable to embrace a phallocentric view of the universe, her existence subverts masculine mythology.

More broadly, tensions between creativity and destruction assume gender characteristics. Typical of female-authored texts, the conflict appears in the emphasis on generativity and reproduction. It reveals a particularly female approach to aggression. Minn admits to having trouble with Freud's death instinct and demonstrates the way in which women turn aggression against themselves. She dreams of an extravagant shopping trip that temporarily satisfies her own desires, but then masochistically balances it by dreaming her children asleep or dead in the bathtub, "curled up like little gleaming fish" (p. 5). She admits that "remembering the dream, her mouth was dry. This was the hardest instinct to face, the destructive one" (p. 5). Yet in spite of the masochism of her dream, and in spite of incidents she recalls of mothers murdering their children, she increasingly associates death with men, with her alcoholic, suicidal father, or with the policemen who enter her house like Nazi storm-troopers. She worries that contemporary fathers, too critical of their sons, will produce men who are programmed to fail. For example, Richard, one of her young boarders, seems totally passive, "pale and unformed" (p. 35), the offspring of a generation whose sons seemed "zonked, dead" (p. 35). Traditional gender roles are not only unpleasant and counter-productive, they are also politically and culturally disastrous. As in *Pandora*, where the patriarchal family proves unbalanced, unfair to women and Fascist, possible annihilation completes culture's current path.

That path Minn and her country face. Yet during her pregnancy, Minn would prefer to forget such issues, to hide, ostrich-like, to focus only on her body, to be dominated by her womb. Although she can think about the larger world, like Canada, she has trouble extending her vision. Immediacy seems more pressing. She wants to believe that "[T]he state of the world is not an appropriate subject for meditation on dark nights. It leads to the picture of a woman and her children fleeing the holocaust and they are not quick enough and she is not strong enough, and which one should she save?" (p. 40). This either-or decision, as dramatically imagined here as it is in Styron's *Sophie's Choice*, seems a basic female dilemma. Yet Minn knows that a mother's role in the contemporary world can no longer afford to end at the doors of her home. Women cannot avoid involvement. Dr. Minnow proves correct:

"'There is no longer any place that is not of general interest'" (p. 135).

A similar tension between creation and destruction occurs in one of Minn's dreams. In the dream, she parallels politics and housekeeping in ways that seem peculiarly fitting to the female consciousness. Imagining her arrest in a police-run campaign to make the inner city cleaner, she hears a policeman announce that "'[M]iddle-class values have got to be imposed in order to get these girls to clean up'" (p. 92). Minn reveals her anxiety about women's traditional roles as housekeepers of society. She is dragged off to jail as a cautionary example of running a filthy home and, as part of her defense, invokes Virginia Woolf. Later, awake, she imagines revisions of Plato's Republic: "In my government there'd be compulsory downstairs bathrooms for all mothers, and a squad of government housekeepers on motorcycles . . . holiday help by lottery, abortion on demand, cheap nationalized shoes" (p. 95). By relating women and politics, Minn's imaginings emphasize the importance of women's participation. Masculine rulers miss important issues, as far as women are concerned, because they do not know enough about women's lives. Minn longs for a society that will make equal male and female perspectives; she suggests a new world vision that, unlike the obsessively Puritan one that became the moral basis for American culture, will alter gender patterns in ways most beneficial to survival.

At the same time, Minn, like most Canadians, is no political radical. Because she is a mother, continuance fascinates her; she concentrates on ways to bring the past and present together, to program a possible future. Even a game of Solitaire allows her to construct a cultural history. The cards become twentieth-century figures, "Gene Autry, Roy Rogers, Sonja Henie," while her wandering mind imagines the "interior landscapes" of different generations: "Alice and Gertrude laughing at Amos and Andy. Talk of Marie Dressler. The first television that came to Godwin: Joe McCarthy with five o'clock shadow interrogating, accusing. In a furniture store window. Grey airwave invasion unwilled. My country tis of theirs" (p. 103). Colonial spatial and temporal restrictions irritate her. The United States leans too heavily on Canada in the twentieth century, and haunting residues of Great Britain's influence remain from the nineteenth. A friend's mother owned a pair of Georgian fire-screens, "Silent Companions," a British housemaid and a wigged serving-man. When she was dying, she took them to her room with her, "sweet vapid faces like her own or General Wolfe's, a conceit in Gainsborough colours" (p. 103). Such a description of a fading empire suggests a certain colonial satisfaction. Yet the satisfaction remains ambivalent. Minn's own toys illustrate the dilemma. They are toy-theatre characters, British, and Minn has given them new faces, a new world; has attempted to "create some kind of concrete landscape of her imagination" (p. 104). Yet, in vital ways, these characters never succeed, for they "remained paper figures, flat, inaccurately cut, with small out-of-scale faces pasted on" (p. 105). This distinctively colonial problem haunts the narrative throughout.

While it articulates the thoughts of a single woman, the novel also allegorically demonstrates Canada's political and cultural dilemmas. Specifically, the text reveals colonialism from the point of view of the colonized. Toward the end of the novel, increasingly terrifying fantasies control Minn's imagination: "[i]t would be something to be beaten physically, broken. No, not masochism: justification. It would be real .... I would not fall back on being middle-class. I swear it. The wounds would be external, visible. I would wear them like stigmata, and say to everyone, 'Look what society has acted out'" (p. 115). Such fantasies seem to characterize victimized people: politically victimized, sexually victimized.

Symbolically, Minn acts out a struggle against world-wide aggression when a young policeman, looking for one of her boarders, enters her home. Pregnant and alone, she tackles him, twisting "as Ben had taught her to twist from a grip. Her eye fixed on the gun in his belt. The bloody Nazi" (p. 117). After the fight, she describes the policeman as if he were an American image: "He stood in the doorway, very Western movie, gun on hip. 'Let's get moving,' he said to his podner" (p. 119). When she wakes in the morning, signs of her mock-epic battle surround her: clutter, broken fingernails, a bad taste in the mouth, some colonial residue that insists "the natives use their mouths so badly" (p. 128). But what remains most clearly is that violence seems to have spilled across the border: "Last night, the cop. Bang-bang you're dead. Where did the children learn it, down here with only me to play with and censored television? In the air, is it? Or in the psyche?" (p. 129). Violence threatens to efface women. When the young policeman had arrived, Minn instantly recognized him, but her face was not "something he noticed. And she had changed from a pretty girl to a pregnant squaw in four, five years. You didn't get any consideration unless you and your house were expensively fixed up" (p. 117). Her fight becomes a woman's fight for recognition.

However, Minn does question the possible success of female revolution. Frequently in literature and often enough in life, "[D]eath in childbed seems to end every feminine revolution" (p. 123). Minn does not believe that the Pill has solved women's fates. When she thinks of her mother-in-law's life she admits that it has been more economically depressed than her own. In her mother-in-law's time, when babies were born at home, disaster was imminent. Women were encouraged to accept martyrdom, to be silent masochists. Yet, at the same time, such women also developed idiosyncratic strengths. In the latter half of the twentieth century, Minn questions those strengths. She imagines the children of contemporary women growing up; the moment when "the dreary mums bloom again. They get new clothes and sprint from job to job singing" (p. 130). But she imagines also the generational problems that will result, the mothers' collisions with "paranoid teenagers." The mothers may fall back "mortally wounded" (p. 130). They have not been trained "like Gertrude, like Norman's mother" (p. 130) to fight for their independent survival.

The Honeyman Festival remains an ambivalent novel. It reflects precisely the cultural and sexual confusions of the early 1970s. Written just as the new wave of feminism was making itself felt, and as Canadian nationalism was becoming pronounced, it fluctuates between a conservative and a radical presentation of gender roles. Minn is still in the house, still tied to her body, still using her imagination as her major escape. Against the eternal truths, her life lacks substance, is politically uninteresting. Minn's own view of the universe consigns her to a certain oblivion: "Whatever happens, the universe will roll on somehow. It's big enough to do without us, there's a comfort. The tides will ebb and flow, the moon rise even if she isn't cheese or snow. *Das ewig Weibliche* will whip us from her dog-cart. *Das ewig Maennliche* will slog across the moor" (p. 131). Nonetheless, Minn is concerned about the continuance of the universe and concludes the novel with a question: "And the morning will come, and so will the night again. Won't it?" (p. 131). The tone is enigmatic, yet not surprising. Minn recognizes the problems but despairs of solutions. Cultural and sexual changes multiply around her. Indeed, not until *Lunatic Villas* will Engel again attempt this kind of analysis. Ten years later, solutions seem more possible.

Lunatic Villas is more consistently allegorical. The setting of the prologue, carefully dated 1967, the year of Canada's centennial, is a typical Canadian city, Toronto, where the population, like Canada's, is made up of a variety of cultural groups that have not been assimilated into a national unity. At one end of the street, "no one has spoken English since 1926" (p. 7). The novel also connects Canada's colonial history with the history of women. Like Minn's house in *The Honeyman Festival*, a house that has been rented "from a woman who had hoped to turn it into a town house, but lost her money on the adjoining member of the row" (p. 12), Harriet's house represents Canada. Wilma Wickwire, a real-estate broker who dominates the prologue and who is responsible for altering the street, is a reconstructor and an historian, a combination peculiarly suited to a country that became a dominion without fighting a war of independence. Wilma preserves the houses she renovates. Harriet Ross is one of the original buyers and the central character of the novel. Her name parodies the name of the famous American nationalist hero, Betsy Ross.

An old lady, the British Mrs. Saxe, introduces further colonial metaphors. Her arrival encourages Harriet to imagine herself a "colonial paying for" her shooting weekend, while Mrs. Saxe, bicycle and all, represents "the mother country's revenge" (p. 18). Such allusions proliferate, reminding Canadians of the mother-daughter metaphor that dominates their history. Repeatedly, Harriet's colonial insecurities surface and, as Dennis Lee argues in an essay about finding a voice, she discovers the necessity of exploring those "obstructions to cadence" that define the "nature of colonial space."[4] In speaking to Mrs. Saxe, Harriet finds herself using language quite different from her own; she worries about the thickness of the towels and defends her colonial status from implied threats: "She's a nice enough old thing but her generation stays for ages. What on earth can I do? If she pulls that old British line that all Canadians are *wet* I'll run after her with an axe" (p. 20). Harriet's family is so differently structured and mannered from a typical British one as to almost defy comparison. Badly organized, occasionally vulgar, her children betray all the characteristics an aristocratic tradition finds most offensive. For Harriet, the laws of inheritance seem meaningless. She acquires her children "'the way some people pick up furniture'" (p. 23). Ancestral time, the smooth flow of generations into each other, is radically altered. And although Mrs. Saxe asserts that the empire is a "good thing," her casual summary of its broken umbilical cord suggests a faltering imperialism, and also the mother country's failure to keep track of her possessions: "Oh, children, lovely. Gone now: grown. On the land, off the land: Australia, India, Cyprus, Egypt, Jo'burg" (p. 23).

When Harriet asks Mrs. Saxe about a daughter purported to be living in Vancouver, the old British woman abruptly informs her that her daughter has died. This statement about the relationship between British Columbia and Great Britain underlines the failure of imperialist countries to become involved in the life of the colonies. The narrator ironically denies the allegorical abstraction: "It would be more amusing to see Mrs. Saxe as a kind of existential mystery, but the world around Harriet as usual refuses abstraction" (p. 50). Great Britain is all too real. Various concrete reminders of the empire crop up in unexpected places throughout the novel. One of the children is compared to the heroine of a Victorian British novel. A crocheted tea cosy depicts Anne Hathaway's cottage. Queen Victoria decorates Babs's bottle of gin. Metaphorically, the novel balances — like Canada — precariously between an idiosyncratic identity and an anxiety that results from the overpowering influence of the mother country.

As well, the current threat of Canadian cultural extinction by American political and economic power informs the allegory of the novel. During the 1960s, Harriet was married to an American draft dodger. Although the figure of the draft dodger perhaps says more about Canada than about the United States, his presence implies violence just across the border. In *Technology and Empire*, a book written during the Vietnam War and a rallying point for many Canadian nationalists, George Grant writes: "The present happenings in Vietnam are particularly terrible for Canadians. What is being done there is being done by a society which is in some deep way our own. It is being done by a society which more than any other carries the destiny of the West, and Canadians belong inevitably to that destiny. Canada could only continue to be if we could hold some alternative social vision of the great republic."[5] Engel struggles with that alternative vision. Yet Harriet's dependence on Tom and her emptiness when he abruptly dies reflect an ambivalent Canadian attitude to the United States. Like Minn in *The Honeyman Festival*, Harriet sees her southern neighbour as masculine and aggressive. Mick, her son by the American draft dodger, is the only one of her children who violently loses his temper. In one of his rages, he threatens to destroy the house. Yet he is also the son who survives most splendidly, finally giving a certain kind of unity to his sprawling country.

As Mrs. Saxe's far-roaming children imply the British Empire, so Harriet's motley crew become a metaphor for Canada. The lack of blood ties and the failure of central identity demonstrate the tenuous connections among Canada's provinces and her simultaneous concern for a singular identity. So does Harriet's own familial past: "They want me not to be anyone's mother because I wasn't anyone's daughter . . . . No, I was Father's daughter. Mother died or was put away . . . . I saw the State standing over me in my father's Sunday suit, in high boots with a whip or a whiplash collar. I hate, I decided, the State" (p. 34). Later, like Betsy Ross, Harriet defies cultural extinction, becomes a woman defending her country: "The State wants Sim, I thought. No. I will stand and be martyred. I will hold him against my bosom as we stand against a wall. They . . . can shoot us both" (p. 34). Yet when Harriet thinks about moving to the suburbs, she recognizes a nostalgia for Great Britain that troubles her. In "the attempt to reproduce the playing fields of England," the new world tenants forget that such fields "were planted and rolled by serfs" (p. 84). Desiring a more communal perspective, Harriet remembers that "[O]ur aristocracy came from manure spreaders . . . and tedders and harrows and the instalment plan" (p. 84).

Finally, some of the male characters negatively portray colonial failings. Harriet is having an affair with "the Man from Montreal," an

English Canadian in Quebec, who "looks like an American football player" (p. 74). Her second husband, the symbolically named Michael Littemore, exemplifies the failing patriarchy described also in *The Honeyman Festival*. Littlemore is a conserver of energy, not a spender. He is an inadequate father and husband; he weighs three hundred pounds; and he is a man who has never been able to leave his mother: "He knows his place, knows she needs him . . . . She's the last of a fine old race, thinks the male of the species is to be indulged. It makes her happy" (p. 79). But such dependence backfires in the colonies. When he goes out, dressed up, he looks out of place, a period piece.

Apart from the usual sexual analogies — that the masculine represents destruction, or at least impotence, the feminine creativity — such metaphors make use of various characteristics of mother-daughter relationships and of the development of the female personality. Canadian history lends credence to such allegorical representation. The emergence of a strong Canadian literature with the rise of the current women's movement allows for the developmental metaphors used by the writers discussed in this collection. Apart from its insistent colonial metaphors, *Lunatic Villas*, like *The Honeyman Festival*, informs the reader of "things about all of us [women] that nobody wants to know" (p. 70). In some respects, the novel becomes an elongated version of the newspaper column written by Harriet entitled "Depressed Housewife." Like that column, the narrative undergoes transformations that result, by its conclusion, in altered interpretations of male and female gender roles. But before that happens, old roles are attacked. The youngest of three sisters, Harriet represents a precarious balance between cultural extremes. Her older sister, the wealthy, hardened, and increasingly mad Madge, represents an aristocratic extreme that seems out of place in Canadian society. She also exemplifies the fate of the isolated and lonely woman. Harriet's other sister, the alcoholic Babs, at one time a brilliant student, is now a deserted wife and a failed, adoptive mother, depressed and unproductive. Other female characters in the novel also serve as warnings. A crippled neighbour raises birds; she treats them as if they were her children and infects the neighbourhood with disease.

Male characters also reveal the disastrous effects of rigid gender stereotyping. Apart from Michael Littlemore, who represents a tiring patriarchal tradition that is almost entirely dependent on women to support it, the writer Vinnie Palmer is also sarcastically characterized: he is the "successful product of a successful mother" (p. 132). Not surprisingly, he is profoundly troubled by women. A man of rigid routine, a "disciplined man" (p. 130), a "creature of habit" (p. 131), he wants to preserve culture unchanged. His exposure to strong, rebellious women especially undermines his writing. This undermining is dramatically enacted when, crossing the street against a red light, Vinnie is rescued from probable catastrophe by Marshallene. As the representative female writer of the novel, a contrast to Harriet who has not yet become a serious writer, Marshallene embodies everything Vinnie finds most disgusting and even terrifying in women. He sees her as "vulgarity backed by truth" (p. 135), a representation of "cultural indelicacies" (p. 136), even though she has been "called 'a sensitive and, what is rarer still, energetic critic of Ontario society,' and 'a poet of super-consciousness'" (p. 136). The rescue exacerbates "the gulping adolescent" (p. 135) in Vinnie, as well as invoking cultural myths that portray women as profoundly destructive. He imagines Marshallene becoming huge, swelling "like the face of the Cheshire cat; her eyes are greener and greener, her curls are aggressive pubic tendrils, her little teeth are pegs" (p. 136). Vinnie's reaction to powerful women seems also cautionary. Women writers are altering the stories of men's lives, are, as Vinnie admits, "rewriting his autobiography by existing" (p. 137).

The novel demonstrates a pervasive concern with the ways in which traditional sexual roles and patterns are changing or need to change. For example, in the British-Canadian marriage between Olivia and Roger, Roger represents the new world. The British Olivia finds her Canadian husband's friends dreary and the demands of motherhood impossible. About her, Roger thinks: "It's because she's English and of the old, upper-middle-class school: she has that confidence they have, that feeling that it was right for them to own the world and tell the rest of us not only how to live our lives but even how, from their point of view (which to them is the only possible point of view, no weak relativity for them), lives in the past were led. So that they incorporated our pasts while they were manipulating our futures" (p. 100). When Olivia agrees to give birth to a baby, it is on the condition that her Canadian husband rear it. His experience with motherhood fundamentally changes him: he undergoes a different struggle with the self, a struggle that reflects the effects of learning to nurture. "He sees himself, then, what he has been and what he is going to be: no longer the tall, sure man who lectures, organizes, mocks, prompts, chairs, chides, but an unsure creature, gangling and awkward and coy . . . unsure, half drunk with fear and discombobulation, pram-pushing, vague, milk-scarred, forever fumbling in his Doctor Spock" (p. 98). Engel demonstrates a radical gender alteration, so radical that it alters the very authority of the patriarchy. In real earnestness, Hercules dons women's clothes.

Roger changes, becomes more human. Before his daughter was born, he confesses, his dream "had been a father's dream, a dream of formation, of education" (p. 99). From another perspective, Roger begins to understand the power that women feel, the knowing about another human being, the total involvement. He compares himself to Alice in Wonderland, a mythic commentary on femininity. Psychological femininity can be understood by men and demonstrated by male literary characters. Feminine, too, is Roger's sense of becoming a garden: "It seems to him, for a moment, that he has become a garden, changeable, flexible, weather-vulnerable; no more the great male rock he is supposed to be, consistent, unchangeable. I will, he thinks again, know the things that women — no, parents — know. And he feels flooded with a great and almost political peace" (p. 101). The correlation between women and political peace stresses a major theme of this allegory and reminds the reader that Canada was named "the peaceable kingdom." Roger seems closer to women's idea of an attractive man than does Michael Littlemore, who quite clearly proves "bad for civilization" (p. 105), among other reasons because he is a man who depends on women to nurture him, a man who takes their jobs but fails to produce. He is the old man, opinionated and domineering; Roger is the new man, translated and reborn.

The tension between destruction and creation is not simplistic. Engel does not categorically dramatize aggression as male, pacifism as female. However, she imagines mothers to be in a better psychological position to prevent total holocaust. Because maternal characters in Engel's novels are committed to generation, they become the central voices. Harriet wants to stay away from countries that are dominantly aggressive; she claims that "[I]t's people without any kids who fool around with the idea of revolution" (p. 114). In this light, the subject of abortion gains resonance, as it does, for example, in Gilligan's study, where the central problem of the moral and cultural prerequisites that determine a woman's approach to aborting her own foetus suggests wide-ranging psychological extensions. If men learn to respect life, as Roger learns to raise and nurture his own child, *Lunatic Villas* implies, revolutions will be less easy to start and abortion not so necessary. And, as Frank Kermode argues about E. C. Bentley's *Trent's Last Case*, "the hermeneutic spawns the cultural."[6] Unlike Great Britain and the United States, Canada is not an imperial power. "Local and provincial restrictions" in the novel help shape the reading.

Lunatic Villas also portrays dramatically the central character's discovery of the woman's voice, a preparation for the understanding of the female novel. As the novel progresses, Harriet more frequently imagines becoming a serious writer. Indeed, the community of lunatic villas, largely a community of women, suggests, as Nina Auerbach argues about literary communities of women, its own "somewhat quirky and grotesque authority."[7] In *Lunatic Villas* and *The Honeyman Festival*, that authority often connects with domesticity. Each develops what Nina Baym refers to as "closed and structured social space," frequently the home, which often contracts into even smaller spaces, "the room of her own that is the heroine's particular territory, identified with her self."[8] Yet within this space, political and cultural metaphors abound. Private space and public space cohere. What has seemed the private language of women metamorphoses into public utterance. The domestic novel's assumed triviality thus comes under attack. Although Engel uses the genre, the characters she creates subvert it, sometimes by parodying it, at other times by turning it into allegory. Like palimpsests, her novels transform tightly controlled space into cultural structures. As a result, the public voice replaces the private and the genre of "women's fiction," where a developmental circularity encloses women characters in the text, becomes political. Correspondingly, this public voice represents Canada's emergence from a closed and private colonized space to one of international importance.

The novel also investigates the process of literary production. Harriet's double, Marshallene, is a serious writer, a woman who lives "with plots" (p. 177), who represents "cultural indelicacies" (p. 136), a politically committed writer who, Vinnie says, has written the only book "about my ancestors that isn't bullshit" (p. 138). Most revealingly, Marshallene gravitates to the secret selves of ordinary people. She shares Munro's fascination with "the lies, the speculations, the slanders" (p. 177) and emphasizes to Harriet "the novels about our darker selves" (p. 177). These two Engel novels are, in fact, about women's darker selves. They imply that women's stories emerge from cultural darkness, from houses that have become private and from bodies that have been denied. Both endeavour to illuminate such spaces. In other Engel stories, Marshallene has demonstrated the career of the contemporary woman writer. In "Marshallene on Rape," in the collection *Inside the Easter Egg*, she concentrates on female bodies, on the fact that "the literature of rape is incomplete from the female point of view, so that how rape affected the brain before 1970 is pretty well unknown," although she recognizes that "the gap is now being filled in feminist papers."[9] Her recognition of the female body as vulnerable reflects, in literary terms, her own sensation of being "a manuscript that's found a publisher."[10]

In another story in *Inside the Easter Egg*, "Marshallene at Work," the writer self-consciously analyzes her artistic development. She acknowledges a commitment to women and recalls the anonymity of female story-tellers from her past: "How she heard, she did not remember. Someone told the stories, which of the old, old women was it, in black stockings and aprons over aprons, worn cardigans, men's slippers, white cataracted eyes?"[11] The reader discovers that the character Marshallene has developed specifically as a woman writer, using stories passed down by women. She is also Canadian, a sensitive reflector of Canada's history and culture. About her country, she says: "They took their bundle of hope and put it on flat clay land, made doctors, engineers and consumptives, rag and bone men, oilmen, Indians, ferrymen. They made these streets I walk, they made the laws, they made the sallow shadow of righteousness I walk in . . . . There ought to be a way of telling it."[12] The way of telling it absorbs her. In *Lunatic Villas*, she imagines herself as Canada, a Canada that refuses a colonial future: "those who want everything both ways get it no way. Two plusses make a minus. I'm therefore an island in spite of myself — as you are, Mrs. Saxe — but, by God, I'm a floating island with a fifty-horsepower motor, and pardon me while I strop my leathers and get out of here" (p. 199).

Images of women, of writing, and of nationalism merge. As in *Bodily Harm*, the colours of the Canadian flag, red and white, metaphorically illustrate the merger. Sitting in the courtroom "on the edge of a white chair," waiting to be judged an inadequate mother, Harriet is "afraid she'll get her period suddenly and soil it" (p. 208). The tenth chapter of the novel offers an overview of Canada, a summary look at the ten provinces. The activity Engel chose to represent this part of the novel's allegory, the trans-Canada bicycle race, allows the two most politically representative characters, Michael, the son of the American draft-dodger, and the British Mrs. Saxe, to co-operate in a gesture that illustrates an evolving Canadian identity that pushes into "the future, rather than away from the past" (p. 234). The novel stresses the importance of a literary tradition in the forming of the national consciousness. As the whole of Rathsbone Place gathers to watch the Great Canadian Bicycle Race, the country's political provinces become literary ones: "They've pedalled through Farley Mowat, L. M. Montgomery, Bliss Carman, Hugh MacLennan, Ralph Connor, Margaret Laurence, Sinclair Ross, W. O. Mitchell, and Ethel Wilson-land" (p. 246). The authority given the Canadian voice as a result of this political-literary race allows Harriet to tell Mrs. Saxe's daughter to leave, a distinctively Canadian victory.

* * *

In spite of the plethora of nationalistic themes and images, *The Honeyman Festival* and *Lunatic Villas* are not narrowly chauvinistic. Both recognize a necessary commitment to international politics. Often, that commitment is revealed in homely images that, as they do in "The Pegnitz Junction," emphasize the preservation of life most involving to women. Minn concocts dinners that bring together various countries around the table. Harriet, recovering from her illness, envisages as world-wide the red and white that symbolize Canada: "Crimson and madder and pink and red creep into the edges of her dreams, like the red that creeps through the white of Rembrandt tulips. A procession of women creeps up the hill, miners' picks over their shoulders, singing 'The Volga Boat Song,' their jeans and jean jackets tinged with gold and a blessedly non-menstrual red" (p. 224). In one of the concluding paragraphs of *The Honeyman Festival*, a similar condensation of women and international politics occurs. Minn imagines Canadians sitting "in a circle longing for the lights of Moscow," but continuing to clean their houses and to make artifacts (p. 131).

As her "Notes in a Future Key" suggests, Jean Baker Miller discusses the importance women place on their ties to other people. The individual's need for those ties has been illustrated throughout the narratives I have discussed. But something else has also emerged: women's voices have become essential to the survival of the planet. Miller writes: "Practically everyone now bemoans Western man's sense of alienation, lack of community, and inability to find ways of organizing society for human ends. We have reached the end of the road that is built on the set of traits held out for male identity — advance at any cost, pay any price, drive out all competitors, and kill them if necessary."[13] These traits Miller believes to be no longer acceptable if human beings are to survive. Thus, she turns to women who, she argues, can effect a "most basic social advance,"[14] not because of their biological differences, but because of their psychological conditioning. At this stage in the world's history, western women understand better than do men the importance of forming connections. Convinced that this knowledge is essential to survival, Miller argues that "[I]t now seems clear we have arrived at a point from which we must return to a basis of faith in affiliation — and not only faith but recognition that it is a requirement for the existence of human beings."[15]

Engel's novels structurally and contextually verify the political necessity of affiliation. At the same time, they never lose sight of the precarious conditions for survival that have evolved in the contemporary world. Minn acknowledges "war and murder," Harriet the insanity of Hitler, the McCarthy era, Vietnam. Both novels dramatize Canada's tendency toward isolation, and the Canadian pretense of "living as if we're trying to finish a nineteenth-century novel when it's been over for nearly eighty years" (p. 239). Involvement increasingly becomes a political as well as a moral necessity. The novels bring together metaphors of childbirth and of nurturing to establish relationships among women and political governance. They demonstrate, fictionally, the necessity of women's participation in the world. Miller acknowledges that most of women's strengths have been "hidden in this culture," that politics has suffered from rejecting the "benefit of women's leadership, the advantage of women's deep and special strengths."[16] Engel's novels suggest a rationale for the female literary character, and a new power for the female writer.

Miller concludes: "A community of purposeful and sympathetic women directed to their self-determined goals is a new phenomenon. It has created an atmosphere and milieu that brings a whole new quality to life. It advances and fosters both attempts at knowledge and a personal conviction about the content and the methods of getting at knowledge. It creates a new sense of connection between knowledge, work, and personal life."[17] Women writers in Canada, even heuristically, need to be perceived communally. As they help to forge their country's literary imagination and to determine many of her metaphors, they also carry political weight. Indeed, as their fictional landscapes become mapped and the hidden stories of their texts articulated more clearly, a new North American ethos begins to take shape. That ethos stresses historical continuity, geographical conservation, communal survival and physical as well as creative generation. It is a profoundly feminine ethos. Two poems by Margaret Atwood isolate such concerns. In the first, "The Red Shirt," from *Two-Headed Poems*, the poet describes a shirt she and her sister make and give to the poet's daughter. The metaphor of the making of the shirt suggests to the poet her own writing, a woman's writing. The covert signs through which women have traditionally communicated she stitches into the shirt, thereby writing them into the language:

> It may not be true   that one myth cancels another.
> Nevertheless, in a corner
> of the hem, where it will not be seen,
> where you will inherit
> it, I make this tiny
> stitch, my private magic.[18]

In the other poem, "Book of Ancestors," from *You Are Happy*, the poet offers a strategy for survival:

> You are intact, you turn
> towards me, your eyes opening, the eyes
> intricate and easily bruised, you open
>
> yourself to me gently, what
> they tried, we
> tried but could never do
> before . without blood, the killed
> heart . to take
> that risk, to offer life and remain
>
> alive, open yourself like this and become whole.[19]

When opened up, the subversions of these novels, their hidden stories encourage new ways of seeing that point toward a more collective human integrity. The silencing of female voices has led to political and sexual division. North America needs to listen to its women writers, to take the risk, to embrace life, to become whole.

Notes

INTRODUCTION

The epigraph is from Annette Kolodny's "Dancing Through the Minefield: Some Observations on the Theory, Practice, and Politics of a Feminist Literary Criticism," *Feminist Studies*, 6, No. 1 (Spring 1980), pp. 6–7.

1. Wayne Booth, "Freedom of Interpretation: Bakhtin and the Challenge of Feminist Criticism," *Critical Inquiry*, 9, No. 1 (Sept. 1982), p. 74.
2. Roland Barthes, *The Pleasures of the Text*, trans. Richard Miller (New York: Hill and Wang, 1975), p. 10.
3. Barthes, p. 37.
4. Barthes, p. 47.
5. Norman O. Brown, *Love's Body* (New York: Vantage, 1966), p. 3.
6. Dianne Sadoff, *Monsters of Affection: Dickens, Eliot and Bronte on Fatherhood* (Baltimore: The Johns Hopkins Univ. Press, 1976), p. 81.
7. Sadoff, p. 107.
8. Sadoff, p. 65.
9. Sandra Gilbert and Susan Gubar, *The Madwoman in the Attic: The Woman Writer and the Nineteenth-Century Literary Imagination* (New Haven: Yale Univ. Press, 1979).
10. Sadoff, p. 167.
11. John Berger, *Ways of Seeing* (Middlesex: Penguin Books, 1972).
12. Sadoff, p. 7.
13. Harold Bloom, *A Map of Misreading* (New York: Oxford Univ. Press, 1975), p. 9.
14. Nancy Chodorow, *The Reproduction of Mothering: Psychoanalysis and the Sociology of Gender* (Berkeley: Univ. of California Press, 1978).
15. Carol Gilligan, *In a Different Voice: Psychological Theory and Women's Development* (Cambridge: Harvard Univ. Press, 1982).
16. Margaret Homans, *Women Writers and Poetic Identity* (Princeton: Princeton Univ. Press, 1980), p. 217.
17. Homans, p. 236.
18. *The Future of Difference*, ed. Hester Eisenstein and Alice Jardine (Boston: Barnard College Women's Center, 1980), p. xvii.
19. Eisenstein and Jardine, p. xx.
20. Margaret Homans, "Her Very Own Howl," *Signs*, 9, No. 2 (Winter 1983), p. 191.
21. Homans, p. 190.
22. Homans, p. 190.

[23] Homans, pp. 190–91.
[24] Eisenstein and Jardine, p. 152.
[25] Homans, p. 198.
[26] Homans, p. 205.
[27] Dennis Lee, "Cadence, Country, Silence: Writing in Colonial Space," *boundary 2*, 3, No. 1 (Fall 1974), 163.
[28] Lee, p. 166.
[29] Leslie Fiedler, *Love and Death in the American Novel* (New York: Delta, 1966), p. 60.
[30] Adrienne Rich, *Of Woman Born* (New York: Bantam, 1976), p. 292.
[31] Kolodny, p. 5.
[32] Robert Scholes, *Semiotics and Interpretation* (New Haven: Yale Univ. Press, 1982), p. 131.
[33] Hélène Cixous, "The Laugh of the Medusa," *Signs*, 1, No. 4 (Summer 1976), 877, n. 1.
[34] Janet Richards, *The Sceptical Feminist: A Philosophical Inquiry* (London: Routledge and Kegan Paul, 1980), p. 267.
[35] Sigmund Freud, *The Standard Edition of the Complete Psychological Works of Sigmund Freud*, trans. James Strachey, Vol. 17 (London: The Hogarth Press, 1955), p. 231.
[36] This is a list of the major novels and short stories discussed in this collection: Audrey Thomas, *Mrs. Blood* (Vancouver: Talonbooks, 1970); Margaret Atwood, *Bodily Harm* (Toronto: McClelland and Stewart, 1981); Audrey Thomas, *Blown Figures* (Vancouver, Talonbooks, 1974); Mavis Gallant, "Its Image on the Mirror," in *My Heart Is Broken* (1957; Don Mills: PaperJacks, 1974); Alice Munro, *The Moons of Jupiter* (Toronto: Macmillan, 1982); Sylvia Fraser, *Pandora* (Boston: Little, Brown, 1972); Mavis Gallant, "The Pegnitz Junction," *The Pegnitz Junction* (Toronto: Macmillan, 1982); Mavis Gallant, *Home Truths: Selected Canadian Stories* (Toronto: Macmillan, 1981); Marian Engel, *The Honeyman Festival* (Toronto: House of Anansi, 1970); Marian Engel, *Lunatic Villas* (Toronto: McClelland and Stewart, 1981).
[37] Annis Pratt, *Archetypal Patterns in Women's Fiction* (Bloomington: Indiana Univ. Press, 1982), p. 10.
[38] Berger, p. 64.
[39] Pratt, p. 11.
[40] Pratt, p. 178.
[41] Frank Kermode, *The Art of Telling: Essays on Fiction* (Cambridge: Harvard Univ. Press, 1983), p. 55.
[42] Booth, p. 76.

CHAPTER ONE

The epigraph is from Jessie Weston's *The Quest of the Holy Grail* (New York: Doubleday, 1957), p. 76.

1. Pratt, p. 178.
2. Margaret Atwood, "Foretelling the Future," in *Two-Headed Poems* (Toronto: Oxford Univ. Press, 1978), p. 10.
3. Atwood, p. 11.
4. Lee, p. 155.
5. Karen Gould, "Setting Words Free: Feminist Writing in Quebec," *Signs*, 6, No. 4 (Summer 1981), 621.
6. Gould, p. 617.
7. Cixous, p. 885.
8. Cixous, p. 878.
9. Lee, p. 164.
10. Audrey Thomas, *Ten Green Bottles* (1967; Ottawa: Oberon, 1977).
11. Pierre Macherey, *A Theory of Literary Production*, trans. Geoffrey Wall (London: Routledge and Kegan Paul, 1978), p. 96.
12. *Women Writing and Writing About Women*, ed. Mary Jacobus (London: Croom Helm, 1979), p. 16.
13. Julia Kristeva, *Desire in Language: A Semiotic Approach to Literature and Art*, trans. Thomas Gora, Alice Jardine, and Leon Roudiez (New York: Columbia Univ. Press, 1980), p. 237.
14. Jessie Weston, *From Ritual to Romance* (New York: Doubleday Anchor Books, 1957). This book was originally published in 1920 and influenced the writing of T. S. Eliot's *The Waste Land*.
15. Audrey Thomas, *Songs My Mother Taught Me* (Vancouver: Talonbooks, 1973).
16. Edward Said, *Beginnings: Intention and Method* (New York: Basic Books, 1975), p. 34.
17. John Irwin, *Doubling and Incest/Repetition and Revenge: A Speculative Reading of Faulkner* (Baltimore: The Johns Hopkins Univ. Press, 1975), p. 162.
18. Susan Gubar, "The Birth of the Artist as Heroine: (Re)production, the *Künstlerroman* Tradition, and the Fiction of Katherine Mansfield," in *The Representation of Women in Fiction*, ed. Carolyn Heilbrun and Margaret Higonnet (Baltimore: Johns Hopkins Univ. Press, 1983), p. 26.
19. Fredric Jameson, *The Political Unconscious: Narrative as a Socially Symbolic Act* (New York: Cornell Univ. Press, 1981), p. 85.

CHAPTER TWO

The epigraphs are taken from *New French Feminisms: An Anthology*, ed. Elaine Marks and Isabelle de Courtivron (New York: Schocken Books, 1981), pp. 174, 177.

1. Berger, p. 47.
2. Audrey Thomas, "Topic of Cancer," *Books in Canada*, 10, No. 8 (Oct. 1981), p. 12.
3. Berger, p. 33.
4. Berger, p. 46.
5. Berger, p. 63.
6. Margaret Atwood, *Survival: A Thematic Guide to Canadian Literature* (Toronto: House of Anansi, 1972), p. 18.
7. *Survival*, p. 17.
8. Margaret Atwood, *True Stories* (Toronto: Oxford Univ. Press, 1981), p. 11.
9. *True Stories*, p. 18.
10. Margaret Atwood, *Life Before Man* (Toronto: McClelland and Stewart, 1979), p. 3.
11. Margaret Atwood, *Surfacing* (New York: Simon and Schuster, 1972), p. 222.
12. Freud, 4 (1953), p. 278.
13. Gilbert and Gubar open *The Madwoman in the Attic* with the question: "Is a pen a metaphorical penis?" p. 3.
14. Cixous, p. 875.
15. Cixous, p. 877. Emphasis added.
16. *True Stories*, p. 51.
17. Cixous, p. 887.
18. Marks and de Courtivron, p. 36.
19. Luce Irigaray writes: "Woman finds pleasure more in touch than in sight and her entrance into a dominant scopic economy signifies, once again, her relegation to passivity." Marks and de Courtivron, p. 101.
20. Pratt, p. 11.

CHAPTER THREE

The first epigraph is from Frances Power Cobbe, *Darwinism in Morals and Other Essays* (London: Williams and Norgate, 1872), p. 338. The second is from *The Madwoman in the Attic*, p. 57.

1. Phyllis Chesler, *Women and Madness* (New York: Avon, 1972), p. 31.
2. Barbara Rigney, *Madness and Sexual Politics in the Feminist Novel* (Madison: Univ. of Wisconsin Press, 1978).
3. Gilbert and Gubar, p. 73.

4. Gilbert and Gubar, p. 77.
5. Rigney, p. 22.
6. Rigney, pp. 126–27.
7. Gilbert and Gubar, p. 16.
8. Sigmund Freud, *Delusion and Dream and Other Essays* (Boston: Beacon, 1956), p. 147. I am using this edition because it includes the text of Jensen's story "Gradiva: A Pompeiian Fancy."
9. Gubar, p. 34.
10. Margaret Atwood, *You Are Happy* (Toronto: Oxford Univ. Press, 1974), p. 68.
11. Gradiva, p. 171.
12. Gradiva, p. 193.
13. Joseph Conrad, "Heart of Darkness," in *Great Short Works of Joseph Conrad* (New York: Harper and Row, 1966), p. 237.
14. This quotation, from Sir Thomas Browne's *Religio Medici* (1642) is from one of the epigraphs to *Blown Figures*.
15. Shoshana Felman, "Turning the Screw of Interpretation," *Literature and Psychoanalysis*, ed. Shoshana Felman (Baltimore: The Johns Hopkins Univ. Press, 1977), p. 135.
16. Felman uses Freud's essay "A Child Is Being Beaten" (1919) in ways that elucidate Thomas' work.
17. See Erik Erikson, "Genital Modes and Spatial Modalities," *Childhood and Society* (New York: W. W. Norton, 1950), pp. 97–108. The discussion is developed further in Erikson's "Womanhood and the Inner Space," *Identity: Youth and Crisis* (New York: W. W. Norton, 1968), pp. 261–94.
18. Judith Gardiner, "On Female Identity and Writing by Women," *Critical Inquiry*, 8, No. 2 (Winter 1981), 355.
19. Gardiner, p. 352.
20. Audrey Thomas, "My Craft and Sullen Art: The Writers Speak," *Atlantis*, 4, No. 1 (Fall 1978), p. 153.

CHAPTER FOUR

The epigraph is taken from Louise Bernikow's *Among Women* (New York: Harper and Row, 1980), p. 103.

1. Elaine Showalter, "Feminist Criticism in the Wilderness," *Critical Inquiry*, 8, No. 2 (Winter 1981), 193.
2. *Home Truths*, p. xii.
3. Geoffrey Hartman, "Psychoanalysis: The French Connection," in *Psychoanalysis and the Question of the Text*, ed. Geoffrey Hartman (Baltimore: The Johns Hopkins Univ. Press, 1978), p. 102.
4. Frank Kermode, *The Genesis of Secrecy: On the Interpretation of Narrative* (Cambridge: Harvard Univ. Press, 1979), p. 141.
5. Kermode, p. 125.

6. Margaret Atwood, *Murder in the Dark* (Toronto: Coach House, 1983).
7. *Murder in the Dark*, p. 330.
8. Peter Brooks, "Freud's Masterplot: Questions of Narrative," *Literature and Psychoanalysis*, p. 288.
9. Pratt, p. 178.
10. W. B. Yeats, "The Shadowy Waters," in *The Collected Plays of W. B. Yeats* (New York: Macmillan, 1934), p. 96.
11. Yeats, p. 99.
12. Mavis Gallant, *A Fairly Good Time* (New York: Random House, 1970), p. 45.
13. John Moss, *A Reader's Guide to the Canadian Novel* (Toronto: McClelland and Stewart, 1981), p. 83.
14. Mavis Gallant, *From the Fifteenth District* (Toronto: Macmillan, 1979), p. 72.
15. Bernikow, p. 82.
16. Bernikow, p. 90.
17. Showalter, p. 192.
18. Frank Kermode, "Secrets and Narrative Sequence," *Critical Inquiry*, 7, No. 1 (Autumn 1980), p. 99.
19. Patricia Spacks, *The Female Imagination* (New York: Alfred A. Knopf, 1975), p. 62.

CHAPTER FIVE

The first epigraph is from Carol Gilligan's *In a Different Voice*, p. 19; the second is from Jane Gallop's *The Daughter's Seduction: Feminism and Psychoanalysis* (Ithaca: Cornell Univ. Press, 1982), p. 112.

1. Hélène Cixous, *New French Feminisms*, p. 95.
2. Cixous, p. 95.
3. Luce Irigaray, *New French Feminisms*, p. 101.
4. Irigaray, p. 104.
5. Alice Munro, *Lives of Girls and Women* (Toronto: McGraw-Hill Ryerson, 1971), p. 141.
6. *Lives*, p. 197.
7. Gallop, p. 12.
8. Gallop, p. 30.
9. Gallop, p. 31.
10. Alice Munro, "Material," *Something I've Been Meaning To Tell You* (Toronto: McGraw-Hill Ryerson, 1974), p. 36.
11. *Lives*, p. 166.
12. Beverly Rasporich, "Child-women and Primitives in the Fiction of Alice Munro," *Atlantis*, 1, No. 2 (Spring 1976), 13–14.
13. *Lives*, p. 146.
14. Michel Foucault, *The History of Sexuality*, trans. Robert Hurley (New

York: Vintage, 1980), p. 48.
15. Chodorow, p. 207.
16. James Joyce, "A Portrait of the Artist As A Young Man," in *The Portable James Joyce* (New York: Viking, 1946), p. 483.
17. Alice Munro, "The Ottawa Valley," *Something I've Been Meaning To Tell You*.
18. Gallop, p. 79.
19. Margaret Atwood, *Bodily Harm*, p. 172.
20. Jean Baker Miller, *Toward a New Psychology of Women* (Boston: Beacon Press, 1976), p. 83.
21. Hélène Cixous, "The Laugh of the Medusa," p. 880.
22. Gallop, p. 112.

CHAPTER SIX

The first epigraph is from Jane Harrison's "Pandora's Box," *Journal of Hellenic Studies*, 20 (1900), p. 99. It is quoted in Dora and Erwin Panofsky, *Pandora's Box: The Changing Aspects of a Mythical Symbol* (New York: Pantheon, 1956), p. 3. The second is from *The Voyage In: Fictions of Female Development*, eds. Elizabeth Abel, Marianne Hirsch, and Elizabeth Langland (Hanover: Univ. Press of New England, 1983), p. 12.

1. Virginia Woolf, *A Room of One's Own* (New York: Harcourt, Brace & World, 1929), p. 36.
2. Juliet Mitchell, *Psychoanalysis and Women: Freud, Reich, Laing and Women* (New York: Vintage, 1974), p. 403.
3. Chodorow, p. 47.
4. Chodorow, p. 54.
5. Sheila Rowbotham, *Women, Resistance and Revolution: A History of Women and Revolution in the Modern World* (New York: Random House, 1972), p. 246.
6. *Feminism and Materialism: Women and Modes of Production*, ed. Annette Kuhn and AnnMarie Wolpe (London: Routledge and Kegan Paul, 1978), p. 65.
7. Catharine MacKinnon, "Feminism, Marxism, Method, and the State: An Agenda For Theory," *Signs*, 7, No. 3 (Spring 1982), 515.
8. MacKinnon, p. 535.
9. MacKinnon, p. 543.
10. Catharine MacKinnon, "Feminism, Marxism, Method, and the State: Towards Feminist Jurisprudence," *Signs*, 8, No. 4 (Summer 1983), 657.
11. Alan Twigg, *For Openers: Conversations with 24 Canadian Writers* (Madiera Park: Harbour, 1981), p. 119.
12. Chodorow, p. 32.
13. Lillian Rubin, *Worlds of Pain: Life in the Working-Class Family* (New

York: Basic, 1976).
[14] Freud, 22 (1964), p. 120.
[15] Gallop, p. 46.
[16] Woolf, p. 80.
[17] Macherey, p. 150.
[18] Susan Lanser, *The Narrative Act: Point of View in Prose Fiction* (Princeton: Princeton Univ. Press, 1981), p. 47.
[19] Lanser, p. 167.
[20] Gilligan, p. 170.
[21] Freud, 21 (1961), p. 145.
[22] Freud, p. 145.
[23] Panofsky, p. 113.
[24] Chodorow, p. 214.
[25] Chodorow, p. 214.

CHAPTER SEVEN

The first epigraph is taken from Mary Daly's *Gyn/Ecology: The Metaethics of Radical Feminism* (Boston: Beacon, 1978), p. 400. The second is from Louky Bersianik, *The Euguélionne*, trans. Gerry Denis, Alison Hewitt, Donna Murray, Martha O'Brien (Victoria: Porcépic, 1981), p. 336.

[1] John Ayre, Rev. of *The Pegnitz Junction*, *Saturday Night*, 8 (Sept. 1977), p. 33.
[2] George Woodcock, *The World of Canadian Writing* (Vancouver: Douglas & McIntyre, 1980), p. 108.
[3] Ronald Hatch, "Mavis Gallant: Returning Home," *Atlantis*, 4, No. 1 (Fall 1978), 99.
[4] Spacks, p. 6.
[5] Bersianik, p. 336.
[6] Kolodny, p. 16.
[7] From an interview with Mavis Gallant by Geoff Hancock. Cited in Woodcock, p. 103.
[8] Woodcock, p. 111.
[9] Barthes, p. 10.
[10] Karen Horney, *Feminine Psychology*, ed. Harold Kelman (New York: W. W. Norton, 1967). The chapter entitled "The Dread of Woman" (pp. 133–46) is particularly relevant.
[11] Bernikow, p. 10.
[12] Bersianik, p. 336.
[13] Daly, p. 400.

CHAPTER EIGHT

The first epigraph is from Marian Engel's *Sarah Bastard's Notebook* (Don Mills: PaperJacks, 1974; original title, *No Clouds of Glory* [1968]), pp. 123–24. The second is from France Vézina's *Les Journées d'une anthropophage* (Montréal: Grandes Editions du Quebéc, 1974), p. 28. It is quoted in its English translation in Karen Gould's "Setting Words Free: Feminist Writing in Quebec," p. 637.

1. William Kilbourn, "The Quest for the Peaceable Kingdom," *Canadian Writing Today*, ed. Mordecai Richler (Middlesex: Penguin, 1970), p. 53.
2. *Sarah Bastard's Notebook*, p. 8.
3. Susan Griffin, *Woman and Nature: The Roaring Inside Her* (New York: Harper and Row, 1978).
4. Lee, p. 154.
5. George Grant, *Technology and Empire: Perspectives on North America* (Toronto: House of Anansi, 1969), p. 74.
6. *The Art of Telling*, p. 60. Kermode calls Chapter Two "Local and Provincial Restrictions."
7. Nina Auerbach, *Communities of Women: An Idea in Fiction* (Cambridge: Harvard Univ. Press, 1982), p. 8.
8. Nina Baym, *Woman's Fiction: A Guide to Novels by and about Women in America, 1820 – 1870* (Ithaca: Cornell Univ. Press, 1978), p. 188.
9. Marian Engel, *Inside the Easter Egg* (Toronto: House of Anansi, 1975), p. 107.
10. Engel, p. 108.
11. Engel, p. 142.
12. Engel, p. 145.
13. Miller, p. 82.
14. Miller, p. 93.
15. Miller, pp. 92–93.
16. Miller, p. 101.
17. Miller, p. 141.
18. Margaret Atwood, *Two-Headed Poems* (Toronto: Oxford Univ. Press, 1978), p. 105.
19. *You Are Happy*, p. 96.

Selective Bibliography

CRITICISM AND CRITICAL THEORY

Abel, Elizabeth. "(E)Merging Identities: The Dynamics of Female Friendship in Contemporary Fiction By Women." *Signs*, 6, No. 3 (Spring 1981), 413–35.
———, Marianne Hirsch, and Elizabeth Langland, eds. *The Voyage In: Fictions of Female Development*. Hanover: Univ. Press of New England, 1983.
Andersen, Margaret. "Feminism and the Literary Critic." *Atlantis*, 1, No. 1 (Fall 1975), 3–12.
Atwood, Margaret. *Survival: A Thematic Guide to Canadian Literature*. Toronto: House of Anansi, 1972.
Auerbach, Nina. *Communities of Women*. Cambridge: Harvard Univ. Press, 1978.
Bakhtin, Michel. *The Dialogic Imagination*, trans. M. Holquist and Caryl Emerson. Austin: Univ. of Texas Press, 1981.
Barthes, Roland. *The Pleasures of the Text*, trans. Richard Miller. New York: Hill and Wang, 1975.
Baym, Nina. *Woman's Fiction: A Guide To Novels By and About Women in America, 1820–1870*. Ithaca: Cornell Univ. Press, 1978.
Berger, John. *Ways of Seeing*. Middlesex: Penguin, 1972.
Bernikow, Louise. *Among Women*. New York: Harper and Row, 1980.
Bloom, Harold. *The Anxiety of Influence: A Theory of Poetry*. London: Oxford Univ. Press, 1973.
———. *A Map of Misreading*. New York: Oxford Univ. Press, 1975.
Booth, Wayne. "Freedom of Interpretation: Bakhtin and the Challenge of Feminist Criticism." *Critical Inquiry*, 9, No. 1 (Sept. 1982), 45–76.
Brooks, Peter. "Freud's Masterplot: Questions of Narrative." *Literature and Psychoanalysis: The Question of Reading: Otherwise*, ed. Shoshana Felman. Baltimore: The Johns Hopkins Univ. Press, 1977, pp. 280–300.
Brown, Norman. *Life Against Death: The Psychoanalytic Meaning of History*. Middleton: Wesleyan Univ. Press, 1959.
———. *Love's Body*. New York: Vintage, 1966.
Brown, Russell. "Critic, Culture, Text: Beyond Thematics." *Essays on Canadian Writing*, No. 11 (Summer 1978), 151–83.
Burke, Carolyn. "Irigaray Through the Looking Glass." *Feminist Studies*, 7, No. 2 (Summer 1981), 288–306.
Cameron, Barry, and Michael Dixon. "Mandatory Subversive Manifesto: Canadian Criticism vs. Literary Criticism." *Studies in Canadian Literature*, Special Issue (Summer 1977), 137–45.
Chesler, Phyllis. *Women and Madness*. New York: Avon, 1972.
Chodorow, Nancy. *The Reproduction of Mothering: Psychoanalysis and the Sociology of Gender*. Berkeley: Univ. of California Press, 1978.

Christ, Carol P. *Diving Deep and Surfacing: Women Writers on Spiritual Quests*. Boston: Beacon, 1980.
Cixous, Hélène. "The Laugh of the Medusa." *Signs*, 1, No. 4 (Summer 1976), 875-93.
——. "Castration or Decapitation?" *Signs*, 7, No. 1 (Autumn 1981), 41-55.
Cott, Nancy. *The Bonds of Womanhood: 'Women's Sphere' in New England, 1780-1835*. New Haven: Yale Univ. Press, 1977.
Daly, Mary. *Gyn/Ecology: The Metaethics of Radical Feminism*. Boston: Beacon, 1978.
Davey, Frank. *From There to Here: A Guide to English-Canadian Literature Since 1960*. Erin: Porcépic, 1974.
——. "Surviving the Paraphrase." *Canadian Literature*, No. 70 (Autumn 1976), 5-13.
Diamond, Arlyn, and Lee Edwards, eds. *The Authority of Experience: Essays in Feminist Criticism*. Amherst: Univ. of Massachusetts Press, 1977.
Dinnerstein, Dorothy. *The Mermaid and the Minotaur: Sexual Arrangements and Human Malaise*. New York: Harper and Row, 1976.
Douglas, Ann. *The Feminization of American Culture*. New York: Alfred A. Knopf, 1977.
Eisenstein, Hester, and Alice Jardine, eds. *The Future of Difference*. Boston: G. K. Hall, 1980.
Erikson, Erik. *Childhood and Society*. New York: W. W. Norton, 1950.
——. *Identity: Youth and Crisis*. New York: W. W. Norton, 1968.
Felman, Shoshana. "Turning the Screw of Interpretation." *Literature and Psychoanalysis*, pp. 94-207.
——. "Rereading Femininity." *Yale French Studies*, No. 62 (1981), 19-44.
Fiedler, Leslie. *Love and Death in the American Novel*. New York: Delta, 1966.
Foucault, Michel. *The History of Sexuality*, trans. Robert Hurley. New York: Vintage, 1980.
Freud, Sigmund. *The Standard Edition of the Complete Psychological Works of Sigmund Freud*, trans. and ed. James Strachey. London: The Hogarth Press, 1962-66.
Gallop, Jane. *The Daughter's Seduction: Feminism and Psychoanalysis*. Ithaca: Cornell Univ. Press, 1982.
Gardiner, Judith. "On Female Identity and Writing by Women." *Critical Inquiry*, 8, No. 2 (Winter 1981), 347-61.
Gibson, Graeme. *Eleven Canadian Novelists*. Toronto: House of Anansi, 1973.
Gilbert, Sandra, and Susan Gubar. *The Madwoman in the Attic: The Woman Writer and the Nineteenth-Century Literary Imagination*. New Haven: Yale Univ. Press, 1979.
——. "Costumes of the Mind." *Critical Inquiry*, 7, No. 2 (Winter 1980), 391-417.
Gilligan, Carol. *In a Different Voice: Psychological Theory and Women's Development*. Cambridge: Harvard Univ. Press, 1982.
Gould, Karen. "Setting Words Free: Feminist Writing in Quebec." *Signs*, 6,

No. 4 (Summer 1981), 617-42.

———. "Spatial Poetics, Spatial Politics: Quebec Feminists on the City and the Countryside." *The American Review of Canadian Studies*, 12, No. 1 (Spring 1982), 1-9.

Grace, Sherrill. *Violent Duality: A Study of Margaret Atwood*. Montreal: Véhicule, 1980.

———, and Lorraine Weir, eds. *Margaret Atwood: Language, Text and System*. Vancouver: Univ. of British Columbia Press, 1983.

Grant, George. *Lament for a Nation: The Defeat of Canadian Nationalism*. Toronto: McClelland and Stewart, 1965.

———. *Technology and Empire: Perspectives on North America*. Toronto: House of Anansi, 1969.

Griffin, Susan. *Woman and Nature: The Roaring Inside Her*. New York: Harper and Row, 1978.

Gubar, Susan. "'The Blank Page' and the Issues of Female Creativity." *Critical Inquiry*, 8, No. 2 (Winter 1981), 243-63.

Hartman, Geoffrey. "Psychoanalysis: The French Connection." In *Psychoanalysis and the Question of the Text*, ed. Geoffrey Hartman. Baltimore: The Johns Hopkins Univ. Press, 1978, pp. 86-113.

Hatch, Ronald. "Mavis Gallant: Returning Home." *Atlantis*, 4, No. 1 (Fall 1978), 95-102.

Hedenstrom, Joanne. "Puzzled Patriarchs and Free Women: Patterns in the Canadian Novel." *Atlantis*, 4, No. 1 (Fall 1978), 2-9.

Heilbrun, Carolyn. "Women, Men, Theories and Literature." *Profession 81* [MLA Publication], pp. 25-29.

———, Carolyn and M. Higonnet, eds. *The Representation of Women in Fiction*. Baltimore: The Johns Hopkins Univ. Press, 1983.

Homans, Margaret. *Women Writers and Poetic Identity*. Princeton: Princeton Univ. Press, 1980.

———. "Her Very Own Howl." *Signs*, 9, No. 2 (Winter 1983), 186-205.

Horney, Karen. *Feminine Psychology*, ed. Harold Kelman. New York: W. W. Norton, 1967.

Irigaray, Luce. "And the One Doesn't Stir Without the Other." *Signs*, 7, No. 1 (Autumn 1981), 60-67.

Irvine, Lorna. "Surfacing, Surviving, Surpassing: Canada's Women Writers." *The Journal of Popular Culture*, 15, No. 3 (Winter 1981), 70-79.

———. "One Woman Leads To Another." In *The Art of Margaret Atwood*, eds. Cathy and Arnold Davidson. Toronto: House of Anansi, 1981, pp. 95-106.

———. "Changing Is The Word I Want." *Probable Fictions: Alice Munro's Narrative Acts*, ed. Louis MacKendrick. Toronto: ECW, 1983, pp. 99-111.

Irwin, John. *Doubling and Incest/Repetition and Revenge: A Speculative Reading of Faulkner*. Baltimore: The Johns Hopkins Univ. Press, 1975.

Jacobus, Mary, ed. *Women Writing and Writing about Women*. New York: Barnes and Noble, 1979.

Jameson, Fredric. *The Political Unconscious: Narrative as a Socially Symbolic Act*. New York: Cornell Univ. Press, 1981.

Jardine, Alice. "Introduction to Julia Kristeva's 'Women's Time.' " *Signs*, 7, No. 1 (Autumn 1981), 5–12.
——. "Pre-texts For the Transatlantic Feminist." *Yale French Studies*, 62 (1981), 220–36.
Jones, Ann. "Writing the Body: Toward an Understanding of L'écriture Féminine." *Feminist Studies*, 7, No. 2 (Summer 1981), 247–63.
Kermode, Frank. *The Genesis of Secrecy: On the Interpretation of Narrative.* Cambridge: Harvard Univ. Press, 1979.
——. "Secrets and Narrative Sequence." *Critical Inquiry*, 7, No. 1 (Autumn 1980), 83–101.
——. *The Art of Telling: Essays on Fiction.* Cambridge: Harvard Univ. Press, 1983.
Kilbourn, William. "The Quest for the Peaceable Kingdom." In *Canadian Writing Today*, ed. Mordecai Richler. Middlesex: Penguin, 1970.
Kolodny, Annette. "Dancing Through the Minefield: Some Observations on the Theory, Practice and Politics of a Feminist Literary Criticism." *Feminist Studies*, 6, No. 1 (Spring 1980), 1–25.
——. "A Map for Rereading: Or, Gender and the Interpretation of Literary Texts." *New Literary History*, 11, No. 3 (Spring 1980), 451–67.
Kristeva, Julia. *Desire in Language: A Semiotic Approach to Literature and Art.* New York: Columbia Univ. Press, 1980.
——. "Women's Time." *Signs*, 7, No. 1 (Autumn 1981), 13–35.
Kuhn, Annette, and AnnMarie Wolpe, eds. *Feminism and Materialism.* London: Routledge and Kegan Paul, 1978.
——. "Introduction to Hélène Cixous' 'Castration or Decapitation?' " *Signs*, 7, No. 1 (Autumn 1981), 36–40.
Lanser, Susan. *The Narrative Act: Point of View in Prose Fiction.* Princeton: Princeton Univ. Press, 1981.
Lee, Dennis. "Cadence, Country, Silence: Writing in Colonial Space." *boundary 2*, 3, No. 1 (Fall 1974), 151–68.
Macherey, Pierre. *A Theory of Literary Production*, trans. Geoffrey Wall. London: Routledge and Kegan Paul, 1978.
MacKinnon, Catharine. "Feminism, Marxism, Method and the State: An Agenda For Theory." *Signs*, 7, No. 3 (Spring 1982), 515–44.
——. "Feminism, Marxism, Method and the State: Towards Feminist Jurisprudence." *Signs*, 8, No. 4 (Summer 1983), 635–58.
Maler, Grazia. *Mavis Gallant: Narrative Patterns.* Ottawa: Tecumseh, 1979.
Marks, Elaine. "Women and Literature in France." *Signs*, 4, No. 3 (Summer 1978), 832–42.
——, and Isabella de Courtivron, eds. *New French Feminisms: An Anthology.* Amherst: Univ. of Massachusetts Press, 1980.
Miller, Jean Baker. *Toward a New Psychology of Women.* Boston, Beacon, 1976.
Miller, Nancy. "Emphasis Added: Plots and Plausibilities in Women's Fiction." *PMLA*, 96, No. 1 (Jan. 1981), 36–48.
Mitchell, Juliet. *Psychoanalysis and Women.* New York: Vintage, 1974.
Morley, Patricia. "Engel, Wiseman, Laurence: Women Writers; Women's

Lives." *World Literature Written in English*, 17 (1978), 154–64.

Moss, John. *Sex and Violence in the Canadian Novel*. Toronto: McClelland and Stewart, 1977.

———. *A Reader's Guide to the Canadian Novel*. Toronto: McClelland and Stewart, 1981.

Northey, Margot. *The Haunted Wilderness: The Gothic and Grotesque in Canadian Fiction*. Toronto: Univ. of Toronto Press, 1976.

Parker, Douglas. "Memories of My Own Patterns: Levels of Reality in *The Honeyman Festival*." *Journal of Canadian Fiction*, 4, No. 3 (1975), 111–16.

Pratt, Annis. *Archetypal Patterns in Women's Fiction*. Bloomington: Indiana Univ. Press, 1981.

Rasporich, Beverly. "Child-Women and Primitives in the Fiction of Alice Munro." *Atlantis*, 1, No. 2 (Spring 1976), 4–14.

Rich, Adrienne. *Of Woman Born*. New York: Bantam, 1976.

———. *On Lies, Secrets and Silence: Selected Prose, 1966–1978*. New York: W. W. Norton, 1979.

Richards, Janet R. *The Sceptical Feminist: A Philosophical Inquiry*. London: Routledge and Kegan Paul, 1980.

Rigney, Barbara. *Madness and Sexual Politics in the Feminist Novel*. Madison: Univ. of Wisconsin Press, 1978.

Robinson, Lillian. *Sex, Class and Culture*. Bloomington: Indiana Univ. Press, 1978.

Rosaldo, Michelle, ed. *Women, Culture and Society*. Stanford: Stanford Univ. Press, 1974.

Rowbotham, Sheila. *Women, Resistance and Revolution: A History of Women and Revolution in the Modern World*. New York: Random House, 1972.

———. *Woman's Consciousness, Man's World*. Middlesex: Penguin, 1973.

Sadoff, Dianne. *Monsters of Affection: Dickens, Eliot, and Brontë on Fatherhood*. Baltimore: The Johns Hopkins Univ. Press, 1982.

Said, Edward. *Beginnings: Intention and Method*. New York: Basic, 1975.

Scholes, Robert. *Semiotics and Interpretation*. New Haven: Yale Univ. Press, 1982.

Schor, Naomi. "Female Paranoia: The Case for Psychoanalytic Criticism." *Yale French Studies*, 62 (1981), 204–19.

Showalter, Elaine. *A Literature of Their Own*. Princeton: Princeton Univ. Press, 1977.

———. "Feminist Criticism in the Wilderness." *Critical Inquiry*, 8, No. 2 (Winter 1981), 179–205.

Spacks, Patricia. *The Female Imagination*. New York: Avon, 1975.

Spivak, Gayatri. "French Feminism in an International Frame." *Yale French Studies*, 62 (1981), 154–84.

Staines, David, ed. *The Canadian Imagination*. Cambridge: Harvard Univ. Press, 1977.

Stimpson, Catherine, and Ethel Person, eds. *Women: Sex and Sexuality*. Chicago: Univ. of Chicago Press, 1980.

Thomas, Audrey. "My Craft and Sullen Art." *Atlantis*, 4, No. 1 (Fall 1978),

152–54.

Todd, Janet. *Women's Friendship in Literature*. New York: Columbia Univ. Press, 1980.

Twigg, Alan. *For Openers: Conversations with 24 Canadian Writers*. Madiera Park: Harbour, 1981.

Wenzel, Helene. "The Text As Body/Politics: An Appreciation of Monique Wittig's Writings in Context." *Feminist Studies*, 7, No. 2 (Summer 1981), 264–87.

——. "Introduction to Luce Irigaray's 'And the One Doesn't Stir Without The Other.'" *Signs*, 7, No. 1 (Autumn 1981), 56–59.

Woodcock, George, ed. *The Canadian Novel in the Twentieth Century*. Toronto: McClelland and Stewart, 1975.

——. *The World of Canadian Writing*. Vancouver: Douglas and McIntyre, 1980.

Woolf, Virginia. *A Room of One's Own*. New York: Harcourt, Brace and World, 1929.

Index

Abel, Elizabeth: *The Voyage In*, 111
Alice in Wonderland (Carroll), 64–67, 66, 164
Among Women (Bernikow), 73
"And the One Doesn't Stir without the Other" (Irigaray), 53, 94
Anxiety of Influence (Bloom), 7
Archetypal Patterns in Women's Fiction (Pratt), 18, 19, 23, 53, 78
Art of Telling: Essays on Fiction (Kermode), 19, 164
Atwood, Margaret: *Bodily Harm*, 14, 15, 16, 17, 18, 31, 37–53, 49, 78, 82, 84, 93, 109, 113, 120, 134, 140, 166; "Book of Ancestors" 169; "Circe poems," 64; "Foretelling the Future," 23; *Life Before Man*, 47; *Murder in the Dark*, 76; "Postcard," 45; "Red Shirt," 168; "Simmering," 76; *Surfacing*, 35, 42, 47, 78; *Survival*, 42; *True Stories*, 44; *The Two-Headed Poems*, 168–69; *You Are Happy*, 168
Auerbach, Nina: *Communities of Women*, 165
Austen, Jane, 6, 12
Autry, Gene, 157
Ayre, John, 133

"Bardon Bus" (Munro), 102
Barth, John: *The End of the Road*, 57
Barthes, Roland: *The Pleasures of the Text*, 3, 140
Baym, Nina: *Woman's Fiction*, 165
Beckmann, Max, 128
Beginnings: Intention and Methods (Said), 31

Bentley, E. C.: *Trent's Last Case*, 164
Berger, John: *Ways of Seeing*, 5, 17, 39, 41, 93
Bernikow, Louise: *Among Women*, 73
Bersianik, Louky: *L'Eugelionne*, 25, 131, 137, 146; *Maternative*, 25
"Between Zero and One" (Gallant), 143
Beyond the Pleasure Principle (Freud), 117
Bible. New Testament, 34
Bible. New Testament. Epistles of Paul, 32
Bible. Old Testament, 34
Bible. Old Testament. Genesis, 67, 123
Bible. Old Testament. Song of Solomon, 34
"Birth of the Artist as Heroine" (Gubar), 35
Bleeding Heart (French), 9
Bloom, Harold: *The Anxiety of Influence*, 7; *A Map of Misreading*, 7
Blown Figures (Thomas), 16, 17, 18, 28, 55–72, 82, 84, 122, 123
Bodily Harm (Atwood), 14, 15, 16, 17, 28, 31, 37–53, 57, 58 84, 93, 109, 113, 120, 140, 166
"Book of Ancestors" (Atwood), 168
Booth, Wayne: *Freedom of Interpretation*, 3, 12, 18, 19
Bronte, Charlotte, 4
Brooks, Peter: "Freud's Masterplot," 76
Brossard, Nicole, 25, 121
Brown, Norman: *Love's Body*, 3

Browne, Thomas: *Religio Medici*, 65

"Cadence, Country, Silence: Writing in Colonial Space" (Lee), 10–11, 23
Carroll, Lewis, 64, 66, 164
Cather, Willa, 101–02
Chaucer, Geoffrey, 93
Chawaf, Chantal: *New French Feminisms*, 37
Chesler, Phyllis: *Women and Madness*, 57
"Child-women and Primitives in the Fiction of Alice Munro" (Rasporich), 95
Chodorow, Nancy: *The Reproduction of Mothering*, 7, 100, 114, 116, 129
Civilization and Its Discontents (Freud), 127
Cixous, Helene, 93–94; "The Laugh of The Medusa," 12, 24, 50, 52, 110; *New French Feminisms*, 93–94
Cobbe, Frances Power: *Darwinism in Morals and Other Essays*, 55
Communities of Women: An Idea in Fiction (Auerbach), 165
Conference of Inter-American Women Writers (University of Ottawa), 72
"Connection" (Munro), 95–96
Conrad, Joseph, 28, 64, 65, 87

Daly, Mary: *Gyn/Ecology*, 131, 147
"Dancing through the Minefield: Some Observations on the Theory, Practice and Politics of Feminist Literary Criticism" (Kolodny), 1, 12, 137
Darwinism in Morals and Other Essays (Cobbe), 55
Daughter's Seduction: Feminism and Psychoanalysis (Gallop), 91, 94, 108
De Courtivron, Isabella: *New French Feminisms*, 37, 53, 94
Desire in Language: A Semiotic Approach to Literature and Art (Kristeva), 29
Dickinson, Emily, 6
Didion, Joan: *Play It As It Lays*, 57
Dostoevsky, Fedor, 57, 58
Doubling and Incest/Repetition and Revenge: A Speculative Reading of Faulkner (Irwin), 35
Dressler, Marie, 157
Duchess of Malfi (Webster), 34
"Dulse" (Munro), 17, 101, 102, 105
Duras, Marguerite: *New French Feminisms*, 37

Eisenstein, Hester: *The Future of Difference*, 8, 9–10
Eliot, George, 4
Eliot, T. S.: *The Waste Land*, 32, 63
Emma (Austen), 12
End of the Road (Barth), 57
Engel, Marian: *The Honeyman Festival*, 16, 17, 149–69; *Inside the Easter Egg*, 165, 166; *Lunatic Villas*, 14, 16, 17, 18, 31, 58, 78, 149–69; "Marshallene on Rape," 165; *Sarah Bastard's Notebook*, 7, 149
Erikson, Erik: "Genital Modes and Spatial Modalities," 70
Eugelionne (Bersianik), 25, 131, 137

Fairly Good Time (Gallant), 82
Faulkner, William, 35, 57
Felman, Shoshana: "Turning the Screw of Interpretation," 69
Female Imagination (Spacks), 78, 135
Feminine Psychology (Horney), 144

Feminism and Materialism (Kuhn & Wolpe), 114
"Feminism, Marxism, Method, and the State: An Agenda for Theory" (MacKinnon), 115
"Feminist Criticism in the Wilderness" (Showalter), 75
Fiedler, Leslie: *Love and Death in America*, 11
For Openers: Conversations with 24 Canadian Writers (Twigg), 116
"For the Etruscans" (collective), 9
"Foretelling the Future" (Atwood), 23
Foucault, Michel: *The History of Sexuality*, 96
Fraser, Sylvia: *Pandora*, 14, 16, 17, 31, 58, 111–29, 140, 156
"Freedom of Interpretation: Bakhtin and the Challenge of Feminist Criticism" (Booth), 3, 12, 18, 19
French, Marilyn, 9
Freud, Sigmund, 3, 5, 13, 48, 57, 59, 93; *Beyond the Pleasure Principle*, 117; *Civilization and Its Discontents*, 127; *Totem and Tabu*, 76
"Freud's Masterplot: Questions of Narrative" (Brooks), 76
From Ritual to Romance (Weston), 29
From the Fifteenth District (Gallant), 86
Frye, Northrop, 42, 45
Future of Difference (Eisenstein & Jardine), 8

Gagnon, Madeleine, 24
Gallant, Mavis, 17, 131–47; *A Fairly Good Time*, 82; "Between Zero and One," 143; *From the Fifteen District*, 86; *Home Truths*, 16, 18; "Its Image on the Mirror," 14, 75–89, 113, 123, 133, 141; "The Moslem Wife," 86; "The Pegnitz Junction," 16, 133, 134, 135, 140, 142, 167; "Voices Lost in Snow," 143
Gallop, Jane: *The Daughter's Seduction*, 91, 94, 108
Gardiner, Judith: "On Female Identity and Writing by Women," 70, 71
Genesis of Secrecy: On the Interpretation of Narrative (Kermode), 79, 88
"Genital Modes and Spatial Modalities" (Erikson), 70
Getty, J. Paul, 127
Gilbert, Sandra: *Madwoman in the Attic*, 4, 55, 58
Gilligan, Carol: *In a Different Voice*, 7, 91, 123, 126, 164
Gould, Karen: "Setting Words Free," 24
Gradiva (Jensen), 58
Grant, George: *Technology and Empire*, 161
Griffin, Susan: *Woman and Nature*, 153
Gubar, Susan, 63; "The Birth of the Artist as Heroine," 35; *In a Different Voice*, 7; *Madwoman in the Attic*, 4, 55, 58
Les/Guerilleres (Wittig), 9, 60
Gyn/Ecology: The Metaethics of Radical Feminism (Daly), 131, 146–47

"Hard Luck Stories" (Munro), 105, 109
Harrison, Jane: "Pandora's Box," 111
Hartman, Geoffrey: *Psychoanalysis and the Question of the Text*, 76
Hatch, Ronald: "Mavis Gallant," 134
Hayworth, Rita, 128

Heart of Darkness (Conrad), 28, 64, 65
Hemingway, Ernest, 35
Henie, Sonja, 157
Hirsch, Marianne: *The Voyage In*, 111
History of Sexuality (Foucault), 96
Hitler, Adolf, 136, 167
Homans, Margaret: "Her Very Own Howl," 9, 10; *Women Writers*, 7
Home Truths (Gallant), 16, 18, 133
Homer, 63, 65
Honeyman Festival (Engel), 16, 17, 148–69
Horney, Karen: *Feminine Psychology*, 142–44
Hughes, Howard, 127

"If One Green Bottle" (Thomas), 25, 26
In a Different Voice (Gilligan), 7, 91, 123, 126
Inside the Easter Egg (Engel), 165, 166
Irigaray, Luce: "And the One Doesn't Stir without the Other," 53, 94
Irwin, John: *Doubling and Incest*, 35
"Its Image on the Mirror" (Gallant), 14, 16, 75–89, 113, 123, 133, 134, 141

Jacobus, Mary, 26–27
James, Henry, 69
Jameson, Frederic: *The Political Unconscious*, 35
Jardine, Alice: *The Future of Difference*, 8
Les Journées d'une Anthropophage (Vezina), 149
Joyce, James, 105, 142

Kermode, Frank: *Art of Telling*, 19, 164; *Genesis of Secrecy*, 88, 79

Kesey, Ken: *One Flew over the Cuckoo's Nest*, 57
Kilbourn, William: "The Quest for the Peaceable Kingdom," 151
Klee, Paul, 128
Kolodny, Annette: "Dancing through the Minefield," 1, 12, 137
Kristeva, Julia: *Desire in Language*, 29
Kuhn, Annette: *Feminism and Materialism*, 114–15

"Labour Day Dinner" (Munro), 14, 99, 102, 105, 110
Laing, R. D., 57
Lake, Veronica, 128
Langland, Elizabeth: *The Voyage In*, 111
Lanser, Susan: *The Narrative Act*, 124
"Laugh of the Medusa" (Cixous), 12, 24, 50, 52, 110
Lear [*King Lear*] (Shakespeare), 34
Lee, Dennis: "Cadence, Country, Silence," 10–11, 23
Life Before Man (Atwood), 47
Linnet Muir stories (Gallant: *Home Truths*), 16, 133, 134, 135, 135, 139–45
Literature of Their Own (Showalter), 75
Lives of Girls and Women (Munro), 94, 95
Lost Lady (Cather), 101–02
Love and Death in the American Novel (Fiedler), 11
Lunatic Villas (Engel), 14, 16, 17, 18, 31, 58, 78, 149–69

MacKinnon, Catherine: "Feminism, Marxism, Method, and the State," 114–15

Macherey, Pierre: *A theoryy of Literary Production*, 25, 122
Madness and Sexual Politics in the Feminist Novel (Rigney), 57
Madwoman in the Attic: The Woman Writer and the Nineteenth Century Literary Imagination (Gilbert & Gubar), 4, 55, 58
Map of Misreading: A Theory of Poetry (Bloom), 7
Marks, Elaine: *New French Feminisms*, 37, 53, 93
"Marshallene on Rape" (Engel), 165
"Material" (Munro), 94
Maternative (Bersianik), 25
"Mavis Gallant: Returning Home" (Hatch), 134
McCarthy, Joseph R., 157, 167
Miller, Jean Baker: *Notes in a Future Key*, 167–68; *Toward a New Psychology of Women*, 109
Milton, John, 35, 156
Mitchell, Juliet: *Psychoanalysis and Women*, 114
Monsters of Affection: Dickens, Eliot and Bronte on Fatherhood (Sadoff), 4
Moons of Jupiter (Munro), 16, 91–110
"Moons of Jupiter" (Munro), 108
"Moslem Wife" (Gallant), 86
Moss, John: *A Reader's Guide to the Canadian Novel*, 84
Mrs. Blood (Thomas), 14, 15, 17, 18, 21–36, 39, 40, 44, 57, 63, 68, 82, 84, 122, 151
Mrs. Dalloway (Woolf), 99
Muir stories (Gallant: *Home Truths*), 16, 133, 134, 135, 139–44
Munro, Alice: "Bardon Bus," 102; "Connection", 95–96, "Dulse," 17, 101, 102, 105; "Hard Luck Stories," 105, 109; "Labour Day Dinner," 14, 99, 105, 110; *Lives of Girls and Women*, 94, 95; "Material," 94; "The Moons of Jupiter," 108; *The Moons of Jupiter*, 16, 91–110; "The Ottawa Valley," 108; *Something I've Been Meaning to Tell You*, 108; "The Stone in the Field," 97, 110
Murder in the Dark (Atwood), 76
"My Craft and Sullen Art: The Writers Speak" (Thomas), 72

Narrative Act: Point of View in Prose Fiction (Lanser), 124
New French Feminisms, 37, 53, 93
"Notes in a Future Key" (Miller), 167–68

Odyssey (Homer), 63, 65
Of Woman Born (Rich), 11, 123
"On Female identity and Writing by Women" (Gardiner), 70, 71
One Flew over the Cuckoo's Nest (Kesey), 57
"Ottawa Valley" (Munro), 108

Pandora (Fraser), 14, 16, 17, 31, 58, 111–29, 140, 156
Pandora's Box (Panofsky), 128
"Pandora's Box" (Harrison), 111
Panofsky, Dora: *Pandora's Box*, 128
Panofsky, Erwin: *Pandora's Box*, 128
Paradise Lost (Milton), 35, 156
Pegnitz Junction (Gallant), 133
"Pegnitz Junction" (Gallant), 16, 133, 134, 135–39, 140, 142, 167
Plato: *Republic*, 157
Play It As It Lays (Didion), 57
Pleasures of the Text (Barthes), 3, 140
Poe, Edgar A., 58
Political Unconscious: Narrative as a Socially Symbolic Act (Jameson), 35

"Postcard" (Atwood), 45
Pratt, Annis: *Archetypal Patterns in Women's Fiction* 18, 19, 23, 53, 78
"Prelude" (Mansfield), 63
Psychoanalysis and Women: Freud, Reich, Laing, and Women (Mitchell), 114
"Psychoanalysis: The French Connection" (Hartman), 76

"Quest for the Peaceable Kingdom" (Kilbourn), 151
Quest of the Holy Grail (Weston), 21

Rankin, Jennifer, 48
Rasporich, Beverly: "Child-women and Primitives in the Fiction of Alice Munro," 95
A Reader's Guide to the Canadian Novel (Moss), 85
"Red Shirt" (Atwood), 168
Religio Medici (Browne), 65
Reproduction of Mothering: Psychoanalysis and the Sociology of Gender (Choorow), 7, 114, 116, 129
Republic (Plato), 157
Rich, Adrienne: *Of Woman Born*, 11–12, 123
Richards, Janet R.: *The Sceptical Feminist*, 13
Rigney, Barbara: *Madness and Sexual Politics in the Feminist Novel*, 57
Rogers, Ginger, 128
Rogers, Roy, 157
Room of One's Own (Woolf), 113, 122
Rowbotham, Sheila: *Women, Resistance, and Revolution*, 114
Rubin, Lillian: *Worlds of Pain*, 116

Sadoff, Diane: *Monsters of Affection*, 4

Said, Edward: *Beginnings*, 31
Sarah Bastard's Notebook (Engel), 78, 149, 151
The Sceptical Feminist (Richards), 13
Scholes, Robert: *Semiotics and Interpretation*, 12
Secrets and Narrative Sequence (Kermode), 76
Semiotics and Interpretation (Scholes), 12
"Setting Words Free: Feminist Writing in Quebec" (Gould), 24
"Shadowy Waters" (Yeats), 79
Shakespeare, William, 34, 57
Showalter, Elaine, 75
"Simmering" (Atwood), 76
Something I've Been Meaning to Tell You (Munro), 108
Songs My Mother Taught Me (Thomas), 30
Sophie's Choice (Styron), 156–57
Spacks, Patricia: *The Female Imagination*, 78, 135
"Stone in the Field" (Munro), 97, 110
"Structures of Patriarchy and Capital in the Family" (Kuhn), 115
Styron, William: *Sophie's Choice*, 156–57
Surfacing (Atwood), 42, 47, 78
Survival: A Thematic Guide to Canadian Literature (Atwood), 42
Sydney, Philip, 72

Technology and Empire: Perspectives on North America (Grant), 161
Ten Green Bottles (Thomas), 25, 26
Theory of Literary Production (Macherey), 25, 122
Thomas, Audrey, 121; *Blown Figures*, 16, 17, 28, 55–72, 82, 84, 122, 123; *Mrs. Blood*, 14, 15, 17, 18, 21–36, 39, 40, 44, 68, 82, 84, 122; "My Craft and Sullen Art," 72; *Songs*

My Mother Taught Me, 30; *Ten Green Bottles*, 25, 26; "Topic of Cancer," 41
Through the Looking Glass (Carroll), 64, 66
Tiger, Lionel, 126
"Topic of Cancer" (Thomas), 41
"Torture" (Atwood), 50
Totem and Tabu (Freud), 88
Toward a New Psychology of Women (Miller), 109
Trent's Last Case (Bentley), 164
True Stories (Atwood), 44
"Turn of the Screw" (James), 69
"Turning the Screw of Interpretation" (Felman), 69
Twigg, Alan: *For Openers*, 116
Two-Headed Poems (Atwood), 168–81

Ulysses (Joyce), 105
Under Western Eyes (Conrad), 87

Vezina, France: *Les Journées d'une anthropophage*, 149
"Voices Lost in Snow" (Gallant), 143
Voyage In: Fictions of Female Development (Abel, Hirsch, & Langland), 111

Waste Land (T. S. Eliot), 32, 63
Ways of Seeing (Berger), 5, 17, 39, 42, 93
Webster, John: *Duchess of Malfi*, 34
Weston, Jessie: *From Ritual to Romance*, 29; *The Quest of the Holy Grail*, 21
Wilde, Oscar, 125
Wittig, Monique: *Les Guerilleres*, 9, 60
Wolpe, AnnMarie: *Feminism and Materialism*, 115

Woman and Nature: The Roaring Inside SHer (Griffin), 153
Woman's Fiction: A Guide to Novels by and about Women in America, 1820–1870 (Baym), 165
Women Writers and Poetic Identity (Homans), 7
Women and Madness (Chesler), 58
Women, Resistance, and Revolution: A History of Women and the Revolution in the Modern World (Rowbotham), 114
Woodcock, George: *The World of Canadian Writing*, 134, 140
Woolf, Virginia, 157; *Mrs. Dalloway*, 99; *A Room of One's Own*, 113, 122
World of Canadian Writing (Woodcock), 134, 140
Worlds of Pain: Life in the Working-Class Family (Rubin), 116

Yeats, W. B.: "The Shadowy Waters," 79
You Are Happy (Atwood), 168

ABA-7224